Bioethics and Secular Humanism:
The Search for a Common Morality

The Park Ridge Center exists to explore the relationships among health, faith, and ethics. In its programs of research, publishing, and education, the Center gives special attention to the bearing of religious beliefs on questions that confront people as they search for health and encounter illness. It also seeks to contribute to ethical reflection on a wide range of health-related issues. In this work the Center collaborates with representatives from diverse cultures, religious communities, health care fields, and academic disciplines and disseminates its findings to professionals and others interested in health, religion, and ethics.

The Center is an independent, not-for-profit organization supported by grants, foundations, private and corporate contributors, and subscribing Associates. Additional information may be obtained by writing to The Park Ridge Center, 676 North St Clair, Suite 450, Chicago, IL 60611.

Bioethics and Secular Humanism:

The Search for a Common Morality

H. Tristram Enge

SCM Press · London

Trinity Press International · Philadelphia

A book from the Park Ridge Center for the Study of Heath, Faith, and Ethics

This edition first published 1991

SCM Press
26–30 Tottenham Road
London N1 4BZ

Trinity Press International
3725 Chestnut Street
Philadelphia PA 19104

British Library Cataloguing in Publication Data

Engelhardt, H. Tristram (Hugo Tristram) 1941-
Bioethics and secular humanism.
1. Health services. Ethical aspects – Christian viewpoints
I. Title
261.8321

ISBN 0-334-02495-1

Library of Congress Cataloging-in-Publication Data

Engelhardt, H. Tristram (Hugo Tristram), 1941–
Bioethics and secular humanism : the search for a common morality
H. Tristram Engelhardt, Jr.
p. cm.
Includes bibliographical references and index.
ISBN 1-56338-000-5 (hard)
1. Bioethics. 2. Secularism. 3. Humanism. 4. Medical policy–
–Moral and ethical aspects. I. Title.
QH332.E54 1991
179'.1–dc20 90-23377

Typeset at The Spartan Press Ltd, Lymington, Hants
and printed in Great Britain by
Clays Ltd, St Ives plc, Bungay, Suffolk

An meine Eltern

O curas hominum!
O quantum est in rebus inane!

Lucilius

Contents

Acknowledgments

For years this volume refused to come about. It has finally gained reality by the grace of the muses in Athens on the Spree, in particular through the heuristic atmosphere and library services of the Institute for Advanced Study of Berlin (Wissenschaftskolleg zu Berlin), where I was a Fellow during the academic year 1988–89. I am indebted also to the Institute and to the Center for Ethics, Medicine, and Public Issues, Baylor College of Medicine, which supported me during my sabbatical. Because of the administrative and other vexations he shouldered during and on behalf of my absence, I am in special debt to Baruch A. Brody. Gratitude is as strongly due and felt to His Magnificence, the Rector of the Wissenschaftskolleg, Wolf Lepenies, for giving intellectual harbor to an unreconstructed Texan.

This volume took shape through conversations and discussions with many colleagues and from the inspiration of many friends. Fellows at the Institute for Advanced Study, directly and indirectly, made suggestions that were important in its writing. Indeed, many of the themes explored in this volume were first articulated years ago in conversation with Gunther Stent, a permanent Fellow of the Institute. Numerous individuals read through this volume in great detail and provided a multitude of helpful suggestions, not all of which I have taken. In many respects, I am an old mumpsimus. The strengths of this volume must therefore be attributed to them, but none of its weaknesses. In this regard, I want to acknowledge my special gratitude to Thomas J. Bole III, Gunther Albrecht-Bühler, Corinna Delkeskamp-Hayes, Edmund L. Erde, Robert H. Haynes, George Khusf, Emilio Lledo, B. Andrew Lustig, Gabriel Motzkin, Michael A. Rie, Kurt Schmidt, Stuart F. Spicker, Stephen Wear, Becky C. White, and Kevin W. Wildes, S.J. But I must in particular underscore my debt to Edmund Erde and Laurence B. McCullough, who helped me rephrase whole sections of this work. Thanks are due also to Elissa Linke, Firooza Kraft, Ulla Moni gatti, Regina Plaar, and Andrea Will, who worked with the manuscript and the computers that harbored it. Most importantly, the book would never have taken on reality without the love, encouragement, inspiration, and patience of my wife Susan.

Finally, I must thank the scholars associated with the Park Ridge Center for the Study of Health, Faith, and Ethics. It is because of their original support and encouragement through their Project X aimed at publishing volumes laying out issues concerning health and medicine in the faith traditions that this volume was undertaken. In particular, it was Kenneth Vaux who first induced me to write a slim volume of this character and focus. This volume has subsequently benefited from suggestions provided by the Park Ridge Center. Most especially, I am in enduring debt to the President of the Park Ridge Center, Laurence O'Connell, for his help and guidance.

Introduction

I begin with a confession. This volume is meant as much to address the fundamental philosophical and cultural challenges of the post-modern age as to give an account of bioethics or to explore the significance of secular humanism. Bioethics has a claim on our attention because it is the critical expression of our interest in properly employing the powers of medicine and the biomedical sciences to provide health care. Secular humanism has a claim on our attention because it is central to our contemporary moral and cultural challenge: justifying a moral framework that can be shared by moral strangers in an age of both moral fragmentation and apathy. But the challenge is defined by the failure of religion or reason to establish a canonical account of justice or morality. Because of the diverse character of traditional, especially religious, moral accounts, and their conflicting implications for health care (e.g., regarding the morality of abortion, the allowability of euthanasia, or the definition of death), there is a natural hope that we may share enough together simply as humans in order to justify a common bioethics. Secular humanism is the attempt to articulate what we as humans hold in common without special appeal to religious or other particular moral or metaphysical assumptions. Secular humanism plays a special role in our culture because it promises to provide the background for much of our contemporary understandings of health and medicine. As we will see, this promise cannot be kept in a content-full fashion.

The problem of articulating a justifiable health care policy will be examined against the background of our major intellectual and moral limitations. First, human reason is not able to provide for morality and political theory what we long took for granted: a rationally justified content-full moral vision. Second, the contemporary world is characterized by moral fragmentation and polarization on the part of some and a moral apathy on the part of others. The moral apathy is in part a socio-anthropological consequence of the limits of moral reasoning, which is an ontological infirmity. The experience of the finitude of human reason, along with the moral fragmentation of the contemporary world, characterizes the age, for which I will use the somewhat ambiguous term "post-modern".

In the post-modern age one has neither the institutions of religious totality that marked the Middle Ages nor the convictions of rational totality that marked the modern age. For over a thousand years the West was Christendom. Despite venality and cynicism, it was consecrated to a concrete, religiously-based moral vision that was sustained, guided, and guarded by an ecclesiastical structure. Though the men and women of the Middle Ages made robust assumptions concerning the capacities of reason, their goal was to make the kingdom of grace incarnate in the social and political institutions of their time. The modern age emerged as these aspirations to totality that had directed the medieval Western mind fragmented. There was no longer Christendom, but Christendoms. The hope of reunion between schismatics at the Council of Florence (1439) was followed by the separation from heretics articulated at Trent (1543–1563). Against the background of religious division, and finally bloody warfare, the modern mind turned to reason for a framework of universal scope that all could recognize as authoritative, as speaking for their true selves.

Such a framework was and is necessary because morality is tied to power. People search out the meaning of the good, not just to live their lives as pious anchorites, but as citizens in societies with others who, among other things, establish health care institutions. As a result, moral discussions must inevitably consider under what circumstances who should conform to whose moral vision. Moral visions provide the foundation for political theory, for the justification of political authority, for the framing of political structures, for the establishment of health care policies. To articulate a moral theory is in the end to select a political structure. To select a political structure, and to hold it to be intellectually justified, is to presume a moral theory. Bioethics justifies health care policy and a justified health care policy presupposes a foundational bioethics. Moreover, integral to giving an account of health and medicine is determining when that account may be realized through coercive state force. The lineaments of permissible political action are central to a secular bioethics which must indicate what moral views may be imposed on whom, by whom, and in what circumstances.

As a result, it will not be enough to react to the post-modern condition by abandoning the encompassing aspirations of reason.

One might be tempted to characterize the difficulties as the result of the totalizing aspirations of medieval Christianity. One might think: why not acquiesce in a world framed by numerous competing visions of rationality, morality, and justice, somewhat as contemporary Christian sects now live side-by-side without the Inquisition or writs for the burning of heretics? The answer is indeed that it is possible, as long as there is no attempt to form a common government. But the framing of a common government (along with, for example, the establishment of particular health care policies) requires deciding what should be (may be) imposed by force.

If one cannot justify public policy imposed by an appeal to a rational argument which shows that all (i.e., as rational beings) should endorse the policy, or the process that produced it, then the policy must in principle be as alien a moral imposition on those who do not share its premises as would be the imposition of a particular religion. When there are numerous unmediateable senses of morality, rationality, and justice, each will have a status analogous to a religious vision of the world; each will depend on special premises not open to general rational justification. As religions depend on endorsing particular understandings of the Ultimate, theories of justice depend on endorsing particular thin theories of the good (e.g., John Rawls' thin theory of the good) or their analogues. What will be the difference, then, between imposing a Rawlsian theory of justice and a Roman Catholic contraceptive policy? What will be the difference between appealing to the divine right of the Pope or to the right of a democratic majority? Why should not the divine right of kings count as much as (or more than) the claims of a 51% majority? If there is no rational perspective that should on rational grounds govern across conflicting moral visions, then the moral fragmentation of the post-modern world is an inescapable element of our ontological condition, not just a sociological fact. There will not be a common moral framework available to be shared by moral strangers.

I use the term "moral strangers" to signal the relationship people have to one another when they are involved in moral controversies and do not share a concrete moral vision that provides the basis for the resolution of the controversies, but instead regard one another as acting out of fundamentally divergent moral commitments. When one meets another as a moral stranger, one meets in circumstances where there is no communality of moral commitment that could in principle resolve the difference and allow the disputants to regard cooperation in the matter at issue as warranted in terms of content-full moral principles. Instead, one regards the other's actions as morally unjustifiable or, worse, as morally reprehensible. Imagine a group of Basque Americans who wish to establish a private school that will admit only children of Basque ancestry and within which the courses will be taught only in Basque, confronting individuals who hold such an endeavor to be racist. Imagine individuals who wish to organize a for-profit surrogate mother service, confronting individuals who hold such an endeavor to be an instance of the exploitation of women. Imagine a group who hold that requiring sexual favors as a condition of employment is not morally different from requiring service in the Armed Forces as a condition for citizenship, discussing such matters with the American Equal Employment Opportunity Commission. Imagine Rawlsians and Nozickians disputing over proper governmental health care policies. Imagine Catholics and committed atheists disputing over proper abortion policies. In some cases of dispute there will be enough shared in common to resolve the controversies. In other cases there apparently will not be sufficient moral premises commonly shared. Is this indeed the case? Do individuals on opposite sides of such controversies in principle share enough simply as rational individuals for one in ideal circumstances to be able to show who is right and who is wrong, or at least how public policy may be established with moral authority that should have a claim on moral strangers? Or will they face each other in such controversies as moral strangers, reciprocally and incorrigibly regarding each other's position as morally misguided and perhaps offensive? Is it in the end just a matter of whose religious, moral, or political vision has power, in the end no definitive moral judgment being possible one way or the other? To be a moral stranger to another is not to share enough of a concrete morality to allow the common discovery of the basis for the correct resolution of a moral controversy.

I use the term "post-modern" to characterize this fragmented character of practical reason. The post-modern age is the age of moral strangers. The modern age had been marked by a faith in reason, by a faith that those who appear to be moral strangers are in fact bound by an implicit web of content-full moral rights and duties. What the Christian faith had failed to provide by grace, the modern age sought through reason. First looking back to the ancient world and then looking towards a future confirmed by scientific and political progress, the modern age assumed that reason could provide a general justification of a moral vision and political power. By demonstrating what is rational to do, one could (1) show in concrete, contentful terms what is rational to accept, (2) dismiss protests to the contrary as irrational, and (3) render the morality imposed by political power implicitly congenial, not alien to, the true nature of those individuals who are forced to conform. The post-modern age is defined by the implausibility of these assumptions. With the loss of the centripetal forces of a concrete moral vision, the moral fabric shatters into disparate moralities.

Still, there is the hope that something can be saved. Secular humanism can be understood as the core of the modern hope to provide a common content-full moral framework for moral strangers. By appealing to human nature, humanism hopes to disclose what men and women share simply as humans. This should cut across religious, ideological, and philosophical communities. Moreover, the adjective "secular" reminds us that the interpretation of humanism, of human nature, which we are seeking, is not that of a particular religious, philosophical, or ideological perspective. It is sought from the most neutral, most secular, most immanent perspective possible — from a perspective that we share in terms of our common world of reality. Though there are good grounds to suspect that the endeavor is doomed to failure (at least insofar as it aspires to establish a single content-full canonical moral vision), the intellectual and cultural stakes are so great that the labor is still worth the undertaking. Against the post-modern moral fragmentation and the consequent concerns regarding the moral legitimation of power, I offer an account of secular humanism with reference to bioethics and health care. Bioethics and health care provide an ideal occasion for this undertaking because they are the source of a wide range of important moral debates involving the interpretation, manipulation, and refashioning of human nature. In addition, health care is important because it consumes large amounts of resources in most industrialized countries, i.e., between five and over eleven percent. To explore bioethics and health care in the secular humanist traditions is to explore the possibility of disclosing a fundamental and implicitly common understanding of human nature and the human condition.

This volume explores the possibilities of understanding bioethics and health care in a secular humanist tradition. Towards this end, an intellectual and a historical account of secularity and humanism are provided. These are elaborated against the background of a diagnosis of the intellectual infirmities of the post-modern age and towards the goal of justifying a secular bioethics. The first chapter introduces the controversial nature of secular humanism and indicates its relationship to the moral fragmentation and apathy of post-modern times. The problem of mediating the diversity of bioethics is then explored. This chapter also introduces the problem of providing an intellectual foundation for a secular bioethics, a bioethics open to moral strangers. The second chapter examines the meanings of secularity and the third chapter the meanings of humanism. The third chapter also scrutinizes the recent interest in the medical humanities. These substantially historical chapters demonstrate the complex character of secularity and the intricate interplay of the ideas and forces that have shaped our understandings of humanism. Against these explorations of secularity and humanism, the fourth chapter analyzes the differences between two key meanings of secular humanism (i.e., secular humanism as a body of content-full moral propositions and secular humanism as a content-less perspective for peaceable negotiation among moral strangers) and their implications for bioethics. The final chapter then shows how a secular humanist bioethics, a secular appreciation of health and medicine, can indeed be secured with intellectual warrant. The intellectual journey is from a background of problems (i.e., the intellectual difficulties of a post-modern age) and an account of two cardinal concepts (i.e., secularity and humanism) to a defense of a secular bioethics.

There is urgency in all of this. The energies and possibilities of medicine must be given direction. We stand on the threshold of new biomedical possibilities from genetic engineering to fetal tissue transplants. We also face well-established challenges such as containing health-care costs and enabling people to control the effects of medical technology in their lives. These are major practical challenges which can only be met by a foundational intellectual response. Yet such a response appears impossible. We are living in a period with similarities to the Renaissance and the Reformation: old belief systems, both Christian and Marxist, are losing their political hegemony and their cultural force. It is unclear how, or indeed whether, we will ever again be able to assemble what appeared in the past to be a seamless fabric of morality and public authority. Much is tearing apart that once seemed quite solid. Unexpected possibilities are becoming real. I do not pretend to like all I see. The conclusions I affirm are not necessarily those I celebrate. Moreover, though faith in reason is largely lost, I have not lost the Faith.

Houston, Texas H.T.E., Jr.
June 3, 1990

I Secular Humanism, Bioethics, and the Post-Modern World

1. Secular Humanism: A Critical Reception

To call someone a secular humanist can be to use fighting words. For many, secular humanism is antagonistic to established traditions and religious commitment. Mincing no words, Bob Sutton characterizes humanism as "satanic in origin."[1] The cardinal sin of humanism is human self-exaltation:

> Humanism is the worship or recognition of man's claim to sovereignty and lordship. Humanism does not always deny the existence of God. In fact, the tempter, the founder of humanism, made no attempt to deny the reality of God. Instead, he held that God seeks to prevent man's self-realization; man must be his own lord or sovereign, choosing, knowing, or determining for himself what constitutes good and evil in terms of his own self-interest.[2]

Humanism is "a rejection of the ultimacy of God's throne and its replacement by the thrones of men."[3] Though humanists are acknowledged as having "promoted the myth of neutrality," this is regarded only as "a facade for the elimination of Christianity."[4] Humanism is "the summation of all anti-Christianity,"[5] and is seen as antithetical to all religion. "The doctrine of humanism is antitheistic; that is, it denies the existence of God, the inspiration of the Scriptures, the divinity of Christ, the existence of the soul, life after death, and the biblical account of creation."[6] Humanism has become for many "the dominant religion of our time, a part of the lives of nearly everyone in the 'developed' world and of all others who want to participate in a similar development."[7] In addition, secular humanism is opposed not just because of its putative hostility to religion, but also because of a supposed hostility to patriotism and nationalism.[8]

Those who oppose humanism need not do so on religious grounds. Many view humanism as displacing the central, decisive, and insightful role of the emotions in favor of a belief in reason. Reason, they hold, has led to a false attempt to overrationalize life. Humanism is regarded by these critics as the source of a disproportionate reliance on technology, a failure to respect the environment, and a reluctance prudently to acknowledge the limited nature of the world's resources.

> . . . we come at once to the core of the religion of humanism: a supreme faith in human reason — its ability to confront and solve the many problems that humans face, its ability to rearrange both the world of Nature and the affairs of men and women so that human life will prosper. Accordingly, as humanism is committed to an unquestioning faith in the power of reason, so it rejects other mythologies of power, including the power of God, the power of supernatural forces, and even the undirected power of Nature in league with blind chance. . . Because human intelligence is the key to human success, the main task of the humanists is to assert its power and protect its prerogatives wherever they are questioned or challenged.[9]

Humanism is regarded as arrogant in placing humans at the center of value and moral considerations.

Though humanism or secular humanism is decried as a dangerous religion, its organized membership is so small that it would appear insignificant.

> Although the American Humanist Association has only 3,500 members after forty years of effort, other groups have not done any better. The American Ethical Union has only 3,500 members after a hundred years, the Society for Humanistic Judaism 4,000 adherents, and the Fellowship of Religious Humanists 300 — and these figures may be on the generous side. Within the Unitarian Church, which is declining in members, humanism is beleaguered and is losing its influence.[10]

Considering the actual number of formal adherents, humanism and secular humanism in particular have evoked reactions totally out of proportion to their numbers. This stark contrast between the paucity of members and the magnitude of the reaction against secular humanism can be explained by the influence of the members of Humanist groups. It can also be explained by the role secular humanist ideas and images play in much of contemporary culture. The so-called religion of humanism, the celebration of human capacities and abilities along with a faith in the powers of reason, became the bedrock of the modern age.

To understand the diverse influence of secular humanism, a distinction is needed. In this volume, I will generally use "Secular Humanism" to identify beliefs or opinions associated with organized humanist movements, especially Secular Humanism. In this respect, I will accept "A Secular Humanist Declaration" as the articulation of some of the core commitments of Secular Humanists.[11] In contrast, I will use "secular humanism" to identify the cluster of philosophical, philological, moral, and literary ideas, images, and commitments, which have been associated with the historical phenomenon of humanism in dissociation from particular religious or ideological commitments. As such, secular humanism comes to identify that body of moral, political, and philosophical claims that can be rigorously justified as integral to a moral language for moral strangers. The term "moral strangers" identifies individuals who in small or large areas do not share a common concrete religious, moral, or philosophical viewpoint. People meet as moral strangers when (1) they have different views regarding the morality of a particular endeavor, such as euthanasia, surrogate motherhood, or justice and health care, and (2) have no common content-full moral or philosophical framework, which would allow a rational, morally content-full resolution of the controversy at issue. People can be both moral friends and strangers to one another, depending on how well embedded they are in their particular moral frameworks. On the West Bank, Hassidic Jews and Shiite Muslims will likely meet as moral strangers under most circumstances. On the other hand, secularized Yuppies may confront one another as moral friends, even when they are nominally separated by confessional differences. When moral strangers meet and cooperate, the question is: what basis can exist for cooperation, other than force and coercion? To find a basis for amicable cooperation, moral strangers must look for some neutral framework (i.e., some secular framework) in terms of which they can discover what they share in common (e.g., perhaps an understanding of what it is to be human) despite their other differences in moral vision. Where useful, through the differential use of upper and lower case letters I will contrast the ideas and images associated with Secular Humanism as a formal organization with the ideas and images associated with secular humanism as a set of phenomena embedded in the last two and a half millennia of the development of Western notions of humanism.

Secular humanism (i.e., as the attempt to ground culture and public policy in non-religious terms by appeal to what we share as humans) has set the tone for much of recent moral reflection. It underlies most contemporary understandings of bioethics and health care. It will be the focus of this volume. The principal concern of this work is to understand the historical and conceptual phenomena that have shaped secular humanism in this broad sense and to give an account of its influence on the character and significance of contemporary health care.

2. The Weakening of Traditional Religious Controls on Western Society

Secular humanism is the result of two major phenomena: the development of secularity and the development of humanism. The first, secularity, evokes much of the reaction against the term secular humanism because of the distress felt by traditional Christians who have experienced the radical secularization of this century. If one understands secularization as the process that occurs "when supernatural religion — that is, religion based on 'belief in God or a future state' — becomes private, optional and problematic,"[12] then Christianity is becoming secular. This secularization has led some Christians to a feeling of cultural crisis. For others, the central structures of their traditional belief are now dubious.

> The Christian revelation, in the form in which it has been handed down to us, clearly no longer provides any valid answer to the questions about God asked by the majority of people today. Neither would it appear to make any contribution to modern man's meaningful understanding of himself in this world and in human history. It is at once evident that more and more of these people are becoming increasingly displeased and dissatisfied with the traditional Christian answers to their questions.[13]

With the collapse of traditional belief structures, there has also been a dramatic transformation of the ways in which the world, society, and the authority of political and social structures are regarded.

> Probably for the first time in history, the religious legitimations of the world have lost their plausibility not only for a few intellectuals and other marginal individuals, but for broad masses of entire societies. This opened up an acute crisis not only for the

> nomization of the large social institutions but for that of individual biographies. In other words, there has arisen a problem of "meaningfulness" not only for such institutions as the state or the economy but for the ordinary routines of everyday life.[14]

There has been a rupture, a break in the perceived significance of social and individual reality.

These changes are part of a social reorientation that has brought into question the relevancy of religion generally. No doubt many of the traditional pieties have remained intact for a wide range of people.[15] However, the experience of secularization has been culturally transforming and individually disorienting, leading to a dramatic decline in traditional faith.[16] For traditional Christians whose faith commitments have not been undermined by these major cultural ruptures, there is still the sense that Christianity has lost its inheritance and been deprived of its rightful place in society. With the West no longer as Christendom, believing Christians have found that "they have become a 'peculiar people', anomalous in their primary beliefs, assumptions, values and norms . . ."[17]

This alienation of religion from contemporary life is not an experience of the West or Christianity alone. In particular, Islam in the late 1970s and 1980s reacted against what had become the destiny of Christianity. To prevent the passing of its religious and cultural traditions, Islamic groups have reasserted old cultural and religious verities. As a consequence, industrialization has not led ineluctably to secularization, nor has economic development always led to the passing of traditional society, as some anticipated in the late 1950s and early 1960s.[18] Instead, in the Muslim world, there has been a massive reaction against secularization. Secular humanism is regarded as an arch-enemy and instrument of Satan not just by fundamentalist Christians, but by fundamentalist Muslims as well.

3. Post-Modernity

There is irony in all of this. Not only has this era been characterized as post-Christian in the sense that Christianity is widely considered irrelevant, but our age is seen as post-scientific and post-humanist. The rationality and humanism that secularized Christian institutions now themselves seem in question. Science has been "relativized as a mode of knowledge" and is regarded as creating more "problems than it can solve."[19] The loss of faith in science has been part of a more fundamental loss of faith in reason itself and in the Enlightenment's commitment to the rational criticism of existing institutions.[20] In post-modern times, "reason is a dropout;" it no longer attends to its post-Renaissance task of providing a unified critical account of human nature and the human condition. As Jean-François Lyotard, the exegete of the post-modern condition, phrased it:

> In contemporary society and culture — postindustrial society, postmodern culture — the question of the legitimation of knowledge is formulated in different terms. The grand narrative has lost its credibility, regardless of what mode of unification it uses, regardless of whether it is a speculative narrative or a narrative of emancipation.[21]

Just as traditional Christianity and Islam have been brought into question by the secular world, and in particular by secular humanism, secular humanism itself has been brought into question. Its general overarching account of reality and values has been subjected to critical reassessment. The very legitimacy of reason's claim to judge the tenets of traditional moral orthodoxies, new cults, or revolutionary political movements has been brought into question. Humanism, indeed the entire task of modernity, can be seen as having lost its original force.

To view this phenomenon within the history of thought, one might use a distinction, shaped by Flavio Biondo (1392–1463), between ancient, medieval, and modern times.[22] The modern period was ushered in by the literary and rational criticism of the Renaissance.[23] Lionel Trilling (1905–1975) considered the modern period as "beginning in the latter part of the eighteenth century and [having] its apogee in the first quarter of the twentieth century."[24] However, following Octavio Paz, the modern age is better characterized as beginning with a "breaking away from Christian society".[25] In this, Paz is closer to the truth. Paz recognizes implicitly the emergence of secular humanist culture as an adversary culture, as one that brought the traditional Christian culture of the Middle Ages into question.[26] After having defined itself against the Christian Middle Ages, the modern age then defined itself in contrast to the ancient vision.[27] Finally, in anticipation of the post-modern age, modernity cut itself off from the past. It was no longer the development out of a tradition but instead something new.[28] Even before the twentieth century, modernism in this sense can be given the characterization that it earned more recently from Marshall Berman as "an unending permanent revolution against the totality of modern existence."[29] However, until the nineteenth century with Protestantism and the twentieth century with Catholicism,[30] Christian culture remained a substantial partner in this adversarial dialogue.

What marks the recent period of modernity is that, in the latter part of the nineteenth and the beginning of the twentieth century, as the cultural hegemony of Christianity collapsed, rational critique lost its substantial traditional target.[31] Bereft of any other significant cultural opponent, it turned against itself.[32] If one regards the post-modern period as having undermined the foundations of rationalism embedded in humanism that have guided us for the last half millennium, then we can see ourselves as looking on a new age in which humanism itself is called into question.[33] The general alienation of art from society[34] and of reason from legitimation[35] tends to uproot the foundations of humanism and to bring all general statements regarding the purposes of society, the meaning of health, and the goals of medicine into question.

In his reflections on the post-modern condition, Ihab Hassan quotes the artist Jean Dubuffet (1901–   ): "I have the impression that a complete liquidation of all the ways of thinking, whose sum constituted what has been called humanism and has been fundamental for our culture since the Renaissance, is now taking place, or at least, going to take place very soon."[36] Hassan characterizes the post-modern condition as springing from the recognition that humanism may no longer be able to play its former cultural role of providing a canonical point of reference. The post-modern age, as a consequence, contrasts starkly with the period between the Renaissance and the end of the progressive era, which focused on man and on the promise of human capacities. In particular, the moral and political catastrophes of the twentieth century present the failure of the modern enterprise in flesh and blood. Strong claims on behalf of reason appear culturally implausible.

> What theorists of the old modern age had to confront were the altogether unexpected disasters of the twentieth century: that after three hundred years of the scientific revolution and in the emergence of rational ethics in European Christendom, Western man in the twentieth century elected instead of an era of

> peace and freedom an orgy of wars, tortures, genocide, suicide, murder, and rapine unparalleled in history.
>
> The old modern age ended in 1914.[37]

The first half of the twentieth century disconfirmed the expectations of reason and progressivism.

On the other hand, the traditional adversarial contrast between secular and religious visions has been muted as the mainline Christian churches of the West have accommodated to the moral sensibilities of the contemporary period (e.g., divorce has been allowed, contraception widely accepted, and female ministers installed). The mainline churches have thus become more concerned with being relevant to the problems of this world (addressing issues such as feminism, sexism, racism, and liberation theology) than addressing the problems of achieving eternal salvation (e.g., preaching hell-fire and damnation or announcing the traditional transcendent truths of Christianity).[38] In a secular world, Secular Humanism does not appear as an enemy to the mildly religious and religion appears to the secular humanist as less of a dangerous superstition in need of rational reformation.[39]

> . . . secular humanism need not be anti-religious in any conscious sense. The aggressive, "secularist" animus of the Enlightenment has given way, in a more pluralistic culture, to philosophical assumptions which weakened religious consciousness not by attacking "religious" modes of thought, but by ignoring them. The traditional imperative to define ultimate reality in supernatural, other-worldly terms, and to ground human systems of knowledge and authority in transcendental principles of one kind or another, has relaxed gradually. Modern preoccupations are less metaphysical, less universal, less abstract. Thus the typical evidence of secularization in a culture based on secular humanism is not a growth of atheism, or even agnosticism, but a general tendency for people ideologically uncommitted on religious issues to become almost entirely alienated from the modes of thought and definitions of reality which have made religiosity explicable and relevant in the past.[40]

These remarks about religion are as true of Secular Humanism or even humanism when it makes special preemptive claims for itself. Humanism itself has been secularized and despoiled of messianic significance.

These changes have taken place along with an abandonment in the academy of the centrality of traditional Western culture and scholarship with their focus on classical languages, classical literature, and a particular tradition of reflections on values and metaphysics. In its place a nascent world tradition has emerged. For example,

> Under the slogan, FOR A NEW ART, FOR A NEW REALITY, the most ancient superstitions have been exhumed, the most primitive rites re-enacted: the rummage for generative forces has set African demon-masks in the temple of the Muses and introduced the fables of Zen and Hasidism into the dialogue of philosophy. Through such dislocations of time and geography the first truly universal tradition has come to light, with world history as its past and requiring a world stage on which to flourish.[41]

Increasingly, there is no unique perspective for critical judgment. An encompassing relativity threatens as a consequence of the failure of the modern rationalist and Enlightenment attempts to step outside of culture, and from beyond culture to criticize and provide it with a rationally justified content. As a result, in the midst of the modern age we have "lost touch with the roots of [our] own modernity."[42] The rupture with our capacities to judge values critically, to assess human purposes, and to make rationally defensible criticisms regarding the human condition, defines the post-modern age and brings humanism, especially secular humanism, into question.

The post-modern age is marked by contrasting forces. There has been a widespread loss of faith in the transcendent as well as in reason, though there remain passionate conflicts among irreconcilable competing moral visions.[43] There has been secularization, but there remains a plurality of faith and moral commitments. There is moral apathy, but there is still intense belief. But in all of this, and most importantly, the possibility of a single morally and intellectually authoritative account of the human condition has been called into question.

4. Bioethics and Secular Humanism

Against these cultural developments, there are major challenges in characterizing a morally canonical policy for health care. Still, one might hope to appeal in some ideologically and culturally neutral fashion to what we share as humans in order to ground a bioethics and a morally justifiable health care policy. The object of this appeal I characterize as secular humanism in the general sense of the attempt to provide (1) a morality for moral strangers without indebtedness to a particular tradition, faith, or ideology, (2) on the basis of rational arguments embedded in a critical account of human nature and the human condition. But, second, given the weakening of traditional understandings of secular humanism, a contemporary account of secular humanism must either sing its own requiem or show how it can survive to serve some of the functions it traditionally claimed. This volume will attempt the latter task. It will show how a coherent understanding of secular humanism can still be articulated so that we can take critical regard of health and medicine. In particular, this work provides a historically embedded account of the possibility of a secular bioethics.[44] It provides a historical perspective on the crisis in culture that requires us to rethink the content of bioethics. It does this by critically examining the possibility of a humanism and the meaning of secularity in the post-modern age.

Bioethics as a field emerged in the 1960s and 1970s, primarily in the United States. It is the attempt critically to assess the significance of medicine in terms of its conceptual and value assumptions. It has included assessments of the concept of health, appraisals of the goals of medicine, explorations of the metaphysical assumptions of traditional medical moral arguments, and attempts to provide the foundations for secularly justifiable health care policies. In the 1980s bioethics as a worldwide phenomenon has taken shape as a part of the broad modern project or assessing culture in terms of reason, and of critically directing biomedical science and biotechnology. Because of its close cultural ties to the traditional endeavors of secular humanism, I shall use the term bioethics in this volume to identify the general critical concerns regarding health and medicine that can be articulated from the standpoint of critical humanist reason.[45]

As will become clear, discussions of humanism are freighted with the ambiguities of the term. Traditionally, "humanism" encompasses (1) concerns with humane or philanthropic actions, (2) the scholarly possession and command of a critical literary tradition, and (3) the development of a moral philosophy grounded in what humans as such can share. This trinity of meanings is recast in the circumstances of the post-modern era and in the context of large-scale states. As a consequence, (1) philanthropy is now primarily realized through welfare systems, within which it is difficult to sustain a sense of fellow feeling or true philanthropy, because, as we will see, there is no shared vision of the good.[46] Indeed, in a tolerant secular pluralist state, philanthropy tends to be transformed into an insurance policy against losses at the natural and social lotteries (e.g., exposures to the risks of health and poverty). In addition, (2) humanism becomes separated from the particular scholarly traditions of the West, which gave it life. The literature of humanism thus becomes a world literature of critical inquiry concerning the nature of man and the human condition that need not be tied to the originative literature of Greece and Rome. Finally, (3) humanism, rather than being a content-full moral philosophy, will have to make do (as we will see) with providing the grammar for the moral discourse of moral strangers. It will show how moral strangers can collaborate peaceably with moral authority, but it will not be able to establish *a priori* what they should talk about or decide to do. But, as such, it will cease to be a humanism and will instead be a general morality that need not be restricted to humans. In the end, all that one can say about the nature of humans with a view to grounding a secular morality will be what can be said about the nature of persons[47] insofar as that nature is the ground of a moral language for moral strangers.

We shall also see that secularity requires tolerance but need not encourage disbelief or be hostile to belief. While Secular Humanism as a particular organization may at times construe itself as in competition with religion, secular humanism as a means for peaceable communication among moral strangers does not presuppose the dissolution of fundamental differences in belief. As we shall see, secular humanism can justify an ecumenical language that does not assume that all will hold the same body of particular beliefs or the same moral perspective — rather to the contrary.

This volume provides an exegesis of the significance of secular humanism for health care policy. Insofar as it reveals the continued viability of secular humanism and its capacities to aid us in achieving a better understanding of the moral significance of health care for moral strangers, it is also a defense of secular humanism. This outcome is not in itself hostile to religion.[48] Instead, it shows the conditions for the possibility of discourse among moral strangers, given (1) the collapse of many of the hopes of the modern age, (2) the persistence of intense belief, and (3) the emergence of widespread indifference to religion and to ultimate values.

5. Pluralism: An Embarrassment of Riches

The world is awash with competing religions, cults, and sects.[49] Anyone seeking salvation has more than enough possibilities from which to choose. Even if one through grace finds a way through this confusion to truth, there is still a multitude of partisans of different religions with which one must deal. Each group has its own understanding of human well-being, of the good life,[50] and of proper health care. Each has its own views on issues of bioethics. The result is an embarrassment of riches. It is like entering an ice cream parlor with a huge selection of flavors, but the choices involve more than matters of taste. One finds mutually exclusive and, indeed, contrary understandings of proper human conduct in health care. It is not at all like diverse flavors one might imagine mixing. As a series of anthropological or sociological studies, the variety and richness are not disturbing: each sectarian bioethics provides an analysis of a particular moral and conceptual perspective on health care shared by an important body of believers. But from a moral and public policy point of view, how does one come to terms with this diversity? With so many contrasting views about what is right to do, how should one act? How could one in principle mediate between such competing viewpoints? It will not do simply to enjoin all to attend the church, synagogue, mosque, or temple of their choice. How does one frame health care policy in the face of such diversity? Where there is no agreement, how does one proceed to agreement? For that matter, what would it mean for a consensus to emerge from such diversity?

The problem is to provide a justification for a way of resolving the moral and public policy controversies occasioned by health care when individuals neither share a particular moral tradition with its commitment to specific moral content nor agree on particular procedures for resolving controversies. If, for example, one is fashioning policy for a hospital that is not allied with any particular faith tradition, how should one adjudicate conflicting views regarding contraception or the definition of death? How should one set policy about the refusal of artificial hydration and nutrition? What should the role of particular traditions be when establishing policies for publicly funded hospitals? For example, is it a good or bad thing to perform a direct abortion to save the life of a mother? Depending on whether one speaks to Roman Catholics or Orthodox Jews, one will get quite different answers.[51]

Outside particular faiths, when faced with the range of possible approaches, it is difficult to know which approach to choose and why. In a society with a plurality of viewpoints (whose institutions are also secular, in the sense that no one viewpoint is established as regnant by appeal to special religious authority or metaphysical considerations), there is the public policy difficulty of establishing a common approach in the face of disputed issues in bioethics.

Secular bioethics (which includes a cluster of investigations of problems in value-theory, metaphysics, the philosophy of biology, and political theory) has been developed to provide the bases for a critical assessment of the concepts of health and disease and of the goals and conduct of health care. The intellectual challenge is to frame a bioethics which can span bioethical discussions engendered within diverse moral communities. This intellectual challenge has practical implications, for as physics is applied in building bridges, moral understandings and authorizations are employed in fashioning public policy. For example, the question of the proper allocation of health care resources is a bioethical question with public policy implications. In the end, public policy will involve the use of coercive state power. One can answer most questions in galactic astronomy without being engaged in moral questions about the proper use of coercive state power. But such is not the case in bioethics, especially secular bioethics, which purports to establish how moral strangers should cooperate over issues in health care. Can one with moral authority fashion public health care policy in a secular, pluralist society?

Pluralism so prevails that we may even doubt whether we can in principle share a common, concrete sense of rationality, not to mention a common sense of grace. The fashioning of a common moral discourse is one of the most serious challenges of the post-modern era. How can public policy in general, or health care policy in particular, be developed with moral authority when there is often little consensus on the meaning of life and death, or the final purposes and significance of human endeavors? It is here that the question of secular humanism arises in earnest: is there enough that we share simply as humans, simply as persons, so that we can resolve disputes with moral authority, even when we do not share a particular faith tradition? The search for that communality, for what we share as a moral foundation, without appeal to religious premises, is the task of secular humanism, or, for that matter, of secular moral philosophy and bioethics. Properly understood, secular humanism embraces the traditional endeavor of Western moral philosophy: to establish a general moral framework by appeal to reason.

Secular humanism as the foundation for a morality of moral strangers is also allied to natural law. As such, it has roots in the Roman Empire, which confronted the challenge of administering an empire that incorporated diverse races, religions, and cultural groups. The Romans drew on a Greek distinction between positive law and what has come to be known as natural law.[52] This distinction had been elaborated by a number of Greek Stoic and Roman thinkers such as Chrysippus (279–206 B.C.) and Cicero (106–43 B.C.). These reflections led the Romans to speak of a *jus naturale* and a *jus gentium*, both in contrast to the positive law of Rome. The *jus naturale* was what reason taught all animals, including humans.[53] It was supplemented by the *jus gentium*, the law of nations, which spanned races and nations.[54] The idea was that reason could disclose criteria for laws, and that one could identify the idiosyncrasy of one's own law by comparing it with the law of nations. More fundamentally, one came to presuppose a morally binding sense of law that transcended particular traditions and groups. This view is underscored by Gaius in the second century (A.D. 161) in his *Institutes*. ". . . [T]he law that natural reason establishes among all mankind is followed by all peoples alike, and is called *ius gentium* as being the law observed by all mankind."[55] The point is that a tradition of natural law emerged that sought to meet the very commonsensical and practical need of providing an intellectual foundation for uniting an empire spanning individuals of diverse religious and cultural traditions.

After the fall of the Roman Empire in the West, Roman Catholic moral theology in great measure absorbed the natural law tradition. Much of natural law exegesis and development, as a result, has taken on a sectarian cast. Yet in its original inspiration and goals, natural law theory was meant to reach across to all in a catholic fashion by appealing to the reason and nature all share in common. It was in this sense secular. Because it was regarded as founded in our nature as humans, it was humanist. Secular humanism in general, and secular humanist approaches to bioethics in particular, attempt to recapture this universalist sense of natural law. Secular humanism can be recognized as responding to an intellectual challenge analogous to that faced by the legal scholars of the Roman Empire, as well as by the apologists of the Catholic Church: the challenge to make its case to individuals of different traditions who do not endorse the same sense of grace or history.

6. Towards a Common Bioethics

Does the very character of moral, philosophical, or religious traditions and visions make it impossible for moral strangers to share a common moral understanding? Is the very meaning of a direct abortion (i.e., the intentional intervention to destroy a fetus) dependent on the religious or moral vision in which it is considered? Is it in principle possible for individuals to resolve a controversy over the moral significance of abortion if they disagree (1) about whether the fetus is a person morally on a par with adult humans or is a mere instance of human biological life morally on a par with other biological life of the same actual functional ability, (2) about whether the meaning of rights and duties is independent of or dependent on consequences, and (3) about whether there is a deity who cares about fetuses or no God at all? Will moral controversies not appear radically different, depending on the moral vision within which each controversy is articulated? Can individuals who face each other from different sides of a controversy characterize what is at stake in sufficiently commensurable terms so that they can be said to participate in one controversy, rather than two controversies conjoined by a furor?

Traditions or moral visions, by binding people over time in a common understanding, separate them from others — Christians from non-Christians, Catholics from non-Catholics, Democrats from Republicans, Marxists from Social Democrats, Social Democrats from Christian Democrats, deontologists from utilitarians, deists from atheists, and egalitarians from defenders of social difference — so that they come to speak different moral languages, making communication difficult (perhaps in some areas impossible). We live in a world fragmented because of the myriad differences in metaphysical and axiological understandings, which lie at the bases of the exemplars and recipes that guide and separate individuals as participants in different moral visions. Consider a controversy between defenders of an egalitarian health care system who deny the existence of inalienably private property and those who affirm stark differences in health care distributions because of irremediable differences in private possessions and because liberty is held to be more important than equality — the groups will be separated not only by divergent accounts of property rights, but by divergent views of the proper ranking of societal goals.

The question is whether we can in principle share enough simply as moral strangers to resolve moral controversies on rational grounds. And if we do share enough, in what would that communality lie? Would it simply be another tradition? And if so, would it then imperiously (but perhaps quite correctly) claim itself to be the one true tradition and others to be only partial or distorted understandings? Or is there a vantage point from which we can cooperate without commitment to yet another concrete or content-full tradition?

Modern Western philosophy has generally attempted to articulate a rationally justified viewpoint without appeal to particular intuitions, religious premises, or moral assumptions. Modern Western philosophers have generally striven to state that which people share simply as humans or persons and to make that the basis for ethics and political theory. The philosophical aspiration has been to transcend particular religions and ideologies, so as to articulate a morally canonical and rationally justified vision for humans as such. From the point of view of a rational morality, if one can state that to which humans or persons should be committed as rational humans or persons, then those who refuse to embrace the conclusions of such successful arguments can be dismissed from rational controversies. After all, if they are rational, they are by their nature committed to the conclusions stated. If they refuse to act rationally, then they have no rational grounds for protest if forced to conform with the lineaments of rational deportment and public policy. What is imposed on them with rational warrant will not be alien to their true selves as humans or rational beings. The traditional Western philosophical approach has thus aspired to establishing a moral account against which there can be no rational protest and the imposition of which would not be alien to the humans or persons involved.

This appeal to rationality in order concurrently to establish morality and morally to authorize public policy is not implausible. A rational perspective is not just one perspective among various alternative possibilities, as an Aristotelian perspective is vis-a-vis a Stoic perspective. Rather, a rational perspective is that which can be defended on the basis of general principles. If one rejects a rational perspective for the resolution of controversies, one can still appeal to force, prayer, inducements, or seduction. But one will not be able to explain why any of these alternative approaches is correct without giving reasons on its behalf. And if one says that one's own sense of rationality is as good as anyone else's, only different, then one can be asked for the reasons that support such a view. And if one attempts to reply, then one will be committed to the terms set by reason in general, insofar as one attempts to give reasons to persons in general. Reason is the forum for all rational questions. Of course, one may in part step back from advancing conclusive rational arguments. Instead, one may say that "the difference between us lies in the fact that God in his grace has given me the true Faith." Or one might say, "compare the moral visions that constitute different traditions, and you will finally understand that the Southern tradition is the most excellent."[56] However, such justifications will not provide warrants, justified in terms that must claim the concurrence of rational moral strangers, for coercive public policy.

An aspiration to a canonical, rational account has characterized secular bioethics. The literature of secular bioethics has for the most part been devoted to establishing what rational men and women should hold to be the case regarding issues such as abortion, euthanasia, and justice in health care.[57] There have been arguments framed in general rational terms about whether fetuses are persons.[58] Governmental commissions have issued documents purporting to show, on the basis of rational arguments, that equity in health care cannot mean equality.[59] Even general ethical guidelines have been elaborated by governmental commissions in order to guide legislative and administrative law.[60] Secular bioethics has been harnessed for the development of a moral foundation for secular public policy.

The secular philosophical approach to issues in bioethics has in general not been intolerant of special religious or cultural traditions, as long as the special claims of such traditions are meant to bind only their own adherents.[61] This toleration has reflected the West's traditional attempt to harmonize religion and reason on the model that grace and special revelation can provide premises that cannot be shown to be false (only beyond rational demonstration).[62] Moreover, the differences among religious and other moral traditions invite the articulation of a secular bioethics. The major practical interest in secular humanism is a perspective from which to mediate in controversies when participants in a health care system are separated by faith, cultural, or moral traditions so that they do not share a common moral vision.

The question of the status of religious bioethics can be viewed from the perspective of a secular bioethics so as to contrast two quite different ways in which a secular humanist perspective can entail consequences for the understanding of health and medicine. The first is secular bioethics as a rival to other bioethics. The second is secular bioethics as a mediator among rival bioethics. These two senses will be explored further in Chapters IV and V. Here it is enough to note that these senses are related to the contrast between Secular Humanism as an organized movement and secular humanism as a body of images and ideas. Secular Humanism tends to include well-articulated, content-full moral claims, but secular humanism need not. However, secular humanism can also embrace a content-full moral view with content-full public policy implications and so enter the field as yet one more moral tradition. After all, secular philosophy can in general be understood as part of the cultural inheritance of humanism and many secular philosophies have robust implications regarding health care policy.[63]

Two senses of a secular bioethics can be contrasted in terms of their commitment to the discoverability of a content-full morality: secular bioethics as a rival to and possible replacement for religious bioethics versus secular bioethics as a neutral framework through which exponents of various religious bioethics can negotiate. The first, in being committed to the possibility of discovering the content for a secular bioethics, is potentially antagonistic to special religious, moral, or philosophical traditions. If there is a rationally defensible and discoverable content-full understanding of morality, it should provide the basis for health care policy. For example, if one can discover the characteristics of the proper content-full policy for the use of prenatal diagnosis (e.g., encouraging its use conjoined with selective abortion), then one is morally obliged to encourage its use and to attempt to reform the views of members of particular moral traditions opposing its use. The first sense of a secular bioethics is thus committed to replacing non-rationally defensible rivals. The second, in contrast, is accepting of the diversity of religious, moral, and philosophical traditions as long as they are peaceable. A diversity of content-full understandings of morality must be accepted because the full content of a moral vision cannot be discovered by appeal to reason alone.

The second sense of secular bioethics does not constitute a complete moral tradition over against already existing traditions.[64] It provides a neutral standpoint to which individuals from various traditions can appeal. It stands in dialectical relationship with particular concrete moral traditions. On the one hand, disputes among members of different content-full traditions require a secular perspective for their resolution; on the other hand, a secular perspective cannot provide all the content required for a complete moral life or for the actual framing of actual health care policy. In short, this second sense of a secular bioethics and health care policy does not possess sufficient content-full metaphysical and axiological commitments to collide with the metaphysical and axiological commitments of many established religious and moral traditions.

These two different senses of a secular bioethics can be contrasted not just in terms of the content-full character of their metaphysical and axiological commitments but also in terms of the social structures they involve. If a secular bioethics (i.e., secular bioethics in the first sense: secular bioethics as a rival to other traditions) can in principle deliver a content-full morality to guide the fine-grained character of health care policy, then all should (as far as is morally feasible) be embedded in the social structures that are entailed. The social structure to which one is implicitly committed as a rational being should then be realized, guided by a content-full notion of proper conduct. The second sense of bioethics (i.e., secular bioethics as a neutral framework) will be less ambitious because of a greater skepticism about the possibility of imposing a content-full bioethics on moral strangers with moral authority. Still, even the second approach will share the presumption of an implicit social structure defined by the character of individuals as humans or persons. It is only if there is some implicit social structure that moral strangers are not irremediably total strangers. If what moral strangers share commits them only to a modest content, or only to some general procedural constraints when they interact, then traditional moral communities and their bioethics need not be abandoned when one appeals to a secular bioethics. The second sense of bioethics (i.e., secular bioethics as a neutral framework) will become relevant only when moral strangers meet.

In anticipation of arguments yet to be developed, it is the second sense of secular bioethics, and of secular humanist appreciations of health and medicine, that will be shown to be central to understanding health care in the post-modern age. After all, the central challenge of post-modern philosophy is to secure some framework through which moral strangers can negotiate and establish common moral undertakings. As we will see in more detail in Chapters 4 and 5, it is only with the philosophical conceits of the modern age that one could have hoped to discover the rational basis for a secular bioethics that could possess a rational warrant to displace its rivals.

II The Secular as a Neutral Framework

1. The Concept of the Secular

The Roman Catholic doxology ends *"per omnia saecula saeculorum,"* recalling that "secular" classically referred to that which took place over a long period of time. It referred especially to the secular games that were held only once in a great interval, ideally every one hundred ten years.[1] The *saeculum civile* was set at a hundred years, while the *saeculum naturale* was set at one hundred ten years; it was the latter that was to govern the dates of the games. A *saeculum* thus indicated an era similar to a century. The interval was perhaps originally seen as also marking the maximum human lifespan and therefore the full scope of one generation, one of the original meanings of *saeculum*. The term also identified the cohort of individuals born at one time, as well as a breed, a race, the contemporary age, or a period of human history (e.g., the Golden Age).[2] For the discussion here, it is important to note that the word came to designate temporal or profane matters, the sphere of human life, the world.

The secular powers for the Christians were the powers of the Roman Empire, which were first hostile and then later themselves nominally Christian. Initially, the Christians, like Romans generally, thought of the Empire as enduring: it existed for this world, even if man's ultimate destiny was with another. Consider, for example, the glowing account of Rome's role in divine providence given by the Christian poet Aurelius Clemens Prudentius (A.D. 348–c.410).

> Shall I tell you, Roman, what cause it was that so exalted your labors, what it was that nursed your glory to such a height of fame that it has put rein and bridle on the world? God, wishing to bring into partnership peoples of different speech and realms of

> discordant manners, determined that all the civilized world should be harnessed to one ruling power and bear gentle bonds in harmony under the yoke, so that love of their religion should hold men's hearts in union . . . Regions far apart, shores separated by sea, now meet together in appearing before one common court of law, in the way of trade in the products of their crafts they gather to one thronged market . . . Rome without peace finds no favour with Thee; and it is the supremacy of Rome, keeping down disorders here or there by the awe of her sovereignty, that secures the peace, so that Thou hast pleasure in it.[3]

As a consequence, the in many ways other-worldly Jerome (A.D. 345–420) cried in his monastery in Bethlehem when he heard of Alaric's sacking of Rome (A.D. 410),[4] for since Virgil's time the city had been synonymous with the societal matrix within which even Christians saw themselves working out their temporal destinies. They were the structures of this age, even if they would one day pass away.[5]

Augustine of Hippo (A.D. 354–430), who lived through the period of the sacking of Rome, forged his metaphors of the city of God and the city of man against the harsh realities of a weakened, failing Empire. Unlike Aristotle, Augustine did not see man as essentially or naturally political, but rather as social. Political structures were necessary, given the fall of man, and would not have existed, had Adam not sinned.[6] Also, the secular world was not the same as the city of man. The city of God, the community of souls dedicated to God who would ultimately be saved, and the city of man, those dedicated to this world who would ultimately be damned, lived together within a secular structure open and beneficial to both. The nominally Christian empire was not the city of man, but neither was it the city of God. *Tertium datur*: the secular city was a neutral place where saint and sinner could meet.

The secular world, the *saeculum*, was the world of ordinary times, not of eternity. The secular authorities, the temporal authorities (as opposed to those that represent the eternal structures of God and the Age that will be after the Second Coming), were those that managed the problems of this age, and as such were useful for saint and sinner alike. Secular came also to refer to the world in general, that enduring external reality within which men and women of all traditions can meet. To be secular was to be in the world, in the fleshy fabric of everyday existence. Of course, one was not to conform to the world (to the *saeculum*), because it was characterized by a range of seductive elements (*et nolite conformari huic saeculo*: Romans 12:2). Yet for those who would not live in monasteries or become hermits, it was necessary to live in the world, within the structures of the age.

In the Middle Ages, the contrast was between the ecclesiastical and the secular powers, both of which were Christian. In the West, the secular authorities were paradigmatically those of the Holy Roman Empire of the German Nation, originally authorized by the Pope and in the end theoretically subject to his authority.[7] In the East, the empire continued until New Rome, Constantinople, fell on May 29, 1453, when Mohammed II defeated Constantine XI. In either case, as with the old Roman Empire, the secular authorities were responsible for the everyday political administration of the lives of citizens, now primarily Christian. The contrast between the ecclesiastical and secular spheres remained, with the Church giving direction to the secular powers. Thus, one finds the Fourth Lateran Council in 1215 providing instructions to the "*saeculares potestates*," the secular powers, on, among other things, the prosecution of heretics and the election of bishops.[8] The secular powers were involved in the wide range of matters that believers and non-believers, saints and sinners, shared.

2. Seven Senses of Secularity

Out of this history, a number of senses of the "secular" and of such allied terms as "secularization" and "secularism" have emerged, each in its own way contrasting a worldly with a religious perspective. "Secular," "secularization," and "secularize" each in different ways draws on notions of rendering worldly something religious or of separating the worldly from the spiritual or ecclesiastical. Seven clusters of meaning are worth underscoring: (1) the secular as a morally neutral framework through which believers and non-believers can collaborate one with another; (2) secular as identifying clerics or the property of clerics who are not bound by religious vows that place them under the rule of an order; (3) secularization as the process by which a member of a religious order, or the property of a member of a religious order, becomes a secular cleric, or a thing becomes the property of a secular cleric; (4) secularization as the process by which the title to church property is transferred to public or private hands; (5) secularization as the attempt to limit or annul the powers, immunities, and influence of the Church; (6) Secularism as a movement aimed at establishing secular societal structures (i.e., structure neutral to religion); and (7) secularization as the process by which a culture's or a society's sense of the religious or the transcendent is transtormed into an immanent, worldly province of meaning.

The first sense is found in the notion of the *seculares potestas*. To be secular is to be of the world, of the fleshy fabric of everyday existence. The secular identifies the worldly structures we all share, as opposed to the spiritual structures we can share only by special grace. One finds this usage in the early sixth century in a constitution of the emperor Justinian (who reigned A.D. 527–565), where reference is made to renouncing the world (*saeculo renuntiare*).[9] It is this first sense of the secular that is most important for this volume. It is this sense of secular that governs in "secular bioethics," a bioethics accessible to peaceable individuals independently of their special moral, ideological or faith traditions. It is also in this sense that the American government represents the emergence of a secular regime, a regime that is neutral in its regard of the various religious sects within its territory.[10] Though in many ways the United States fail to have a truly secular government, still they provide a neutral framework through which both religious and non-religious individuals can collaborate.[11]

The second sense, which opposes the secular to the spiritual, does so within the confines of Roman Catholic canon law.[12] Here secular refers to clerics who live outside the vows and rules of a religious order. The contrast is between *regularis* (i.e., a cleric who is of a religious order, that is, under a religious rule) and *secularis* (i.e., a cleric who is of this world, that is, who lives outside of the monastery, ungoverned by the rules of a religious order). Secular clergy are immersed in the things of this age, of this generation, even though they may in a general sense be very religious (i.e., they are in the world, but not of it). It is only that secular clergy are not specially separated from the world by the rules of a religious order.

The third sense derives its meaning from the second. It is a term to identify a process in Roman Catholic canon law: the process by which a religious cleric is rendered a secular cleric (or the property of religious clerics is given to secular clerics).[13] In particular, secularization relieves a cleric who is a member of a particular religious order from the special vows and obligations of that order. Somewhat loosely, one might also refer to a priest being secularized who moves from his monastery to become a bishop and therefore lives outside the monastic life of his order. Secularization must be contrasted with one meaning of laicization: the process by which a Roman Catholic cleric is released from all duties and obligations as a cleric and is reduced to the status of a layman (e.g., a secularized Dominican priest is still a priest, but no longer bound by the rules of the Dominican order; a laicized Dominican priest is dispensed from the obligations of a priest and may enter the world and marry).

Secularization has also been used to identify various steps in a legal process that transformed Christian Europe into contemporary Europe by seizing the extensive property holdings of the Catholic Church. This fourth sense is a worldly political one. The Catholic Church brought considerable property with it into the Middle Ages. Moreover, the established Church of the Middle Ages (i.e., the Catholic Church) and its clerics were immune from the laws of particular countries.[14] They were bound first by canon law, though they could be handed over to secular authorities for punishment. As an international tax-exempt organization that received compulsory contributions in addition to numerous gifts, the Church was able to amass very extensive holdings, through which it engaged in numerous activities, including the provision of charity and education. Given the Church's affluence, there was always a significant interest on the part of temporal or secular powers in acquiring some of the Church's holdings for secular uses. This interest was pronounced as early as the eighth century.[15]

During and after the Reformation, and with the formation of the Church of England, secular interest in Church property had dramatic manifestation in the large-scale seizure of the holdings of monasteries, convents, and other Church institutions.[16] The sixteenth and seventeenth centuries were marked by the taking of Church property (e.g., by the Treaty of Passau [1552] and the Peace of Augsburg [1555]) and by attempts at restoration (e.g., the Imperial Edict of Restitution of 1629). Even in Catholic countries, the argument was made that in times of necessity a sovereign could use (under a number of restrictions) Church property in order to defend the realm against non-believers.[17]

The conversion of Church properties into state possessions took on its current designation (i.e., secularization) on May 8, 1646, during discussions in Münster preparatory to the *Pax Westfalica*, which treaty in 1648 brought an end to the Thirty Years' War. It would appear that the term secularization (i.e., the term in the German language) was then used for the first time to convey the sense of the Latin *incorporatio bonorum ecclesiasticorum* (the incorporation by the state of ecclesiastical goods). The point at issue was the transfer of Catholic Church property into Evangelical hands. The term appears to have been suggested by the French.[18]

Not all support for secularization was adversarial or aimed at economic advantage. Many devout Catholics regarded the involvement of the Church in secular affairs since Emperor Constantine (324–337) as a moral error. One of the most interesting reflections in this vein was developed by the Landgraf Ernst von Hessen-Rheinfels (1623–1693) in 1656. The Landgraf argued that the worldliness of the ruling bishop-princes of Germany conflicted with the primarily spiritual mission of the Church. To remedy the corruption from luxury and temporal power he proposed a secularization (more particularly, a divestiture by the Church of much worldly property and power) to the benefit of society.[19] In so doing, he anticipated, however inchoately, the virtues of distinguishing and separating ecclesiastical and secular power, a distinction that underlies the sense of secular in this volume's use of "secular humanism" and "secular bioethics."

If the United States represent the emergence of a secular political compact in the first sense of secularity, then the French Republic that came into being on September 22, 1792, was secular in the fifth sense, that of being hostile to the established Christian religion, in particular the Catholic Church. Even before the Republic, the traditional Church was replaced by a Constitutional Church through the Civil Constitution of the Clergy (July 1790). The new Church was placed under state authority and the clergy paid through state funds partly in recompense for the seizure of Church property and partly in order to ensure control. The secularity of the Republic was particularly expressed in the establishment of the Cult of Reason in autumn, 1793.[20] The cult's hostility to Catholicism was demonstrated in the looting of church vestments, vessels, and ornaments, and in such de-Christianization ceremonies as the Feast of Reason held in the Cathedral of Notre Dame de Paris on November 9, 1793. The Republic attempted to remove, as far as possible, the influence of the Church from French life. This included, among other things, establishing marriage as a civil act, encouraging the Catholic clergy to marry, and suppressing religious orders.

The actions of the Republic had some precedents in European history. In 1438 a national council assembled at Bourges, France, in order to limit a wide range of assorted papal prerogatives. Its proclamation of "Gallican Liberties" became a theme in the subsequent history of French church-state relationships. Gallicanism had its analogues in Austrian Josephism, named after Emperor Josef II of Austria (ruled 1765–1790), who attempted in 1790 to interpose his sovereignty between that of the bishops of Austria and that of Rome. In addition, Josef II initiated his own secularization, closing up to 700 religious houses and limiting the number of religious clerics allowed to reside in Austria.

Still, the French Republic and the First Empire were unique in the high-scale drama they engendered in the conflict between Church and civil authorities. In February 1798 the French arranged the proclamation of a Roman Republic, and in the subsequent year Pius VI (1775–1799) was carried to France as a captive, where he died. Then his successor, Pius VII (1800–1823), was persuaded to travel to Paris in order to crown Napoleon Emperor (though Napoleon rebuffed the Pope and crowned himself on December 2, 1804). The drama of papal abduction was repeated again in May, 1809, when the Papal States were assimilated into the French Empire. The doors of the Pope's apartments were broken down on July 6, and Pope VII was taken as a prisoner to Paris. Against this background, the traditional relations of the secular and spiritual were shattered as Napoleon imposed his political and legal reforms on the Europe he conquered.

Concurrently with and influenced by the events in France, the old Holy Roman Empire experienced secularization. As the Empire entered the nineteenth century, it was still marked by a number of territories ruled by sovereign bishops. These episcopal principalities appeared to reformers and German nationalists as relics of the past and stumbling blocks to modernization. In their organization and structure they carried much of the Middle Ages with them and were major obstacles to a secular political structure in Germany. This entire structure was swept away as one of the last acts of the Empire. An extraordinary *Reichsdeputation* was assembled on August 24, 1802, to compensate German sovereigns who had lost territory to the French on the west bank of the Rhine. The *Reichsdeputationshauptschluss* dissolved the remaining episcopal principalities and in 1803 gave their holdings as compensation and as spoils to other German sovereigns.[21] In many Catholic areas an iconoclasm or *Bildersturz* ensued, somewhat as had occurred after the beginning of the Reformation with the plunder of churches and the destruction of art. The impact on Catholic charitable and educational institutions was dramatic. The number of Catholic theological faculties was reduced significantly. There were acts of supreme indifference to cultural treasures. For example, the cathedral of Freising came into the hands of a butcher, and monastic libraries were sold by weight as cheesepaper.[22] The result was a profound dislocation of the traditional expectations from the Church and a secularization of educational and charitable undertakings.[23]

Secularization in this context was a robustly adversarial response to the political, moral, and economic domination of the Church. For many, secularization was experienced as a liberation from the past and as a realization of the modern age. Secularization in this adversarial sense incorporates the more neutral sense of secularization (i.e., as the seizure of Church property *simpliciter*; see sense 4 above) within a frankly anti-clerical program of removing or radically diminishing the influence of the Church. Secularization in this sense has occurred in many countries, including the Soviet Union and Mexico. This anti-clerical sense of secularization is often captured by the term laicism.[24] Laicism (*laicisme*) became a part of French cultural debates especially after 1879, in the political discussions regarding the removal of all church influence from French schools. Thus, Jules Ferry (1832–1893) laicized the French schools in 1886.[25] It is important to note that laicization carries meanings and connotations that range from a commitment to extirpating the cultural influences of the church to an attempt to create a separation of church and state in which societal undertakings, such as public schools, are devoid of any commitment to any particular religion, as in the United States.[26] In its more adversarial forms, laicism captures much of the spirit of Gallicanism and Josephism. In other forms it is equivalent to the first sense of secularity.

In the course of the 19th century, the meaning of "secular" developed under the influence of various cultural and political movements, which were aimed at the liberation of societal and political structures from the influence of religion, especially established religion. In the English-speaking world the most notable example of this sense of secularity (the sixth in my list) was shaped by George Jacob Holyoake (1817–1906) in 1849.[27] Holyoake, following a long philosophical tradition, argued that it is possible to base morality on concerns regarding the well-being of men in this life without any consideration of God or immortality, without addressing the claims of either theists or atheists. He wished to craft what was tantamount to a morality for moral strangers, or at least for those who do not agree about the existence of God and the significance of religion.[28] In this respect he elaborated some of the implications of the first sense of secular. But he did so against the dramatic events of secularization that had occurred in the previous three quarters of a century on the Continent.

Through *The Reasoner*, a magazine he established in 1846, as well as through other publications, he fashioned a social movement he termed "Secularism."[29] Holyoake hoped to employ a non-controversial term to unite free-thinkers and others interested in working for the general material good of citizens and society. He gave the following characterization of Secularism:

> Secularism is the study of promoting human welfare by material means — measuring human welfare by the utilitarian rule, and making the service of others a duty of life . . . inculcating the practical sufficiency of natural morality apart from Atheism, Theism, or Christianity . . . Secularism is a series of principles intended for the guidance of those who find Theology indefinite, or inadequate, or deem it unreliable. It replaces theology, which mainly regards life as a sinful necessity, as a scene of tribulation through which we pass to a better world. Secularism rejoices in this life, and regards it as the sphere of those duties which educate men to fitness for any future and better life, should such transpire.[30]

As this passage shows, Holyoake's interest ranged from supporting a neutral this-worldly understanding of human well-being to a somewhat partisan, mildly anti-religious moral vision which he incarnated in his quasi-political movement.[31] The first charmed even some theists; the second led to attempts to form a "secular guild."[32] It was the second that conveyed a sectarian connotation to the term "secular," a connotation it previously did not possess. This sectarian character was heightened by associates of Holyoake who were outspoken atheists. This sense, with its critical stance vis-a-vis religious belief, resonates with many of the sentiments that drive Secular Humanism and Secular bioethics.

There is a final sense of secularity, in particular of secularization, as the retreat of religious significance from the key symbols and social structures of a culture.[33] Secularization as a social phenomenon and as an object of sociological study is both complex and controversial. In order better to manage the ambiguities, Larry Shiner has proposed five different construals of secularization as a sociological phenomenon:

1. "Secularization . . . as the decline of religion,"
2. "secularization . . . as conformity with the world,"

3. "secularization . . . as the desacralization of the world,"
4. "secularization . . . as the disengagement of society from religion," and
5. "secularization . . . as the transposition of beliefs and patterns of behavior from the 'religious' to the 'secular' sphere."[34]

This classification displays a rich fabric of interweaving social changes. Even where some characterizations of secularization may be controversial, such disputes themselves confirm the ambiguity of the contemporary religious condition.

In *The Secular City*, Harvey Cox characterizes secularization as "the liberation of man from religious and metaphysical tutelage, the turning of his attention away from other worlds and toward this one."[35] Elements of secularization have been integral to the modern vision, in terms both of philosophy and of science.[36] With the modern age, Europe reoriented its culture and social structures from religious and transcendent goals to worldly ones.[37] In part, this was a reaction to the religious wars on the Continent and in England during the seventeenth century. In addition, from Thomas Hobbes (1588–1679) to Immanuel Kant (1724–1804) and Adam Smith (1723–1790),[38] major thinkers and social theorists were only tangentially concerned with the theological interests that had structured the Middle Ages. The result was the fashioning of a secular cultural understanding, within which the concerns of this world, not the next, became more prominent. Each of these changes contributed to a process through which the established Christian religion of Europe was marginalized.

This marginalization was most pronounced with the weakening of the Catholic Church's influence as a result of the French Revolution and the German Secularization of 1803. Here, again, we find that secularization was first directed to the Catholic Church, which was *de facto* and *de jure* the established religion of Europe for 1200 years. However, as Protestant churches became established in their own right, they came under the shadow of this history and were in their own ways subject to nearly the full range of secularization. Moreover, secularization in both Catholic and Protestant countries was not just directed against the political and financial power of the Churches, but against their cultural centrality. An established religion centers a culture on a language so that the onus is not on the believer but on the non-believer. When religious symbols are integral to a society's established moral language and symbols, the religious symbols command the culture without any presupposition being made about depth or sincerity of belief. As a result, believers find themselves in a cultural and linguistic environment where their sacral language of expression is not deviant or exotic. Secularization is thus often best appreciated in terms of the changes in the centrality and significance of religious structures and symbols in officially endorsed spheres of a culture.

The secularization of Church institutions and property in France and Germany, as well as movements of a utilitarian and positivist variety in both England and the Continent, generated a language of secular social concern, often expressed in utilitarian terms, that was innocent of a religious valence. Holyoake's Secularism is but one example of the wide range of movements that framed the progressive and revolutionary sentiments of the nineteenth century.[39] Here one would need to include Karl Marx (1818–1883) and his followers, who came to construe religion as a form of false consciousness born of man's social alienation. Religion in this light was not seen as a source of transcendent truths but as a fully immanent cultural phenomenon open to scientific study. Secularization as a social phenomenon came to be associated with modernity, industrialization, urbanization, and with the two concomitants of the last, anonymity and mobility.[40] The contemporary secular city is the outcome of a complex interplay of ideas and social structures.

As the result of these changes, the traditional morality and usages of the Judeo-Christian heritage were no longer sufficient to the moral needs of modern men and women. This was expressed in the Catholic Church by modernism, in Judaism by the Reform Movement, and in Protestantism by an emphasis on the social gospel. Traditional orthodox beliefs were no longer acceptable to a wide range of individuals.[41] As Emile Durkheim phrased it, "We can no longer impassionate ourselves for the principles in the name of which Christianity recommended to masters that they treat their slaves humanely, and, on the other hand, the idea which it has formed of human equality and fraternity seems to us today to leave too large a place for unjust inequalities."[42] In appreciation of this secularization, Durkheim added, "the old gods are growing old or already dead, and others are not yet born."[43] Similar observations were made by Max Weber (1864–1910), who sketched the secular function of religion at the beginning of the twentieth century.[44] Indeed, by the end of the nineteenth and the beginning of the twentieth century, there was an appreciation that the established Christian sects of Europe were undergoing decay,[45] that in structure and belief they were being rendered worldly,[46] and that the appreciation of history had not been religious for a long time.[47] Moreover, the basis for peace that had in the past been sought through the Papacy now was sought in fully secular terms through political alliances.[48] For that matter, justice was now construed through a social gospel that did not depend on the transcendent claims of religion.

These processes of secularization have shaped contemporary health care institutions. The great preponderance of health care is now delivered outside of institutions directly controlled by religious groups. A well-articulated language of secular moral and legal analysis has developed to serve as the basis for the secular discussion of health and medicine. Health, disease, medical care and bioethics can all be analysed and discussed without reference to religious or transcendent goals or values. Contemporary bioethics is in large measure the product of secular forces, even when it does not recognize itself as such. In Chapter IV and especially Chapter V, the task will be to characterize a bioethics that takes seriously its secular nature.

3. The Secular as a Neutral Moral Framework for Health Care

Against this history of the seizure of Church property, the annulling of Church privileges, and the attenuation of religious faith, all of which have been placed under the rubric of secularization, one can understand why "secular" and its derivatives are seen to have an anti-religious valence by many believers. The forces of secularization have removed not just the Roman Catholic Church but religion generally from the privileged positions it traditionally possessed in Western European life. Even a defense of secularity as a neutral moral framework is antagonistic to many of the traditional privileges of religion in the West, which have included the definition of the meaning of good public morals, which definition has had an immense influence on the law. Moreover, to seek a secular moral language for moral strangers is to endorse a moral sphere beyond the traditional religious mores of the West. However inescapable a neutral secular bioethics may be, it is still a challenge to the ways in which mores and moral reflection have traditionally been understood.

Despite our rich fabric of contemporary usages, a dimension of the medieval contrast between the religious and the secular has maintained its currency. The secular allows us to distinguish between those spheres of political and moral concern that must be articulated in terms of special articles of belief or gifts of grace, and those that identify the worldly fabric that believers and non-believers, men and women of all traditions, can share and understand in common. We distinguish, for example, between a religious hospital and one with only secular concerns. Holyoake recognized this when he distinguished between the secular and his sectarian understanding of Secularism. For example, in speaking of secular education, he argued that:

> Secular education is by some confounded with Secularism, whereas the distinction between them is very wide. Secular education simply means imparting Secular knowledge separately — by itself, without admixture of Theology with it. The advocate of Secular education may be, and generally is, also an advocate of religion . . .[49]

In this volume, unless I explicitly state to the contrary, I will use "secular" as Holyoake does in the phrase "secular education," not as the term is developed under his rubric of Secularism, because the latter constituted a particular philosophical sect with a particular view of the good life. I will use "secular" in a way that incorporates part of Holyoake's intentions, namely, to identify what is open to all, independently of a particular moral or religious tradition, but not in explicit opposition to religion. This sense is embodied in a secular health care policy that incorporates no hostility to particular religious views.

The distinction between the religious and the secular is essential to ethics in general and to health care policy and bioethics in particular. To apply Augustine's metaphor somewhat recast, the various religious traditions provide different accounts of ethics for the city of God. Or rather, they provide competing views of the city of God and the health care policy and bioethics it requires. Again, the question is whether one can identify and characterize a secular structure, not a city of man destined for damnation, but a neutral structure, which believers and non-believers, as well as believers of different sorts, can use in common, especially in the case of health care. But then the problem arises of giving moral content to policies that govern secular health care institutions. For example, how ought one to justify rules for conduct in a secular, as opposed to a religious, hospital? To what kind of moral standards should a hospital be held if it belongs to no particular moral tradition and serves physicians and patients from diverse faith traditions, as well as those who belong to no religious tradition at all? Or more generally, how does one fashion a secular policy for health care delivery?

4. The Yuppie as Prophet of a Secular Tradition for Health Care

The problem of reconciling conflicting bioethics embedded in different faith traditions may be easier than first anticipated. Over against the plurality of competing faith traditions, there is now also an established secular social matrix in terms of which to assess the role of a secular bioethics. A secular bioethics must be placed vis-a-vis the secularity of the age, not just against the plurality of concrete, transcendently based understandings of health and medicine that derive from the various faith traditions. Though a secular bioethics will have its rationally justifiable character in independence of contemporary secularity, the full social significance of secular bioethics can only be appreciated in terms of what is a *de facto* general secular moral tradition or vision. Secular bioethics as a social phenomenon is not just a way of spanning the plurality of religiously-based medical moral traditions, it is also an expression of the secularity of post-modern times.

In the modern West with its ecumenism and general disbelief, contrasts between moral friends and strangers are muted. The differences between many religiously affiliated hospitals and explicitly secular hospitals are minimal to non-existent.[50] Given the spirit of our times, few would dare (or for that matter be inclined) to say, as Boniface VIII (Pope 1294–1303) once did, that outside of the Church (narrowly construed) there is no salvation.[51] Indeed, as many have noted, a large proportion of American college-age students have little knowledge of their traditions as Protestants, Catholics, or Jews.[52] In contemporary Western society nominal membership in a sect or identification with a particular faith tradition appears to have little impact on behavior, as the use of contraceptives by Catholics suggests.[53] Except for groups such as the Hassidim, the Amish, Traditionalist Catholics, and Fundamentalist Protestants, many members of the faith traditions (that is, primarily, the "main line" religions) of the West feel embarrassed if the particularity and exclusivity of their own traditions are stressed.[54] As in America where passing acquaintances are considered friends, it is often difficult for the young of the modern West to identify either moral strangers or moral friends on the basis of religious beliefs, for many have little clear-cut, concrete, content-full commitment to any faith tradition. With the exception of such traditions as Islam and the Sikhs, the phenomenon is global. Just as popes lament the fact that congregants arrive for Mass *post coetum noctis prioris* diaphragm still in place, Mao Tse-Tung bemoaned the passing of revolutionary fervor, and the Soviet bloc has witnessed the large-scale collapse of commitment to the metaphysics of Marxism-Leninism. Eclecticism rather than purity of dogma appears generally to have the upper hand: the lukewarm are regarded as apostles of moderation. Secularity rather than religious faith is in the ascendancy.

The emphasis on faith traditions may indeed be misleading. Many individuals in the Americas, Europe, and the Pacific basin, though nominally members of particular faith or moral traditions, make few of their choices informed by them. As Alasdair MacIntyre suggests, they live in mosaics of meaning assembled from the sundered bits of once robust moral institutions and traditions.

> A key part of my thesis has been that modern moral utterance and practice can only be understood as a series of fragmented survivals from an older past.[55]

A contemporary individual's moral vision will rarely be developed whole and intact within a moral tradition. Instead, it will usually be a pastiche constructed more by accident than by forethought from the bits and pieces of previously vital and integral faith and moral traditions.

The result is that individuals inherit isolated moral tenets sundered from the frameworks that developed them and gave them context and justification. Thus, many have a vague moral revulsion at the practice of selling human organs for transplantation or hiring surrogate mothers. They feel that it is morally wrong to tie welfare payments or state assistance to limiting reproduction, as occurs in the People's Republic of China. These moral sentiments are frequently not given even an attempt at a systematic justification. Practices are rejected on the basis of free-floating moral intuitions, which were once well-argued moral conclusions to arguments set within the ethical reflections of believing Christians and Jews. Indeed, many physicians, patients, hospital administrators, and governmental bureaucrats are largely left to assemble their own bioethics out of pieces and bits.

Following the suggestions of Nietzsche, some may attempt explicitly to fashion moral visions of their own, given the "death of God" (i.e., the collapse of traditional groundings for the moral enterprise).[56] Even where there is no explicit faith or moral tradition, there will still be a concrete view of what is proper, good, or at least attractive behavior. It is not only faith traditions that can provide a content-full moral viewpoint. Various other moral or quasi-moral traditions, or shades of traditions, exist, each with its own understanding of bioethics, however formally, informally, or vaguely articulated. Nor are there clear boundaries between the traditions. Instead, the boundaries are imprecise and shifting. In these circumstances of significant secularization, the moral purchase of attenuated traditions on individual lives tends not to be strong.

For many in the post-modern world, the weakening of faith traditions will mean a sense of moral rootlessness, a sense of purpose denied or a feeling of moral vacuity. The result may be a passing exploration of religions and cults, as well as political or social movements in a search for purpose and moral substance. But most of the fully secularized will find in their circumstances a comfortable ultimate meaninglessness, not a loss of meaning. God is dead, but it doesn't really matter. Theirs is a sense of making do with instrumental significance, where meaning is found in the pursuit of means.

In all of this, the yuppies (young urban professionals) may be the prophets of a coming worldwide secularity in public policy in general, and health care policy in particular, both East and West. Or at least yuppies can serve as a token for an international class of individuals whose vision of the good life and of proper health care is neither tied to a particular, morally instructive history, nor constrained by a set of transcendent values. These individuals, young and old, yuppies *grosso modo*, from Europe, the Americas, and the Pacific Basin, belong to no particular people, but to humankind, to this earth and to its enjoyment. They are citizens of the world for whom notions of a homeland, *Heimat*, Fatherland, Motherland, or a particular sacred place are at best relics of the past and at worst dangerous and divisive. To see oneself bound irrevocably to a particular land is, for them, as anachronistic as orienting one's map to Jerusalem or considering Mount Moriah to be the *omphalus mundi*.

Yuppies can be politely involved in the destinies of the corporations, bureaucracies, or nations within which they work but without the profound commitment and allegiance that one associates with the civil servants of the British Empire or the Kingdom of Prussia. They see themselves morally justified in their muted moral commitment. Their tolerance born of lack of belief can be advanced as the necessary secular cement of a world-wide peaceable community. Yuppies on principle lack the sense of unqualified dedication once found with true communists and National Socialists.[57] Instead, their morality and politics are characterized by a vague liberality.[58] Tendentiously, one might state that the essence of Yuppiedom is a journey to goals that cannot have final definition without changing the meaning of the journey itself. As the stereotype goes, yuppies pursue means for attaining satisfaction, status, and comfort without explicitly endorsing any of those goals as ultimates.[59] There is immanence without a hint of transcendence. Though power, status, and money may be the *de facto* ultimate goals, they are rarely acknowledged as such.

Yuppies usually have more that binds them together in secular terms in the pursuit of success than what separates them in terms of their commitment to different religions. Interest in income, pleasure, and status transcends political boundaries and unites where faith once separated. Even when metempsychosis and new-age religions are given a peripheral place, they are usually commitments of the sort that affirm without defining and allow without condemning.[60] Though yuppies belong to no organized group as such, they can recognize themselves across the world through shared values and style of life. The paradigmatic social institutions in which they work are multi-national corporations in which the standards of communication are "internationalized languages of modernity." The paradigmatic, ceremonial meal for the affluent yuppie is not the Eucharist or the Symposium but a meal in a good restaurant, or, for those less affluent, a meal in one of the fast-food chains available from Kyoto to Brasilia. The yuppie is an individual at home in the general rootless commercial culture of our times, where health care (as insurance) is a commodity to purchase like a hamburger or sushi.

Because of both the narrowness and broadness of the term "yuppie," the term cosmopolitan is, perhaps, to be preferred. I will use the term "cosmopolitan" to identify those individuals who see themselves unconstrained by particular parochial, history-bound traditions or visions, who regard themselves as belonging not to any one people, but rather to the world, to mankind. The vision of the cosmopolitan is one in which membership in a particular family, race, religion, or nation is without substantial significance. Cosmopolitans define their values, especially health and well-being, in terms of this world and without reference to transcendent values.

They even eschew the pursuit of an immanentized eschaton, underscore religious and ideological toleration, and seek to make their lives rich with the goods and pleasures of this world. Yuppies often paradigmatically incarnate these characteristics and can serve as an easily recognized exemplar. By employing the term "cosmopolitan" I have expanded on some images associated with yuppies and included the mature and elderly, not just the young, thus focusing not just on young urban professionals, but on those who embody a stereotypical set of attitudes and values. Indeed, critique is meant or implied of the many virtuous young urban professionals who are not yuppies in my special sense. For example, there are young urban professionals in Tehran, Jerusalem, Dallas, and Paris who are devout Shiites, Orthodox Jews, born-again Christians, or Lefebvre Catholics. These are not yuppies or cosmopolitans in my specially crafted usage.

The image of the cosmopolitan is a device by which to portray the secularity of modern times and within which to understand the social possibilities of a secular bioethics.[61] Secularity exists over against and in competition with a plurality of moral commitments, many of them structured in terms of transcendent religious goals. The post-modern world is a secular pluralist world. On the one hand, there is a plurality of competing moral viewpoints, but no final rational canonical perspective. On the other hand, there is a pronounced secularity within which traditional metaphysical or transcendently grounded moral disputes have lost their force. As Harvey Cox noted, secularization "has relativized religious world views and thus rendered them innocuous."[62] The image of the cosmopolitan is a presentation of the social reality of secularity. The cosmopolitan is as much the paradigmatic patient or physician in the post-modern world as is the divergent true believer. The post-modern world is characterized as much by a loss of belief as by an intellectually unresolvable diversity of beliefs.

For those who can live at peace with the pluralism, unoffended by the secularity, theirs is the life of the cosmopolitan. They are at home in the world and with the general lineaments of secular bioethics. Believers who are confronted with conflicting beliefs may in despair turn to a secular bioethics as a means of reaching across the moral differences separating the bioethics of different faith traditions. But for those who expect neither God nor Reason to establish a canonical concrete normative non-permissive understanding of human well-being or of the proper delivery and conduct of health care, secular bioethics will be an expression of their moral commitments. For them, the absence of tradition and revelation is not a loss but a liberation.

Alasdair MacIntyre has recognized this loss of moral content and interest under the rubric of "internationalized languages of modernity." These are languages that no longer tie the speaker to a particular community of discourse with its background beliefs and commitments. One might contrast the Gaelic of the west coast of Ireland with the English of international trade and commerce, the latter having been purified of particularistic or parochial values.[63] Such languages are "the languages of everywhere and of nowhere."[64] They are the languages of individuals despoiled of a firm place in a tradition with a non-instrumentalist, non-hedonist understanding of well-being.

> [T]he social and cultural condition of those who speak that kind of language, [is] a certain type of rootless cosmopolitanism, [it is] the condition of those who aspiring to be at home anywhere — except that is, of course, in what they regard as the backward, outmoded, undeveloped cultures of traditions — are therefore in an important way citizens of nowhere . . . It is the fate toward which modernity moves precisely insofar as it successfully modernizes itself and others by emancipating itself from social, cultural, and linguistic particularity and so from tradition.[65]

The language of the cosmopolitan gains generality at the price of becoming rootless.

This phenomenon has also been described as modernity. It unites men and women throughout the world and destroys the traditional content of morality and aesthetics, leaving its partakers without ultimate anchor. Marshall Berman recognizes this unifying and destroying maelstrom as characteristic of our time. In its full development and consequences, modernity loses its moral content and shatters into the multiple competing visions of post-modernity.

> There is a mode of vital experience . . . that is shared by men and women all over the world today. I will call this body of experience "modernity." To be modern is to find ourselves in an environment that promises us adventure, power, joy, growth, transformation of ourselves and the world — and, at the same time, that threatens to destroy everything we have, everything we know, everything we are. Modern environments and experiences cut across all boundaries of geography and ethnicity, of class and nationality, of religion and ideology: in this sense, modernity can

> be said to unite all mankind. But it is a paradoxical unity, a unity of disunity: it pours us all into a maelstrom of perpetual disintegration and renewal, of struggle and contradiction, of ambiguity and anguish. To be modern is to be part of a universe in which, as Marx said, "all that is solid melts into air."[66]

The men and women who can live in peace and provide health care in this world without fundamental moral conflicts are the cosmopolitans. They are the contemporary realization of Nietzsche's "Superman." They can look upon the destruction of the old traditions and flourish in the thin air of post-modern times.

For the cosmopolitan, suffering has no transcendent meaning. It cannot, for example, as for the traditional Christian, be regarded as a punishment from God, as an opportunity to witness one's faith or as a means of discharging the temporal punishment due to sins. Health is highly valued by cosmopolitans simply because it is a condition either directly or indirectly for achieving satisfaction. That is, the ill, the deformed, and the disabled will have greater difficulty achieving money, power, status, and fame. Moreover, they will not have full access to the range of immanent pleasures. In this vision suffering, anxiety, deformity are surd hindrances that should as far as possible be set aside. Because of the inability to discover any essential constraints, health and well-being take on an instrumental meaning.

For cosmopolitans, the human exemplar is not *homo romanus* or *homo Christianus*, but rather *homo technicus*. Humans by nature manipulate nature, including now human nature itself. To make human reproductive capacities serve the wishes and desires of humans is thus, in this light, to humanize human nature. The cosmopolitan worldview is not committed to traditional Judeo-Christian concerns about abortion, sterilization, and contraception; quite the contrary. After all, cosmopolitans have come into their status and power through and during the development of modern medical technology. Technological interventions, which treat disease, augment health, or realize reproductive plans, are *prima facie* humane. Initial fears concerning technology tend to be dispelled in a revaluing of the artificial. For a generation that has grown up with and works through computers, much of the artificial has become the truly human word incarnate, a triumph of human will over the often alien and independent forces of nature, including human biological nature. Rather than being alienating, medical technology offers the possibility of rendering human nature congenial to human purposes. It is difficult to imagine that cosmopolitans would decline genetic engineering, even germ-line engineering, when it can ensure them of the perfect child or grandchildren. In fact, cosmopolitans look with suspicion on those who would not seek an abortion when it is socially convenient, and with deep concern on those who would not accept life-saving treatment on religious grounds (e.g., a Catholic refusing a direct abortion when a pregnancy is life-threatening).

In short, an international secular culture has emerged. It conceives of itself as the culture of the new age, the culture of today and of the future. Its members are at home with the contemporary developments in science, technology, and medicine. The ethos of the cosmopolitans has become something like an international civil religion.[67] In particular, it provides guidance for the managers and the employees of many multinational corporations (including health-related corporations). Though possible risks or dangers from medicine, science, and technology are recognized, they are not regarded as involving transcendent moral dangers. Their propriety can be gauged through impact studies and technology assessments. The proper use of medicine and of health care generally is to be understood within a commitment to human well-being construed as human satisfaction or preference maximization. The cosmopolitan is a utilitarian with style. Moreover, the reluctance to underscore transcendent commitments or particular historical attachments allows cosmopolitans to cooperate in and share a world with individuals who belong to robust moral communities with transcendent commitments (e.g., Orthodox Jews, traditionalist Catholics, fundamentalist Protestants, devout Sikhs, and Shiite Moslems) and who by and large regard cosmopolitans as morally vacuous. But even so, as secularity spreads, the future belongs to the yuppie.

5. Towards a Secular Vision of Health Care Delivery

Because of the weakening of traditional morality, despite the persistence of a plurality of living faith traditions, one would expect, as one does in fact find, the salience of procedural norms in contemporary secular bioethics. Free and informed consent becomes a cardinal bioethical practice precisely when one no longer knows what one ought to do and seeks to derive moral authority from the consent of those involved. The focus is on the instrumental character of health care decisions: aiding patients in becoming clear about what they are choosing. If one cannot discover who is *a* moral authority or who is *in* moral authority, one creates answers through mutual negotiation. Rights to privacy become central because they mark the limits of the authority of others to interfere. Accordingly, the right to make choices concerning one's own reproductive future or to refuse life-saving treatment gains a negative rather than a positive justification. As the meaning of good public morals is brought into question, either by cosmopolitans or by disputing true believers, the burden shifts to the state to show that it has a justifiably compelling interest that would warrant coercing the free choices of non-consenting individuals. A bioethics embedded in a culture that possesses both (1) a secular tradition that eschews transcendent goals, affirms immanent pleasures, renounces actions smacking of fanatic commitment, and emphasizes individual fulfillment, but (2) is still marked by the persistence of a plurality of moral communities with transcendent commitments, should accent rights to forbearance over rights to beneficence and make welfare rights refusable. As we will see in Chapter 5, large elements of contemporary American bioethics are not just a reflection of a particular moral vision, but the unavoidable intellectual consequence of not being able to justify in general secular terms a concrete morality that can transcend the controversies that separate competing moral visions.

The problem of articulating a secular bioethics is the central challenge of this volume: how in an increasingly secular world, marked by both religious disbelief and a diversity of religious commitment, do we fashion a health care policy that can be intellectually justified in general secular terms? A secular justification of health care institutions and policies will need: (1) to establish what bioethical issues even the disbeliever must take seriously, and (2) to justify a neutral language within which not only partisans of various faith traditions can meet, but through which both believer and disbeliever can cooperate in the enterprises of health care.

One of the alluring strategies has been to appeal to the character of human nature. If one can read off from human nature what the true human goods are, then perhaps one can establish a common secular morality and provide the foundations for a content-full secular bioethics. In fact, a number of authors in the field of bioethics appeal either directly or indirectly to the goods of human nature in order to establish the goals and purposes of good medical practice and of a justifiable health care system.[68] Appeals to the good of patients, to doing what is best for patients, or to meeting the needs of individuals through a better health care system are often only indirect appeals to a set of goods held implicitly to be grounded in human nature.[69] It is here that an interest in humanism (the study of *humanitas*, that which is characteristically human) is tied to the concerns of secularity. Perhaps an appeal to the interests that we share as humans and to the goods that define a human life of excellence can provide a basis for secular cooperation. It is to this issue that the next chapter turns.

III Humanism, Humaneness, and the Humanities

1. A Cluster of Visions

"In what does the humanity of humans consist?"[1] Martin Heidegger (1889–1976) repeats this perennial and urgent question, asked for more than two and a half millennia. The puzzle is metaphysical, moral, and aesthetic. Its answer is central to understanding the proper focus of medicine and the proper character of bioethics because both concern the nature of human well-being. The question springs from a time before boundaries separated etiquette and ethics, good breeding and good education. When we reflect on this tradition and trace its roots, we tend to see them, if we are not careful, through our post-Enlightenment democratic eyes. In so doing, we typically fail to recognize the intricate interweaving of intellectual, moral, and aesthetic concerns, which we now attempt to separate for moral, political, and social reasons, but which often, in our living culture, still resist compartmentalization. In its origins the question about the humanity of humans was unabashedly élitist, male-oriented, and undemocratic.[2] But its significance reaches beyond its parochial origins and gives voice to concerns about humans as such. "*Homo sum, humani nil a me alienum puto* [I am a human, anything that happens to a human touches me]."[3] Humanism involves not only an interest in exemplary intellectual and aesthetic accomplishment and well-being, but also a concern for others.

When we take stock of the words and ideas that cluster around humanism, it is important to appreciate the power of the original insights given articulation by aristocratic, often slave-holding men whose visions still inspire and liberate twentieth-century men and women of both democratic and socialist societies. The élitist character of the original tradition has taken on an intellectual rather than a political and social cast, and the ties to the past remain for the good. They nurture a breadth of vision and purpose supported by the initial ambiguities of the Latin terms cognate with *humanitas* that suggest a bond among intellectual and moral virtues and among canons of morality, grace, and etiquette.[4] The various elements of human excellence were not compartmentalized but interwoven. This evocative ambiguity, this fertile marriage of interests in beauty, goodness, learning, poise, grace, and kindness, is at the root of both the ethos of medicine and the endeavors of bioethics. This rich and complex vision of human excellence is still of significance in medical education, because the vision of the good physician is not simply a moral vision.[5] Moreover, understandings of health care are based on often only implicitly articulated views of human excellence and well-being.[6]

English contains a cluster of words diverse but related in meaning, which are cognate with the Latin *homo* (human): humanities, humane, humanely, humanitarian, humanism, and humanity. The ambiguity of these English terms reflects the ambiguity of somewhat equivalent words in Latin: *humanitas, humaniter, humanitus, humanus, humane*.[7] Each of these terms in a different way sheds light on the significance of a humane medicine and the project of framing a justifiable bioethics. The terms have similarly a complicated and often obscure history in English, Italian, German, and other languages.[8] In fact, the roots of some of the unclarities go deep into ancient Greece. They are the product of a two-and-a-half-millennia-long project of justifying a morality, developing an appreciation of the ideals and exemplar capacities of humans, and maintaining a learned appreciation of the roots of our culture. As a result, it is not possible to give an account of secular humanism, or of the vision of bioethics it can or should sustain, without examining this collage of ideas, images, and recollections. In particular, the role of one of the connotations of humanism, that of an attempt to establish a philosophy or morality on the basis of commonly shared or justifiable ideals concerning man and the human condition, can only be understood against the history out of which this cluster of meanings arose. History reveals an intricate web of rhetorical and conceptual forces that have shaped an extraordinarily vague but still fruitful notion.

In anticipation, it is important to distinguish nine preliminary major clusters of meanings that have been important in the history of humanism, each of which can be gathered under a term or phrase. In each case, one must recognize that there are important time- and location- determined ambiguities, for each term has a meaning that has changed through time and been shaped by local usages and institutions.

1. *Humanitas.*[9] In the Graeco-Roman world *humanitas* identified that which marks humans apart from animals: refined learning.[10] The term borrows meaning from the Greek concept of *paideia*, which can with difficulty, or at least some qualification, be rendered as culture or education.[11] This sense of education comes closer to the German word *Bildung* in identifying refinement of taste and intellectual appreciation. *Humanitas* might also in part be translated as "genteel, learned urbanity," but it also means the human race, refined manners, and a cultivated taste and way of life. The same range of meanings is associated with the cognate term *humanus*, which can be translated not only as mankind and humanness in the sense of finite human mortality, but also as human dignity, nobility, humaneness, gentility, courtesy, erudition, and educated refinement.[12] One thus finds already in the Latin many of the ambiguities of current terms. *Humanitas* and *humanus* identify a bundle of positive meanings and connotations associated with an exemplar notion of human well-being. The remaining eight headings identify developments of some part of the original notion of *humanitas*. Many physicians, in their attempt to establish a special place for their learned profession, have seen the ideal physician as marked by this consummate refinement of *humanitas.*[13]

2. Humane as philanthropic or humanitarian. Even in the time of the Romans, *humanitas* indicated not only educated refinement, but a certain bearing towards one's fellow-man, which Cicero described as *clementia.*[14] The humane individual showed a mildness, a gentility, which became associated with philanthropy. Philanthropy was one of the marks of an ideal Hippocratic physician.[15] It is used also by St. Paul to convey in Greek the notion of "lovingkindness."[16] As I will show, this elision of intellectual and moral concerns was appreciated by Aulus Gellius (c. 130–170). At stake here is more a distinction of the will and of affect than an intellectual virtue.[17] This sense of being humane underlies many of the senses of being humanitarian that concern the disposition to act to relieve suffering and need. But the terms humanitarian and humanitarianism also reflect an interplay among a complex of interests involving not only humans but animals as well.[18]

3. Humanity as nobility. The word "humanity" also reveals a strategic ambiguity.[19] On the one hand, it can be used as a collective noun to identify humans generally. Yet it can also be employed

honorifically to identify morally or intellectually praiseworthy traits.[20] One might think of Napoleon's remark with regard to Goethe, "Voilà un homme!"[21] Obviously, Napoleon was not engaging in species identification. Instead, he was attributing to Goethe the nobility of intellect, education, sentiment, and cultivation that is embodied in exemplar humans. Similarly, compare the sentences, "Humanity is in need of a moral language that can be shared by all" and "She showed her humanity by treating the patient without charge." The second usage is not merely descriptive but evaluative. It suggests that the physician not only has the biological characteristics of a human, but characteristics of will and inclination that realize certain human moral ideals. In many of its uses humanity carries connotations of philanthropy as outlined above.[22]

4. The humanist as a teacher, scholar, or student. In the latter part of the fifteenth century, the Italian Enlightenment introduced the term *umanista* to identify a teacher of the humanities.[23] In the course of time, this term, as well as the new Latin term *humanista*, also came to identify students of the humanities. As children of the Renaissance, American medical schools even today pay at least lip service to the ideal of their students being humanists in the sense of becoming acquainted with the major ideas of Western culture, and of culture generally, in order better to understand their patients and to provide humane care.

5. Humanities. This term has been as difficult to define as any of the previous. It was originally used to identify the liberal arts and *belles lettres*, the *humanae litterae*, which were the focus of Renaissance scholarship. Broadly, one might think of the humanities as those studies that are appropriate to *humanitas*. Thus, one could speak of a professor *humanarum litterarum*.[24] Later in this chapter, a vignette from Sidonius will present "humanists" of the fifth century (if one might use the term anachronistically) engaged in a discussion of the humanities, those writings that help us better to understand our own condition and the ideas and ideals that shape its possibilities. Currently, the term humanities is used broadly, so that bioethics is embraced as "one of the medical humanities." In the Renaissance, however, the *studia humanitatis* included only the study of the standard writings in Latin and Greek in the subjects of grammar, rhetoric, history, poetry, and moral philosophy.[25]

6. Humanism as scholarship. At the beginning of the Renaissance, humanism identified an interest in the authentic original writings of Rome and of Greece (though originally the term

appeared not to include Greek literature). It also embraced an interest in antiquities and gave birth to the Platonism that marked the Renaissance. Because of the fascination of humanism with things pagan, it was associated with anti-Christian sentiments, as well as with a veneration of the literature of the Greeks on a par with the Judeo-Christian Scriptures. The *humanae litterae* suggest a contrast with the *litterae divinae*, though the Renaissance interests that we associate with humanism came to support a command of Hebrew and Bible scholarship. Since the Renaissance there have been a number of periods of humanism in the sense of pronounced interest in the literature of the ancients.[26] Horst Rüdiger has characterized these periods in Germany as the humanism of the Renaissance, the new humanism, and the third humanism.

> By humanism in the strict sense one usually means the period of time between the first decades of the fourteenth century, that is, the appearance of Petrarch, and more or less the last decades of the sixteenth century. This was followed later in Germany by the new humanism, between approximately 1760 and 1830. This was followed — especially in Germany — by the so-called third humanism at the end of the nineteeth century, some twenty years after the entr'acte of culture-historical humanism.[27]

Over time, humanism as scholarship has been expanded to include works in any of the humanities.

7. Humanism as poise or balance. *Humanitas* and *paideia* both include a sense of proper bearing, a sense of balance or *sophrosyne* that cultivation should produce. Irving Babbitt (1865–1933), for example, associated humanism with decorum and a sense of measure and proportion.[28] He also associated humanism with leisure.[29] Here the bond is an ancient tie that associates liberal arts, leisure, and those who live a life of *otium cum dignitate*. As the realization of a sense of how to live life, humanism is based on intuition[30] and gives a style to action,[31] rather than being just an intellectual virtue.

8. Humanism as a creed or a set of values. As with Holyoake's use of secularism, so, too, individuals have framed humanist philosophies and, in fact, movements which they have articulated in terms of their own particular ideals. They have read their own ideals into a vision of human nature and human deportment, and in terms of that vision often provided particular responses to the controversies in bioethics. In addition, humanism has been interpreted as a set of values within which important human endeavors, such as

science, medicine, and technology, are to be understood.[32] These visions of the moral life and human well-being have usually drawn at least some distant inspiration from the confidence in human capacities and individual abilities that marked the Renaissance.

9. Humanism as a philosophical basis for common moral understanding and negotiation between moral strangers. Here the aspiration is to find something that humans share in common, which can serve as the basis for a general morality, for resolving bioethical controversies, including controversies in health care policy. Only if this last sense of humanism can be justified will individuals who meet as moral strangers find that they share enough to frame common health care policies, which they should recognize as having moral and intellectual authority.[33]

In what follows, I will take seriously the warning of Paul O. Kristeller (1905–) regarding the strategic ambiguities in the concept of humanism.

> The term "Humanism" has been associated with the Renaissance and its classical studies for more than a hundred years, but in recent times it has become the source of much philosophical and historical confusion. In present discourse, almost any kind of concern with human values is called "humanistic," and consequently a great variety of thinkers, religious or antireligious, scientific or antiscientific, lay claim to what has become a rather elusive label of praise. We might ignore this twentieth-century confusion, but for the direct impact it has had upon historical studies. For many historians . . . have cheerfully applied the term "humanism" in its vague modern meaning to the Renaissance and to other periods of the past, speaking of Renaissance humanism, medieval humanism, or Christian humanism, in a fashion which defies any definition and seems to have little or nothing left of the basic classicist meaning of Renaissance humanism.[34]

The problem that Kristeller identifies for the historian is a problem for the bioethicist as well. To make sense of a humanist morality or a secular humanist bioethics, one will need at the very minimum to note the ambiguities and the richness of the terms that cluster around "humanism." The nine clusters of meaning just listed, which are important from a historical perspective, can somewhat Procrusteanly be brought under three rubrics in order to show more clearly the philosophical and moral issues they raise for bioethics:

A. Humanism as humane concern which can be expressed in the character and quality of health care. Here the second cluster of meanings and elements of the third can be interpreted in terms of a cardinal moral and practical goal of medical education and bioethics: the provision of health care in a way that attends to and takes seriously the needs, concerns, and desires of patients. This is a theme that weaves its way through much of the history of humanism and of medicine. It involves a beneficent regard of, and commitment to, patients and those in need of health care. This may also require humanism (*vide* Babbitt) as poise (cluster 7), expressed in a physician's sense of proportion when deciding how far to rely on high-technology medicine or in a physician's facility in translating into human terms the implications of high-technology diagnosis and treatment.

B. Humanism as a body of learning, a community of teachers, scholars, and students, and/or a genre of intellectual refinement, which can provide the intellectual, moral, and aesthetic context within which a humane medicine, one attentive to the full range of human concerns, can be developed and maintained. Here clusters 1, 4, 5, and 6 can be expressed in terms of goals of health care education. There has always been some acknowledgement that medicine constitutes one of the three learned professions. But now nearly uncontrollable forces tend to estrange patients from the institutions and persons who provide health care. Rapid technological advance, with consequent subspecialization of health care professionals, has made health care and hospitalization frequently an alienating experience. Moreover, it is difficult for health care providers, who themselves can often no longer understand the full range of a patient's complicated problems in depth without the aid of a consultant and whose very knowledge is being quickly outdated, to achieve a perspective within which they can understand their own professional lives. The humanities have been brought within health care education as the medical humanities (e.g., bioethics and history of medicine) because, by charting the ideas and images that are foundational to our culture, a perspective is gained that can aid both health professionals and patients. The contribution the humanities offer is an intellectual one: a breadth of vision, an integrated perspective, a more refined understanding of the human condition within which individuals are born, develop, become ill, are treated, grow old, and die. The collection of images and ideas that are part of the fuzzy-bordered intellectual tradition of the humanities is sustained by visions of the intellectual life that share vague but still compelling consanguinities. Certain ancient texts serve as exemplar objects of proper interest. A high value is assigned to the learning associated with studying the ideas and images that shape our culture. A vague sense of common purpose is often felt by those who revere *humanitas*, or study the humanities with zeal. In short, a number of visions of the good intellectual life share sufficient family resemblance to be treated as *a* vision, and to exert a synergistic force on culture generally, and medicine in particular.

C. Humanism as a body of philosophical and moral theory in terms of which a bioethics can be justified. Clusters 8 and 9 both concern the possibility of grounding a secular morality, and thus a secular bioethics. They differ in terms of their possible generality. The former is not only embedded in, but is essentially conditioned by, a particular history and a particular set of ideas. It is often expressed in a cluster of formal organizations (sense 9). The latter raises the question whether a morality for strangers, with true generality, can be intellectually justified in terms of the nature of man and the human condition. Both share the goal of disclosing a set of fundamental moral constraints and, if possible, a generally justifiable hierarchy or account of moral desiderata. They both benefit from exemplar attempts to articulate a common basis for cooperation among moral strangers. One might think, for example, of Immanuel Kant's proposal of a league of nations in *Perpetual Peace*.[35] But they differ in that particular associations of humanists have by the very fact of their particular social organizations a particularity. They are always one organization over against others. However, if there is a common basis for cooperation among moral strangers, it will provide the foundations for a moral community that will exist always first as an intellectual possibility, of which moral strangers should understand themselves as being a part, and through which they can have a justified moral basis for cooperation simply because they are humans or persons.

These three fundamental clusters of ways of understanding humanism (i.e., humanism as humane concern, humanism as a body of learning or a community of scholars or a genre of intellectual refinement, and humanism as a body of philosophical and moral theory) turn on different visions of human well-being and how it is to be achieved. The first, which accentuates humanitarian action, ranks the needs of individuals over the study of the classics or the grounding of a philosophical account of ethics and justified public policy. The disagreement between the first vision and the second, which gives precedence to the study of the classics, and the third, which accentuates the need for grounding a philosophical account, is usually not simply axiological. It is not simply a disagreement about the proper ranking of values but turns also on various assumptions about the influence of learning or the direction that can be given from a clear well-founded philosophy and moral theory. Each of these visions makes plausible a different understanding of how health care can achieve human well-being. The first presupposes a direct connection between the enlightened commitment to do good and its achievement through technology. The second presupposes that only out of a careful reflection on the best that is human, a reflection rooted in a tradition of scholarship and thought, can human endeavors, and technology in particular, be well-directed to the alleviation of suffering and the achievement of human well-being. The third accentuates the need for understanding what binds moral strangers together in order to envision the possibility of a common human endeavor of alleviating suffering and achieving human well-being.

Each of these clusters of understandings of humanism has had a secularizing force. The fact that there was a tradition of humanitarian action prior to and independent of Christian charity has allowed individuals in the West to have a paradigm of philanthropy that does not depend on the established Christian church. Moreover, in the nineteenth and the twentieth centuries, secular understandings of humanitarian action were seen as a force to bring the other-worldly concerns of Christianity to bear on the this-worldly needs of men and women.[36] Philology and study of the classics had the effect of binding the intelligentsia of the West to a pagan culture. They also provided intellectual, aesthetic, and moral ideals which were independent of the Christian establishment. Thus, alongside the traditional biblical and scholastic concerns of Christianity, there was a rival tradition of learning within which individuals could understand themselves. That tradition in the end proved strong enough to cast its shadow over Christian self-understanding as illustrated by the development of biblical textual criticism. Finally, humanism as an attempt to understand the world, morality, and aesthetics from the point of view of human reason, created an intellectual standpoint independent of the Christian orthodoxy of the West. More than simply a tradition of bookish, philological, or exegetical study, humanism in this sense is a philosophical project that can be identified generally with the Age of Reason and the Enlightenment, as well as with contemporary attempts to construe the world from the point of view of reason. These three interweaving clusters of senses of humanism have transformed Western self-appreciation and created not just the modern Western world but the modern world itself. They have set the modern context within which health and medicine are to be understood.

Each of these genres of construals of humanism has had an influence on contemporary health care policy. That influence has been mediated by a complex history in which the various meanings of humanism have interacted and been mutually supportive. Contemporary humanism can be understood only against an account of this intricate interweaving of forces and ideas.

2. Human Thought and Human Form: The Historical Roots of Humanism

Are there messages from God or characteristics of the human mind, nature, or condition that can provide the bases for intellectually justifying an ethics, in particular, a secular bioethics? The responses to these questions, within the Western context, have been complex. The Jews sought an answer from a transcendent God, from the message and meaning God gave in a particular covenant. The largely secularized Greeks sought truth and meaning in this world and through human reason.[37] The God of the Jews was not to be pictured,[38] kept his own counsels,[39] and required his people to follow 613 commandments, the ultimate justification for which was not to be disclosed through the light of human reason.[40] Moreover, for the Jews, God had broken into and shaped history. God had revealed his truth in a particular, written form, so that their Scriptures played a central role in all of their subsequent discussions of the significance of the world and of morality. For the Greeks there were no such scriptures. Or, to put the matter metaphorically, the original scriptures of secular Greeks were the human mind, the human flesh, and the world of men. Without a doubt, there was a profoundly mystical element in Greek culture. But this mysticism was often tied to a faith in ideas and mathematics (e.g., Plato and Pythagoras), so that the writings of its major exponents influenced science and philosophy as much as mysticism.[41] With time, the literature of ancient Greece took on a role distantly analogous to the Bible. Homer's *Iliad*, Plato's *Republic*, Aristotle's *Nicomachean Ethics*, Sophocles' *Oedipus Rex*, the writings of the classical age of Greece came to be revered as a revelation of the creative capacities of the human spirit.

This literature was to become the focus of a future humanism and provide the basis for understanding culture, philosophy, and ethics. But the differences between a revered body of literature and inspired writings are, as Josephus (A.D. 37–100) stressed, immense:

> We have given practical proof of our reverence for our own Scriptures. For, although such long ages have now passed, no one has ventured either to add, or to remove, or to alter a syllable; and it is an instinct with every Jew, from the day of his birth, to regard them as the decrees of God, to abide by them, and, if need be, cheerfuly to die for them . . .
>
> What Greek would endure as much for the same cause? Even to save the entire collection of his nation's writings from destruction he would not face the smallest personal injury. For to the Greeks they are mere stories improvised according to the fancy of their authors . . .[42]

Though the literature of the Greeks, which became the foundation of the humanities, may not have prompted many martyrs,[43] still, its culture has been and is venerated as a model, a unique exemplar of human intelligence and learning. The Greeks provided what was in the end an immanent basis for justifying ethics, including bioethics.

The literatures of the Greeks and the Jews developed against radically different metaphysical backgrounds. The heaven of the Jews had Jehovah (Yahweh) in the central place. It made room for angels, but the centrality of the one God was never challenged. It was instead constantly reaffirmed.[44] On the other hand, though Zeus was nominally the ruler of the Olympian gods and goddesses, their world was as disunited and conflict-ridden as was the world of the Greeks. It also bore great similarities to the intellectual life of the Greeks, which sustained endless contentions between rationalists and empiricists, skeptics and metaphysicians, in a fashion that still marks the character of contemporary Western thought in general and bioethics in particular. Moreover, the gods and goddesses of the Greeks were of human form, and the beauty of the human body, male and female, was the delight of their painting and their sculpture.

These differences in background views about the nature of reality were reflected in and reinforced by the ambience in which each of the literatures developed. Greek learning was pursued in the midst of numerous social practices which were at home with and which valued the fleshy beauty of this world. Jewish learning was undertaken in the face of the revelation and presence of a transcendent God, and the life of scholars was structured by the observation of an all-encompassing set of rules for moral rectitude and ritual purity. Moreover, the intellectual culture of the Jews developed from discussions in synagogues and schools or communities of scholars dedicated to reflection on the Law of God.

In contrast, the two most famous institutions of ancient Greek learning were associated with the celebration of the human body and the veneration of pagan gods. The Academy was named after a grove, sacred to the hero Academus, near Plato's country-house.[45] It was, in fact, a gymnasium, a place where young men exercised in the nude, while philosophers and rhetoricians sat on the stone seats of the *exedrae* of the external colonnades. So, too, the Lyceum in which Aristotle taught for thirteen years was a gymnasium.[46] Gymnasia, which had been the traditional place to develop physical excellence and prepare for the Olympics, thus took on an intellectual significance.[47] The goals of physical and mental excellence were in this way deeply intertwined and were for many inseparable as constituting a unitary sense of human well-being. Consequently, Greek culture often brought with it values that conflicted profoundly with those of the Jews. When Greek culture was imposed on Israel by Antiochus IV Epiphanes (215–164 B.C.), many Jews adopted Greek customs with the result that some Jewish youths sought cosmetic reversal of their circumcision in order to appear "normal" in the gymnasium, that is, to cure what in Greek terms could only be viewed as a deformity or injury.[48]

> Accordingly, [some Jews] petitioned [Antiochus IV] to permit them to build a gymnasium in Jerusalem. And when he had granted this, they also concealed the circumcision of their private parts in order to be Greeks even when unclothed, and, giving up whatever other national customs they had, they imitated the practices of foreign nations.[49]

The Jews saw Greek culture as seducing them away from the Law. The very beauty of Greek culture was a temptation to adopt the pagan balance and celebration of human mind and body as the criterion of human well-being, which defined human well-being in terms of this world and the cultivation of human capacities. The veneration of the human in literature and art marked the Greeks over against Jewish and later Christian and Muslim religious traditions and understandings of bioethics. Here one already sees the gulf still felt by many between secular humanist bioethics and the bioethics of particular faith traditions.

The ideal of the cultivated man which the Graeco-Roman world produced has become integral to the model of the well-educated physician. It sprang from the secularized culture of Greece. Its classical statement is given by Hippocrates (c.460–377 B.C.), who likened to a god the physician who was also a philosopher: ". . . translate wisdom into medicine and medicine into wisdom. For a physician who is a lover of wisdom is the equal of a god. Between wisdom and medicine there is no gulf fixed; in fact medicine possesses all the qualities that make for wisdom."[50] Over time, this image of the physician has been supported by those who needed to distinguish themselves from mere empirics, physicians trained through preceptorships without a university education, those who received their medical training without cultivation or education in the humanities. The salience in the English-speaking medical world of the physician Sir William Osler (1849–1919) may in part be explained by this specially reinforced reverence for the genteel physician who has a knowledge of the humanities.[51] In his erudition and demeanor, Osler incarnated this ideal, which has been explicitly endorsed since the beginning of Western medicine, and which still lays claim on medicine's self-image.

Besides humanism identifying a concern for philanthropy, an interest in the humanities, and a refinement of taste, it came to be understood as a philosophy that justified morality in terms of human nature and the human condition. Unlike the natural-law theorists of the Catholic Church who understood human nature as a creation of God, and then through natural law indirectly elaborated a divinely oriented account of human nature and consequently of morality, humanists in this sense have considered man and the human condition apart from concerns that transcend this life. The classical statement of the foundation of morality in man and the human condition was given by Protagoras (c.480–410 B.C.), who, according to Diogenes Laertius (late second or early third century A.D.), began a work with the assertion that "Man is the measure of all things, of things that are that they are, and of things that are not that they are not."[52] In his account of morality, Protagoras was very clear to prescind from considerations of religion and the Divine. "As to the gods, I have no means of knowing either that they exist or that they do not exist. For many are the obstacles that impede knowledge, both the obscurity of the question and the shortness of human life."[53] Since the Sophist Protagoras held that one could argue both sides of any question,[54] and was a thorough-going moral and epistemological relativist,[55] he concluded that truth depended on the observer and had no objective non-relativist meaning. In short, to quote a gloss by Sextus Empiricus, he understood that "man is the criterion of all objects."[56] Protagoras regarded truth as embedded in individual opinions.[57]

Because of their relativism, the Sophists gave place to process of argument over correctness of conclusion. They did not regard themselves as "scientific" experts, but rather as experts in the use of language and ideas. As such, they were central to the development of the cultured rhetoric of the Greeks. The goal was to be beautiful and eloquent in argument, not to demonstrate "the truth," for the latter was impossible. The Sophists played a major role in removing the gods from the central stage of Greek affairs and replacing them with humans. The Sophists helped to secularize Greece. The myths and rituals remained, but for many they became social conventions, much as Christmas and Easter are for some Western countries today. Protagoras in many ways anticipates the humanist moralists of the twentieth century, who attempt to ground bioethics in the human situation. Indeed, Protagoras can be seen as offering a foundation for the situation-ethics orientation of the bioethics of Joseph Fletcher.[58]

The physicians of Greece, it should be noted, played a role analogous to that of the Sophists. To begin with, Sophists and physicians were the first professionals to gain a place in Greek society by virtue of their special art.[59] They each regarded their art as distinguishing men from animals. Each also considered the customs of the Greeks to be the result of a cultural development, not as given by the gods.[60] In this the physicians, as the Sophists, can in anticipation be seen as underscoring an element of humanism in stressing the human origin of culture. But more than that, as Laszlo Versenyi observed, the physicians also contributed to the secularization and rationalization of Greek life by arguing against the view that some diseases are of divine origin.[61] The most important work in this regard is the Hippocratic text, *On the Sacred Disease*, in which the author attacks the traditional view that epilepsy was due to a special divine cause.

> But this disease [epilepsy] is in my opinion no more divine than any other; it has the same nature as other diseases, and the cause

> that gives rise to individual diseases. It is also curable, no less than other illnesses, unless by long lapse of time it be so ingrained as to be more powerful than the remedies that are applied. Its origin, like that of other diseases, lies in heredity.[62]

Human well-being, health, disease, and suffering were construed in terms of human nature and culture, not divine interventions.

The concept of the normatively human gained a currency so that in Rome it was possible to use as a salutation "*humanissime vir*," "most humane sir," and convey the sense of "most learned sir" as well as the connotation "most benevolent sir."[63] *Humanus* and *humanitas* identified that which was proper to humans: both a development of the special capacities of humans and a concern to do good to one's fellow-man. This central ambiguity was recognized in Graeco-Roman times.

> Those who have spoken Latin and have used the language correctly do not give to the word *humanitas* the meaning which it is commonly thought to have, namely, what the Greeks call "philanthropia," signifying a kind of friendly spirit and good-feeling towards all men without distinction; but they gave to *humanitas* about the force of the Greek *paedeia*; that is, what we call *eruditionem institutionemque in bonas artes*, or "education and training in the liberal arts." Those who earnestly desire and seek after these are most highly humanized. For the pursuit of that kind of knowledge, and the training given by it, have been granted to man alone of all the animals, and for that reason it is termed *humanitas*, or "humanity."[64]

As Aulus Gellius (c.130–170) argues, the term "*humanitas*" most properly designates not humane dispositions, but education in what we would now understand as the humanities. However, because of the rich interplay among the meanings of "*homo*," "*humanitas*," and "*humanus*," there was an intertwining of the meanings and connotations of being human, showing humanity, and possessing the learning, cultivation, nobility, and beneficence which are human in an exemplary fashion. The complex connotations that were engendered in the Latin still resonate in contemporary English usages. They still sustain the assumption that an individual (here a physician in particular) educated in the humanities will have a greater disposition towards being humane and will better understand the nature of man and the human condition.

For Aulus Gellius as well as for the tradition, there was little attempt to derive a proscriptive natural law theory from a concept of the normatively human, as occurred in the Middle Ages (as examples of the latter, one might think of arguments against abortion and contraception[65]). Instead, the accent was on the intrinsic value of being well educated and refined in tastes and way of life. In this vein one finds the view of Aristippus (c.435–350 B.C.) that "it is better . . . to be a beggar than to be uneducated; the one needs money, the others need to be humanized."[66] To be humanized was to show a sort of good breeding, a certain refinement. As Marcus Terentius Varro (116–27 B.C.) argued,

> . . . we wish to have a house not merely that we may be under a roof and in a safe place into which necessity has crowded us together, but also that we may be where we may continue to experience the pleasures of life; and we wish to have table-vessels that are not merely suitable to hold our food, but also beautiful in form and shaped by an artist — for one thing is enough for the human animal, and quite another thing satisfies human refinement [*humanitate*]: any cup at all is satisfactory to a man parched with thirst, but any cup is inferior to the demands of refinement [*humanitate*] unless it is artistically beautiful: — but as we have digressed from the matter of utility to that of pleasure, it is a fact that in such a case greater pleasure is often got from difference of appearance than from likeness.[67]

To be humanized was to have an appreciation of the better things in life. A distinction was drawn between the cultivation of the human animal and that which is distinctively human, a quasi-dualistic theme that we will see rearticulated throughout the history of humanism, as for example by Immanuel Niethammer (1755–1848) in the nineteenth century and by Irving Babbitt (1865–1933) in the twentieth. Moreover, the canons of cultivation were Roman. As Heidegger observes, the *homo humanus* (i.e., the man who realizes the normatively human), who was the *homo romanus*, was contrasted with the *homo barbarus*. *Humanitas* was understood a *romanitas*, the marks of a cultivated Roman gentleman.[68]

Rhetorical skill became a mark of cultivation, so that the Romans praised the Greek schools of philosophy as much for being schools of rhetoric as for being schools of metaphysics. These schools and the skills they taught became central to a critical understanding of culture. Education was not regarded simply as the communication of particular truths. Consider the following comparison by the rhetorician Quintilian (A.D. 35–100) of the schools of Plato and Aristotle.

> Some authorities hold that the Academy will be the most useful school, on the ground that its habit of disputing on both sides of a question approaches most nearly to the actual practice of the courts. And by way of proof they add the fact that this school has produced speakers highly renowned for their eloquence. The Peripatetics also make it their boast that they have a form of study which is near akin to oratory.[69]

Moreover, the rhetorician is seen as not needing a particularly philosophical commitment: "there is no need for an orator to swear allegiance to any one philosophic code. For he has a greater and nobler aim, to which he directs all his efforts with as much zeal as if he were a candidate for office, since he is to be made perfect not only in the glory of a virtuous life, but in that of eloquence as well."[70] Beauty and grace of expression take on a meaning of their own. In this the Sophists anticipated a central element of the humanities, including the medical humanities: grace of expression. Such grace continues to play no small role in idealized pictures of the bedside manner of the genteel physician.

In one sense, the Sophists are not representative of Greek culture or of our traditional understandings of Greek culture. Socrates, Plato, Aristotle, and the Stoics, among others, took the conclusions of their own arguments to disclose objective timeless truths. Moreover, the philosophers' reverence for truth, for culture-independent ideas, and for non-relative understandings of reality, is traced with perennial celebration to the Greeks. On the other hand, the conflicting assertions of the truth forwarded by modern philosophy and bioethics sound like the state of affairs that someone with a sympathy for Protagoras would have anticipated. There are arguments on both sides of every question. All appears to be relative to the first premises and presuppositions of the particular philosopher. There appears to be a chaos in bioethics through which one can negotiate one's way peaceably only with rhetoric, not with conclusive rational argument. Yet the whole, this corpus of conflicting viewpoints and contradictory but passionately held philosophies, has an attractive beauty of its own. Moral reflection perennially inspires men and women across the generations to contemplation, analysis, and eristics. It has become a form of learning that can be admired, enjoyed, and valued in its own right, even if it does not disclose a truth beyond the texts, their interpreters, and their dialogues. In this sense, Protagoras, the Sophists, and the rhetoricians have triumphed. They seem vindicated by the very character and state of the humanities, including moral theory and bioethics especially. In fact, they have been vindicated by the state of all modern, liberal cultures, each of which traces its roots in part and indirectly at least to the humane culture of the Greeks.

What has been said about Graeco-Roman culture in general can be said as well about its reflections on issues of medical ethics: there is again embarrassment of riches. One finds Aristotle ill-disposed to infanticide as a means of controlling population growth, but recommending it for children born with severe physical handicaps:

> Let there be a law that no deformed child shall be reared; but on the ground of number of children, if the regular customs hinder any of those born being exposed, there must be a limit fixed to the procreation of offspring, and if any people have a child as a result of intercourse in contravention of these regulations, abortion must be practised on it before it has developed sensation and life; for the line between lawful and unlawful abortion will be marked by the fact of having sensation and being alive.[71]

Because Aristotle endorsed only first-trimester abortions as a means of population control, he was later to receive qualified praise from St. Thomas Aquinas.[72] Plato recommended infanticide as part of a program of eugenics (*Republic* V, 460c). However, both a general condemnation of killing as well as a specific condemnation of abortion can be found in the Hippocratic Oath: "Neither will I administer a poison to anybody when asked to do so, nor will I suggest such a course. Similarly I will not give to a woman a pessary to cause abortion."[73] Actual practice was quite diverse. By the second century, Christians had already condemned abortion and infanticide: "thou shalt not procure abortion, nor commit infanticide."[74] Indeed, Soranus (A.D. 98–138) in the first extant textbook on gynecology notes the heterogeneity of viewpoints and practice with respect to abortion, including abortion simply for matters of convenience.[75] There was, in short, a wide range of opinions, much as today.[76] The Graeco-Roman legacy with regard to issues of medical ethics resembled its legacy to philosophy: it provided a model of learned discourse, analysis, and argument, but without established conclusions.

Significant differences separate contemporary from ancient understandings of moral and philosophical issues in medicine.

Chief among these differences is the fact that the Mediterranean world lacked a concept of rights as grounded in the decision of an individual not to convey authority, as limits on the authority of the state or the physician. Consequently, much of contemporary discussions regarding patients' rights and free and informed consent would have been difficult to articulate. Nor did the Mediterranean world have a developed notion of limited democracies or of limited social institutions as existed at least among some of the German tribes of the north.[77] Rights to privacy thus also had no easy means of articulation. Roman and Greek moral discourse was framed around concepts of rights as powers (*potestates*) and duties as services (*officia*) that existed within particular social structures (e.g., the city of Rome). The Greeks understood the *polis* as a somewhat Hobbesian solution to the threat of external danger and internal anarchy. In the *polis*, one lived one's life and made one's claims in a web of functional reciprocity with one's fellow citizens.[78] Ultimately, this Graeco-Roman vision was transformed by the Protestant-Germanic vision of northern Europe to give us the context of discourse for health care policy and bioethics we possess today.[79] As a result, modern discussions of secular humanist bioethics can draw upon rich reflections on rights that had not yet matured as the Renaissance gave birth to its interests in humanism.[80]

3. Zeal for the Divine versus Zeal for *Humanitas*: Competing Bases for Health Care Policy

Modern notions of humanism developed out of a struggle to rearticulate a secular notion of human well-being after over a millennium during which a Christian understanding was the regnant vision. That millennium began with a departure from the classical understanding of human well-being and of the human context. That vision regarded God and the picture given by revelation as the fundamental structure of reality in terms of which any account of human well-being and human suffering was to be articulated. The Christian vision contrasted with the humanist, which was skeptical of knowledge of things divine and was concerned instead with the immanent character of human well-being. For the Christians, the world and the flesh defined the origin and context of human suffering, and the world of the Divine that of human well-being. For the ancient humanist view, human well-being was to be defined in terms of the world and the flesh.

Moreover, the city of man was not the community of individuals destined for damnation, but the *polis* of culture within which human well-being was to be realized. For the new vision, exemplar knowledge was found in the Bible and in the creeds and canons of the ecumenical councils, as opposed to the old vision, within which exemplary knowledge was found in philosophical debate and mathematical analysis. Within the new vision, the Eucharist was contrasted with the Symposium, and the social structure of the Church with the informal structure that bound scholars and rhetoricians in the examination of human well-being and the human context.

With the establishment of Christianity, the intellectual focus shifted to theology. The changes took place slowly, but by 529 the Emperor Justinian (483–565) had seized the endowments that supported pagan professorial salaries and the Academy itself, ordered the closing of the Academy, and forbidden the teaching of pagan philosophy.[81] In the same year St. Benedict (480–543) founded the monastery of Monte Cassino and implemented his paradigmatic monastic rule.[82] Despite bitter, often bloody disputes among theologians, an age began in which there was a basis for resolving scientific, moral, and political controversies. The established Church provided rules of evidence and procedure that were held in principle to be reliable and sufficient for resolving disputes about faith and morals. And, as Galileo discovered, matters of faith could include matters of science as well. Christian faith also gave substantial place to reason and came to have a greater confidence in the capacities of reason than is generally the case in contemporary philosophy. In fact, in the context of medieval Christianity, the rationalist aspiration of the Greeks took on a quasi-canonical status.

This faith in reason contrasts with the Jewish orientation out of which Christianity originally sprang. The Jews for the most part lacked secular metaphysical assumptions about the role of reason.[83] As the Christians were articulating their dogmas against the background of Greek philosophical theories of reality, the Jews developed applications of holy scripture to concerns of morality and ritual purity. Argumentative exposition of scripture established a history of reflection, which served as a precedent. The result was a complex moral analysis in which reasoning functioned without explicit, general philosophical and metaphysical principles. Consider, for instance, a passage from the Talmud that reports an argument about whether an oven was kosher.

On that day R. Eliezer brought forward every imaginable argument, but they did not accept them. Said he to them: "If the *halachah* agrees with me, let this carob-tree prove it!" Thereupon the carob-tree was torn a hundred cubits out of its place — others affirm, four hundred cubits. "No proof can be brought from a carob-tree," they retorted. Again he said to them: "If the *halachah* agrees with me, let the stream of water prove it!" Whereupon the stream of water flowed backwards. "No proof can be brought from a stream of water," they rejoined. Again he urged: "If the *halachah* agrees with me, let the walls of the schoolhouse prove it," whereupon the walls inclined to fall. But R. Joshua rebuked them, saying: "When scholars are engaged in a *halachic* dispute, what right have ye to interfere?" Hence they did not fall, in honour of R. Joshua, nor did they resume the upright, in honour of R. Eliezer; and they are still standing thus inclined. Again he said to them: "If the *halachah* agrees with me, let it be proved from Heaven!" Whereupon a Heavenly Voice cried out: "Why do ye dispute with R. Eliezer, seeing that in all matters the *halachah* agrees with him!" But R. Joshua arose and exclaimed: "*It is not in heaven*." What did he mean by this? — Said R. Jeremiah: That the Torah had already been given at Mount Sinai; we pay no attention to a Heavenly Voice, because Thou hast long since written in the Torah at Mount Sinai, *After the majority must one incline*.

R. Nathan met Elijah and asked him: What did the Holy One, Blessed be He, do in that hour? — He laughed [with joy], he replied, saying, "My sons have defeated Me, My sons have defeated Me."[84]

Though the conclusion was resolved by argument and by vote, the initial premises, the basic materials available for exposition and discussion, were for the most part accepted as constraints imposed by divine revelation. Moreover, the arguments within this tradition remained closely tied to scriptural, precedential, and expositional concerns. Though there was significant cabalistic and other speculation, metaphysical philosophical argument never played the central role it did for Christian thought.[85] Moreover, the Jewish moral tradition, and the bioethics it spawned, was not articulated against a prior historically secular rational tradition. Nor did it possess a prior, independent and secular sense of *humanitas*. Moral rectitude, not the refined secular learning and deportment of a Cicero was central to the characterization of the just man of the Jews.

Greek faith in the *logos*, which had already made its way into the Jewish wisdom literature and the reflections of individuals such as Philo Judaeus (c.20 B.C-mid-first century), was used by Christians to place their faith in the God of the Jews within Greek philosophical terms. There are many qualifications that would need to be made. Many Christian theologians also maintained a profound appreciation of the transcendence, mystery, and inscrutability of God and His ways. Still, Christians in general came to see themselves as having a message for all that could in part be philosophically justified to everyone. After all, "In the beginning there was the Word [*logos*]" (John 1:1).[86] As a consequence, contemporary Roman Catholic and, to some extent, much of Protestant bioethics is pursued in a fashion quite different from bioethics within the orthodox Jewish tradition. The Christians, like the Jews, presuppose a particular revelation by a particular God. But the encounter with Greek philosophy recast much of Christian moral reflections, including those on bioethics, in terms of arguments that are meant to appeal to persons generally (often presupposing a concept of human nature, of the *humanum*). The philosophical arguments of the Graeco-Roman world were appropriated and recast to do service for bioethical arguments regarding the nature of duties to patients and the morality of abortion, to note only a few issues. *Pace* Luther and Calvin, the Christians emerged into the modern world from their attempt to come to terms as Greek rationalists with the revelation of Jesus Christ.

Theology, which combined both reason and revelation, became the queen of the sciences, the most certain avenue to reliable truth and the method through which true human well-being was to be understood and the ultimate meaning of human disease and suffering to be comprehended. As the rational life became absorbed with the task of understanding the transcendent, the *studia divinitatis* became the central endeavor of the culture and the *studia humanitatis* fell into desuetude; the Latin *humanus* ceased (until the Italian fifteenth century) to mean erudite. The once vital scholarly discussions of *belles lettres* were muted;[87] the bookstores of the Empire began to close; the interest in medicine as a scientific pursuit slacked; and a new set of interests dominated. Man was no longer the measure of all things, but the true measure was God. Moreover, theology gave an account of God, his moral requirements, and the meaning of life. As a result, one no longer needed to fear irresolveable disputes about the very character of morality or, for that matter, of bioethics. Final answers to the meaning of reality and criteria for proper conduct could in principle be secured.

A grand cultural synthesis emerged from Jewish religious views, Greek philosophy, and Roman law. Remnants of old pagan festivals and pieties were transformed, absorbed, and preserved, and doctrine was expressed within the emerging theology. Within the first four centuries after the establishment of the Church, a series of ecumenical councils gave theological articulation to the doctrines of the Trinity and the Incarnation: Nicaea I (325), Constantinople I (381), Ephesus (431), Chalcedon (451), Constantinople II (553), Constantinople III (680), and Nicaea II (787). Each of these was convened by imperial order. The development of theological orthodoxy was equivalent to the development of an official state worldview. In and through all of this, the rhetoric and learning of the ancient world was being brought to the service of divine goals. Moreover, a new learning, the theology of the Christians, was being developed, which would in the end occasion many of the contemporary quandaries of bioethics.

The new worldview, unlike the previous one, was monotheistic, not polytheistic. In its logic and metaphor, it underscored a singularity of vision. Though the new moral and metaphysical vision was introduced officially on a note of tolerance with the Edict of Milan in 313, it proved at least over the ensuing millennium and more to be highly intolerant of ideological deviation or heresy. It brooked diversity at first when it had no ability to extirpate it. But when it gained firm control, intolerance was officially lauded, as when the Fourth Lateran Council (1215) held that "Catholics who truly take up the cross and give themselves over to the extermination of heretics, shall enjoy the same indulgence, which is given by sacred privilege to those who go to the Holy Land."[88] While the polytheistic environment of Rome tolerated a plurality of bioethical viewpoints, the Christians were not that accepting. It was against this intolerance that the humanists of the Renaissance would define themselves and their understanding of human well-being. It is also this interest in imposing a moral understanding by means of the secular powers that continues to engender controversies in health-care policy.

Despite the dramatic shift in worldview and despite the chaos engendered by the invasions and destruction of the imperial structure in the West, much of the learning and civility of the ancients lingered. Sidonius Apollinaris (430–483) gives an account of this period of transition.[89]

> I have spent the most delicious time in visiting two charming properties and two most sympathetic hosts . . . Well, I was hurried from bliss to bliss. Hardly had I entered one vestibule or the other when behold! . . . [in one] part were books in any number ready to hand; you might have imagined yourself looking at the shelves of a professional scholar or at the tiers in the Athenaeum or at the towering presses of the booksellers . . . it was a frequent practice to read writers whose artistry was of a similar kind — here Augustine, there Varro, here Horace, there Prudentius . . . We would all join in a discussion, expressing our various views just as we felt inclined. We debated why Origen was condemned by some of our chief hierophants as an inept and dangerous expositor, and yet his works had been translated into Latin with such faithfulness to the letter and the spirit . . . [T]he head cook had his eye on the passage of the hours as marked by the water-clock, and as the fifth hour was just departing he was proved to have arrived just at the right moment. The luncheon was at once short and lavish, in the style of senators, who have an inherited and established practice of having abundant viands served up on few dishes, although the meal is varied by having some of the meats roasted and others stewed . . . To sum up, our entertainment was moral, elegant, and profuse.[90]

One must remember that this description was given in the final years of the Roman Empire of the West, probably between A.D. 462 and 467.[91] It shows that the *humanitas* so valued by Cicero and Varro had not vanished. It was, however, being absorbed into the emerging Christian culture.

During the Middle Ages, learning did not cease. Its locus shifted from the academy to the monastery and the cathedral school, and then in the thirteenth century to the university.[92] The intellectual milieu also changed from tolerating a great number of moral viewpoints to establishing an orthodoxy that narrowed the domain of legitimate discourse. But within the general constraints of this orthodoxy, there was a rich and varied literature, shaped by intense debates. These debates included the controversies engendered by Peter Abelard (1079–1142), whose worldly individualism and rationalism anticipated that of the Renaissance. As universities were established, the intellectual life strengthened and theological reflection took on a depth and vigor that compared favorably with the philosophical disputations of the ancient world. For example, at the University of Paris, founded in 1208, St Albertus Magnus

(1206–1280) taught St Thomas Aquinas (1225–1274).[93] The university in the thirteenth century also counted among its faculty St. Bonaventure (1221–1274) and Duns Scotus (1270–1308), and among its students Roger Bacon (1214–1294).

During the millennium of Christian hegemony under Rome, and against the background of intense theological investigations, the bases for many contemporary bioethical discussions were laid down. Catholic moral theology concerning abortion was under development, though from the thirteenth century until 1869 first-trimester abortion was not considered the taking of the life of a person.[94] There was also interest in other bioethical issues, including concerns about medical treatment for the poor. St. Thomas Aquinas articulated the distinction between direct and indirect killing which would influence not only Catholic and Protestant bioethics but also secular law and public policy.[95] In addition, the rich inheritance of scholastic philosophy provided a basis for reflection on the often aggressive medical treatments of the fifteenth, sixteenth, and seventeenth centuries. For example, Thomas de Vio Cajetan (1480–1547), whom the Pope sent to cross-examine Luther, published on the bioethics of medical experimentation.[96] The scholastic tradition also fashioned the still widely current distinction between "ordinary" and "extraordinary" treatment. This distinction establishes a line between morally obligatory and non-obligatory treatment in the refusal of life-saving medical intervention. It turns not simply on what is usual or unusual but on considerations of costs, including psychological burdens.[97] In short, Christian theology articulated a view of human well-being that gave precedence to maintaining the moral life over preserving life in this world. The result was a doctrine that resembled the Greek notion of *sophrosyne* (i.e., balance or temperance, here in the treatment of patients), but for otherworldly reasons.

Though the scholastic intellectual tradition would continue to have significant influence, by the beginning of the fourteenth century the social structure which supported the medieval Christian synthesis was showing serious signs of strain.[98] In this period, Francesco Petrarch (1304–1374) was one of the first voices of Renaissance humanism, employing the Ciceronian idea of *humanitas* in his reappropriation of antiquity. Born three years before Pope Clement V moved the papacy to Avignon, Petrarch died four years before the Great Schism began.[99] During this period, the papacy lost its capacity to provide Christendom with effective moral guidance or a point of cultural synthesis. The papacy failed to respond effectively to the societal and cultural needs of the times and became a source of scandal with putative popes in Rome, Avignon, and Pisa. In an attempt to remedy the situation, the Council of Constance (1414–1418) deposed popes Benedict XIII (1394–1417) and John XXIII (1410–1415), and accepted the resignation of Gregory XII (1406–1415). However, Martin V (1417–1431) and his successors were not able to institute needed reforms. Instead, a conflict ensued between the papacy and the Church: the Council of Constance's assertion of the sovereignty of an ecumenical council over a pope was reaffirmed by the Council of Basel, which in 1431 refused to adjourn on the orders of Pope Eugene IV (1431–1447).[100]

These events reflect a disintegration of medieval social structures and a change in attitudes foreshadowing the emphasis on individuals found in the humanism of the Renaissance. In 1434 there was even a short-lived Roman Republic, necessitating the Pope's flight to Florence (where the Renaissance would flourish after the fall of Constantinople on 29 May 1453, with the consequent movement of scholars and original texts to the West). Out of this age of corruption and chaos the Renaissance interest in humanism emerged, giving hope of reorientation and rediscovery of man.

The humanism of the Renaissance involved reaching back to pre-Christian visions of man and to the original pagan writings, which had been the foundations of Western culture.[101] "The general tendency of the age" was, as Kristeller has noted, "to attach the greatest importance to classical studies, and to consider classical antiquity as the common standard and model by which to guide all cultural activities."[102] As a result, the style of good prose became Ciceronian.[103] Moreover, the return to classical roots led in the fifteenth century to contrasting the *studia humanitatis* with the *studia divinitatis*.[104] The Renaissance again saw man as the measure of reality and morality. As in Giovanni Pico (1463–1494), Count of Mirandola's *Oration on the Dignity of Man* (1486), there was a celebration of humanity and of the human condition.[105] The Renaissance's emphasis on individuality, liberty, and the capacities of humans was as much a reaction against the past with its corruption and restrictions as a return to the *humanitas* of the Graeco-Roman world. The humanism of the Renaissance attempted to step free of many of the constraints of the theologically oriented world of the Christian millennium so as to reclaim, clear and undefiled, the original secular scriptures of the West.

The Renaissance's exultation in the beauties and pleasures of this life had a frankness unknown since pre-Christian times. The Renaissance restated a pagan understanding of human well-being. As Kristeller acknowledges, several of the famous humanists were "violent critics of medieval learning."[106] As a result, humanism took on an adversarial character, however qualified, with respect to Christianity. This was so understood by many of the figures of the Renaissance. For instance, Pope Paul II (1464–1471) felt compelled to forbid the reading of morally objectionable classical texts (1468) and finally to arrest leaders of the Roman Academy, humanists who had been critical of the Church. A reestablished Roman Academy found a much more congenial reception from the Medici Pope, Leo X (1513–1521), and even had future cardinals as members. Humanism both challenged Christianity and attracted its members.

4. Human Well-being in Human Terms

In the century following the fall of Constantinople, the European vision of reality changed dramatically. The Renaissance, with its interest in Graeco-Roman pagan literature and its exultation of man, with its archaeological rediscovery of the monuments and sculpture of the past, transformed art and literature. But already the vision of the times had outstripped that of the ancients. The printing press (invented in 1456) allowed the wide dissemination of texts by humanists, scientists, and physicians. The perceived scope of the world, of the human context, was also dramatically altered. Between March 15, 1493, when Columbus returned to Spain with news of the New World, and April 27, 1521, when Magellan died (ten days after the first questioning of Luther at the Diet of Worms), the horizons of earthly possibilities expanded dramatically. Further, a radically new vision of man's place in the cosmos was offered in 1543 by Copernicus (1473–1543).[107]

Significant change took place in medicine as well. One might think of Andreas Vesalius's *De humani corporis fabrica*, published in the same year as Copernicus's *De Revolutionibus*. Written with the style of a humanist, it revolutionized anatomy and served as a major demonstration of errors in Galen.[108] The result was that men began not to look backwards to a Golden Age, but ahead to an age of progress and reason. It was within this context of unexpected possibilities and growing nationalism that significant moral reflection was brought to bear on the role of health care in the maintenance of the state. This spawned a special genre of medical moral works, the *medicus politicus* literature, focused on the political usefulness of medicine.[109]

In spite of the superiority of the new sciences over the knowledge of the Greeks and Romans, the veneration of their literature continued. It provided contact with the roots of civilization and with literary works equal or superior to any of the time. Moreover, interest in the humanities continued to mark the educated physician. There were not only humanist physicians but also surgeons who tried to recapture the learning of the past. Nutton, in an essay entitled "Humanist Surgery," argues that "By an alliance with the humanism of some physicians, the academic surgeon [of the Renaissance] could further strengthen his own position within the academic hierarchy."[110] The learning of the humanists was seen to be integral to human well-being, to convey both intellectual ability and moral character, so that "the surgeon, possessed of a proper morality, reinforced by Galenic precept, [was] led towards kindness and charity to his colleagues; [he was seen to] preserve a decent semblance of order, as well as being right in his judgments and advice. Traditional craft loyalty is here being strengthened by classical precept, and Guy's heroic surgeon becomes a sort of Galenic saint."[111] One finds again the association of learning and moral excellence, which existed in the ancient world, and which continues today in medicine. By the early eighteenth century, *humanitas* was listed as one of the virtues that a physician should possess.[112]

In the late eighteenth and the nineteenth centuries, especially in Germany, there was a strong movement once again to associate the classics with learning itself. This was particularly due to the centrality of the *humanistisches Gymnasium* in German secondary education, and the general resurgence of interest in Greece. Education was again rooted in Greek and the classics. In this, Wilhelm von Humboldt (1767–1835)[113] and Friedrich Immanuel Niethammer (1766–1848) played central roles.[114] Horst Rüdiger (1908–) termed this Second Humanism the *neues Humanismus*.[115] In this period, physicians who possessed learning in the humanities were able to cater more effectively to the affluent classes, for they were able to project themselves as learned gentlemen, not just craftsmen.[116] Coeval with these developments was a secular emphasis on the capacity of humans as such, a focus that was born of the Enlightenment and the writings of individuals such as Voltaire (1694–1778). It was nurtured by the French Revolution, reinforced by the positivist thought of Auguste Comte (1798–1857) and expressed in a *réligion de l'humanité*. By the end of the nineteenth century, a vague notion of humanism as a concern for the needs of man and for human values became associated with elements of the progressive sentiments of the time. There was a firm conviction of the possibility of articulating and realizing a concept of human well-being in human terms alone. There was also a feeling of and commitment to progress.

This sense of progress often had religious roots. For example, aspirations for a universalistic statement of religious and progressive sentiments free of a commitment to belief in Jesus Christ as the Messiah produced from Unitarianism the Free Religious Association (which began from discussions in 1866) and the publication of *The Radical* (already in publication that year). The result was a progressive humanistic gospel that maintained theistic elements.

> Brothers and sisters, we want to work for humanity. We have a new gospel to proclaim — the gospel of religion and science, two in one — the gospel of faith in man carried out to its extremest consequences . . . We have a new gospel of good news, a radical gospel, the gospel of the "enthusiasm of humanity." God grant us . . . a new Pentecostal outpouring of courage and fidelity to truth![117]

The goal was a rational religion of progress.[118]

These universalist aspirations to progress were not only expressed in scientific theistic terms. Consider, for example, J. Howard Moore's optimistic assessment of the inevitable results of human progress.

> But the world is growing better. And in the Future — in the long, long ages to come — IT WILL BE REDEEMED! The same spirit of sympathy and fraternity that broke the black man's manacles and is today melting the white woman's chains will tomorrow emancipate the working man and the ox; and, as the ages bloom and the great wheels of the centuries grind on, the same spirit shall banish Selfishness from the earth, and convert the planet finally into one unbroken and unparalleled spectacle of PEACE, JUSTICE, and SOLIDARITY.[119]

There was a feeling of history leading to the full realization of human ideals.

In the first four decades of the twentieth century and especially immediately after the First World War, there was a reaction against the materialism and positivism of the time. Rüdiger termed this intellectual reaction the Third Humanism.[120] The reaction included Werner Jaeger's call for a return to the serious study of the humanities. Jaeger (1888–1961) saw a danger in the emerging mass culture, which he characterized as an Americanization. "The percentage of the population that has a truly internal share in the ancestral intellectual assets of our nation decreases from year to year as indicated by the factory-like mass production of popular science and the introduction of the cinema, radio, and pocket microscopes in the school."[121] The reinvocation of the intellectual and moral importance of the study of Greek and the classics at times took on a chilianist cast that can only be understood against the economic and political circumstances of the 1920s and 1930s. Many, like Ernst Robert Curtius (1886–1956), sought from humanism a full, spiritual revival. "If humanism is to live again in the second third of the twentieth century, it can only be a total humanism: one that is sensual and spiritual, philological and touched by the muses, philosophical and artistic, pious and political, all in one."[122]

In the United States an analogous phenomenon appeared before the First World War and came to be styled the New Humanism. Led by such individuals as Irving Babbitt (1865–1933) and Paul E. More (1864–1937), it was a response to a loss of meaning felt within industrial urban mass society.[123] It was also a response against the vocationalism of the time. The New Humanists sought to recover the bond of culture to permanent, universal values. Though the New Humanists were at times critical of religion, they saw themselves endorsing the cardinal, enduring values of the Judeo-Christian tradition.[124] Out of ancient Roman understandings, as well as from the Christian heritage, the New Humanism derived a dualism that contrasted higher human refinements with the animal and physical world.[125] The movement was culturally, much more than politically, conservative.[126] It was also reactionary; it was a response against pragmatism as well as against the scientific and technological infatuations of the time. Here was an attempt to frame a concept of human well-being embedded in the most excellent expressions of refined culture over against a concept of human well-being articulated in terms of the emerging mass culture. In the concerns of the Third Humanism and the New Humanism about a value-free science and technology one can see anticipation of the concerns of the 1960s to recapture commitments to enduring values and purpose in medicine under the rubric of the medical humanities.

Against this background, one can also better understand the sympathy that the medical humanities have had with theology and religious studies as custodians of important values relevant to health care. In particular, the debate about the place of religion became integral to New Humanism's attempt to recapture a sense of balance, proportion, and enduring values. T. S. Eliot (1888–1965) was a major figure in this debate. Eliot argued that religion and humanism should supplement each other. This supplementation was seen to be needed because religion without humanism lacks *humanitas*. Without humanism, religion "can be, and usually is . . . vulgar; it can be equally narrow and bigoted: with the alternative that when it is not narrow and bigoted it is liberal, sloppy, hypocritical and humanitarian."[127] On the other hand, Eliot held that, in the modern world, cultivation of the emotions can be achieved only through dogmatic religion. "The need of the modern world is the discipline and training of the emotions; which neither the intellectual training of philosophy or science nor the wisdom of humanism, nor the negative instruction of psychology can give."[128] Like the New Humanists, Eliot struggled to bring together the discipline and values drawn from the heritage of the Greeks with those taken from the Judeo-Christian tradition.

The New Humanists expected that humanism could serve not only as a field of scholarship and as a source of intellectual and moral renewal, but also as a medium for improving individuals and society. Abraham Flexner (1866–1959), for example, regarded humanism as key to maintaining a human context for the sciences. Flexner, whose report for the Carnegie Foundation directed the scientific focus of twentieth-century American medical education,[129] argued in his 1928 Taylorian lecture that true humnism must be distinguished from philology pursued as a technical scholastic endeavor.[130] He held that humanism is properly understood as the critical appraisal of values. "[T]he assessment of values, in so far as human beings are affected, constitutes the unique burden of humanism."[131] Flexner envisaged humanism having a scope far beyond its traditional role as an intellectual endeavor worth pursuing in its own right, or as a personal moral or aesthetic refinement. For Flexner, humanism should "charge itself with the appreciation of the present as well as of the past, of the value of science, of the value of industry, of the soundness, comprehensiveness, justice, fairness, worth-whileness of government, ours, yours, other nations."[132] In many ways Flexner, who had a profound impact on modern American medical education, anticipated contemporary reflections in bioethics in rejecting notions of a value-free science current in the 1920s.

As shown above, ambiguities of the various terms that have clustered around the concept of humanism have persisted to the present unclarified. A twentieth-century translation of Oxford University's course "*Litterae humaniores*" as the "humane literature", and the traditional styling of the professor of Latin in Scotland as the professor of "humanity," mark the continued interplay of a resonating cluster of concepts and words. These words and ideas bear at least a family resemblance to each other. They have shaped modern academic institutions.[133] The influence of the Renaissance and its rekindled interest in *humanitas* and the human condition have been so pervasive and persuasive that the term humanism has come to identify not just learning associated with the study of the humanities, but a focus on the human individual, a faith in human capacities, and an interest in human values. Kristeller seems correct in saying that the humanists of the Renaissance were not "philosophers with a curious lack of philosophical ideas and a curious fancy for eloquence and for classical studies, but rather professional rhetoricians with a new, classicist ideal of culture, who tried to assert the importance of their field of learning and to impose their standards upon the other fields of learning and of science, including philosophy."[134] However accurate this may be as a description of the humanism of the Renaissance, "humanism" has now come to identify a collection of very influential ideas that constitute a philosophy, a cluster of visions of human well-being, as well as a set of leitmotifs that mark a number of disparate philosophical standpoints. Many of them have had, and continue to have, an influence on understandings of health and medicine.

Appeals to the humanities in part represent a reaction to the secularization of the West and the fragmentation of post-modern times. As the traditional Christian culture of the West loses its grip on social and political institutions, the humanities offer a non-theistic tradition, bound to pre-Christian times, which provides for many a hope for social and political stability in a post-Christian era. The humanities come to be identified with disciplined reasoning itself, thus shoring up the central Enlightenment commitment to reason against the centrifugal forces of the post-modern era. Consider, for example, Albert Levi's definition of the humanities.

1. The humanities are not the natural sciences, the social sciences, or the fine arts.
2. The humanities are identical with the liberal arts.
3. The liberal arts are three, that is, the arts of communication, the arts of continuity, and the arts of criticism. (This means, respectively, the languages and literatures, history, and philosophy.)[135]

This broad construal of the humanities would make them indispensable to the conduct of the lives of men and women in general, and physicians and health care policy makers in particular.

However, many sense a loss in the academies of the West of a commitment to a particular body of learning or to a particular set of intellectual skills. Indeed, there is a sense that the intellectual culture of the West has abandoned its own history, its own values, and its own philosophy. This impression is the result of the fragmentation of the post-modern era in which individuals generally, and in the West in particular, can no longer see themselves as a part of a particular, canonical, rational tradition. There is, as a result, a plaintive tone in the crusade begun by William J. Bennett, when he was Director of the National Endowment for the Humanities of the United States Government. He lamented that one can graduate from 86% of American colleges without having studied the civilizations of classical Greece and Rome.[136] The report issued under Bennett's name is the result of a Study Group on the State of Learning in the Humanities in Higher Education, convened under the auspices of the National Endowment for the Humanities. The Study Group concluded *inter alia* that the "study of the humanities and Western civilization must take its place at the heart of the college curriculum."[137] The Study Group's report has many of the characteristics of the laments by modern church groups that attendance has diminished and the social influence of their denomination has weakened. Still, this loss of cultural orientation has profound implications for the possibility of developing general cultural judgments regarding the significance of health and medicine.

Bennett expands the meaning of the humanities so that they are no longer necessarily bound to the particular literature of the West. Instead, Bennett touts a commitment to reason that developed out of the West but need not be bound to the particular cultural peculiarities of the West.

> Expanding on a phrase from Matthew Arnold, I would describe the humanities as the best that has been said, thought, written, and otherwise expressed about the human experience. The

> humanities tell us how men and women of our own and other civilizations have grappled with life's enduring, fundamental questions: What is justice? What should be loved? What deserves to be defended? What is courage? What is noble? What is base? Why do civilizations flourish? Why do they decline?[138]

The humanities are here tantamount to the cultivation of the skills necessary to be a rational and humane individual. Put in this fashion, it is difficult to reject the humanities without rejecting (as do many post-moderns) the commitment to reason that is so much a part of modern self-understandings.

Christians,[139] Communists,[140] and existentialists[141] all claim that they have articulated the true humanism. Each argues they have correctly taken man's natural and human interests seriously. The claim by Christianity to be the true humanism shows the extent to which, after the Renaissance, the *studia divinitatis* were redefined in terms of the *studia humanitatis*. The inclusion of religious studies as a part of the humanities, especially the medical humanities, is an index of the triumph of the Renaissance, of modernity, of the human-oriented present over the God-centered world of the Middle Ages. The transcendent is treated not in its own terms, but as a set of ideas and images for secular rational analysis. Religion in this context is secularized.

A similar triumph of humanist vision has occurred with respect to the economic forces that were set loose with the Renaissance, leading to capitalism. Capitalism has itself been described as a form of humanism. For example, Bernard Murchland equates capitalism with humanism, because of its immense positive social consequences: the development of political freedoms, an enhanced sense of individual worth, and a higher standard of living. Surely, "the concomitant growth of democracy and capitalism added rich new meanings to the traditional concept of humanism."[142] Moreover, the economic success of capitalism has led to unparalleled support of the intellectual life. "Capitalism is, then, a humanism on empirical grounds."[143]

As is clear from the foregoing broad interpretations, humanism has come to mean much more than an interest in the literature of Greece and Rome. Humanism has come to express a faith in progress and a general, vague affirmation of the human enterprise and of the human individual. The *Great Soviet Encyclopedia* defines humanism as

> a system of historically changing views that recognizes the value

> of the human being as an individual and his right to liberty, happiness, and the opportunity to develop and express his capabilities. It regards human welfare as the criterion in evaluating social institutions and regards the principles of equality, justice, and humaneness as the desired norm in relations between people.[144]

The passage does not provide any precise definition of the crucial terms of the definition. Here Kristeller appears to be vindicated. Whatever humanism means, even in the twentieth century, it does not identify a single system of values, or a philosophical doctrine through which one can understand how to judge competing claims regarding the value of human individuals for medicine, or in general. Nor does humanism provide an unambiguous moral and philosophical basis for a particular bioethics. Still, the general affirmation of the value of individuals and of rights to liberty, happiness, and opportunity resonates, however obscurely, with so many elements of our general culture that it would appear "inhumane" and garishly out of step with the times, were one to reject out of hand the positive connotations attendant to the term humanism.

Those few who do not join in the general praise of humanism and the humanities tend most prominently to be members of fundamentalist religious groups (or of specially orthodox varieties of mainline religions) or to condemn humanism for a onesided accent on reason over the non-cognitive elements of the human enterprise (see Chapter I). The critics have also included certain Marxists as well as certain interpreters of the Post-Modern condition. In the 1950s and 1960s these Marxist critics regarded the individualism of humanism as incompatible with Marxist-Leninism[145] and saw "socialist humanism" as a deplorable distortion.[146] They judged humanism to be a threat to human well-being. Consider, for example, the October 1963 speech by Chou Yang, one of Mao Tse-tung's chief propagandists, to the Chinese Academy of Social Sciences.

> The modern revisionists and some bourgeois scholars try to describe Marxism as humanism and call Marx a humanist. Some people counterpose the young Marx to the mature proletarian revolutionary Marx . . . In particular they make use of certain views on "alienation" expressed by Marx in his early *Economic and Philosophic Manuscripts, 1844* to depict him as an exponent of the bourgeois theory of human nature. They do their best to

> preach so-called Humanism by using the concept of alienation. This, of course, is futile.[147]

Bourgeois talk of humanism was regarded as an attempt to bandage over alienations engendered by capitalism. For some Marxists, the standard notion of humanism had to be recast because Marxism aimed at remaking humanity, not at coming to terms with the human condition. It was in terms of the goal of remaking humanity that revolutionary terror was accepted as having a humane purpose.

> For it is certain that neither Bukharin nor Trotsky nor Stalin regarded Terror as intrinsically valuable. Each one imagined he was using it to realize a genuinely human history which had not yet started but which provides the justification for revolutionary violence. In other words, as Marxists, all three confess that there is a meaning to such violence — that it is possible to understand it, to read into it a rational development and to draw from it a humane future.[148]

This account of Marxism was provided by Merleau-Ponty (1908–1961), while others contrasted the early and late Marx. For example, Louis Althusser (1918–) distinguished the early Marx (pre-1845) from the later Marx (post-1845). The earlier Marx, who was still in the grips of Hegel, gave prominence to themes of humanism. The later Marx discovered the materialistic science of Marxism. It was only the later Marx who was the true Marxist.

In one perspective, these criticisms were not fundamentally opposed to humanism.[149] That is, they were not a criticism of humanism such as one might find from a post-modern viewpoint.[150] Rather, these Marxist criticisms were for the most part embedded within a rationalist understanding of philosophy and science. The difference between the humanists and the Marxists lay in the Marxist affirmation of human nature as it would appear in the future. They rejected contemporary human nature as normative. But faith in science and in the capacity to know remained intact, or was, if anything, exaggerated.

Criticisms of humanism have also been a part of recent French philosophical reflections. Some of these tie humanism to a teleological or idealist vision of history. Others have reacted against the subjectivity and individualistic orientation of humanism. Still others articulated the fundamental post-modern critique against the rationalist assumptions of the modern age.[151] Most significant in this view is Michel Foucault's (1926–1984) recasting of Nietzsche's

(1844–1900) statement that "God is dead" into "man is dead."[152] Interpreted somewhat broadly, this statement claims that not only is the linchpin of the *studia divinitatis* gone, but that of the *studia humanitatis* as well. Man is no longer the master or the criterion of history or culture, but rather the servant of the structures of language and society.[153] There is no *humanitas* to which one can appeal as the foundation of the humanities. This criticism, if it is regarded as part of the post-modern doubts about the possibility of knowledge and culture, has a force beyond its particular articulation.[154] It poses questions about the possibility of humanism, already raised in the preface of this book. It brings into question the possibility of a coherent intellectual standpoint in terms of which the human condition and human well-being can be understood and interpreted. It undercuts the feasibility of articulating a coherent notion of human excellence, of *humanitas*. I shall return to this problem in the final chapter.

Despite the aforementioned criticisms, Marxists have for the most part found the metaphors of humanism congenial. Even Althusser has argued that at least under a true dictatorship of the proletariat a humanistic social condition would obtain.[155] In general, Marxists attempted to characterize their own approaches to morality as marked by a true humanism or simply asserted that "Marxism is humanism."[156] The quasi-official position has been that:

> Marxism rejected the abstract supraclass approach to the problems of humanism and placed them instead on a realistic historical foundation, formulating a new conception of humanism, that of proletarian, or socialist, humanism, which included in itself all the best achievements of humanist thought of the past. Marx first showed the realistic way toward realizing the ideals of humanism by linking it with the scientific theory of social development, with the revolutionary movement of the proletariat, and with the struggle for communism.[157]

Note the appeal to a scientific theory of social development. The problems of humanism and the problems of values generally are rendered problems of science.

As a result, ethical problems become scientific problems. As Loren Graham has shown: "In the Soviet Union . . . ethics and values are considered to be no less a subject of scientific study than is biology. As a Soviet author wrote . . . Marxists believe that, in principle, values can be submitted to 'strict scientific research.'"[158] An account of human well-being is thus a scientific account.

Generally, Marxists are like traditional Roman Catholic moral theorists in holding that a definitive, rational answer can be given, at least in general terms, to most, if not all, moral questions, including those of bioethics.[159] One finds here a special continuation of the medieval Christian faith in reason, inherited from Greek rationalist thought, and bequeathed to this secular Judeo-Christian heresy. The recent collapse of faith in Marxism in the Soviet bloc as well as the phenomena of glasnost and perestroika can be understood, using this metaphor, on an analogy with Vatican II and its consequences. There has been a widespread weakening in the commitment to the metaphysics that sustains the Marxist worldview and its special understanding of humanism. However, the positive valence of the term humanism persists.

Over the past two-and-a-half millennia the various terms that cluster around *humanitas* have been employed in approbation by pagan and Christian, by capitalist and communist, by conservative and revolutionary, each claiming to embody the true humanism. Each party has been engaged in articulating a vision of human well-being. Over this long history, the ambiguities of *humanitas* have not been dispelled. If anything, they are now more pronounced. Yet the concept of humanism is still attractive. This remarkable phenomenon can be explained in terms of the powerful synergy among the intellectual, moral, and aesthetic goals arrayed around the ideal image of human excellence or well-being: *humanitas*. We must fashion societies, develop cultures, apply technologies (such as those in medicine), and eventually reshape ourselves. What more inviting point of departure is there than reflections on our human nature and human condition? What more common goal or aspiration than the realization of our distinguishing capacities? The interest in turning to the normatively human to discover foundations for our culture has taken on an urgent character, given the collapse of old certainties, major social upheavals, as well as today's rapid and seemingly relentless pace of science, medicine, and technology. As the very character of the human condition is being transformed, it becomes ever more urgent, and ever more difficult, to understand the nature of the human enterprise and to characterize the essence of human well-being.

5. The Medical Humanities

In 1940, the United States invested about 4% of its Gross National Product in health care. That had risen by 10% in 1950 (4.4%).

Between 1950 and 1960 the percentage increase was over 20%, so that the share of the Gross National Product became 5.3%. Between 1960 and 1965 the increase was over 15%, bringing the portion of the GNP devoted to health care to 6.1%. In the next two years alone the increase was nearly 5%. The realization of human well-being was pursued through an aggressive investment in health care. But the changes have not been simply economic. The 1960s were a period in which medical technology developed rapidly, intensive care units became commonplace, and the public expectations from medicine became substantial. The year 1967 marked the first successful heart transplant. Indeed, the expectation of the ability of humans to avoid suffering and achieve well-being took on Promethean overtones.[160]

The 1960s were also a period of dramatic social change, which brought established views of human well-being into question. Toffler captured the sense of over-rapid pace and cultural disorientation in the metaphor "future shock."[161] Moreover, there was a concern about an alienation of science and technology from culture. The immense popularity of C.P. Snow's 1959 Rede Lecture is an index of the perceived importance of this issue. In addressing the gulf between the preponderant culture of contemporary science and the traditional literary culture of the West, Snow spoke to a problem that many felt to be crucial: the problem of bridging between the sciences and our sustained reflections on values.[162] Others attempted to bridge the gulf by denying its existence. Instead, they attempted to establish that science itself was embedded in and committed to human values.[163] Yet others reacted by incorporating within their view of science an attention to values and life-experiences, as occurred in the case of humanistic psychology.[164] Still others saw the difficulty as a crisis in the humanities stemming from a failure to take human values and the perennial human questions seriously.[165] There was a perceived need to understand the place of science and technology in culture and the academy.[166]

There was also a realization in the 1960s that the general culture of the West, particularly of Europe, had changed and the political structures had finally become post-Christian. There was a new moral challenge. Just as science and technology allowed manned space exploration, so that man began to leave the earth, the fabric of traditional values was dissolving into a relativism within which neither the goals of science and technology nor a concept of human well-being could unambiguously or univocally be stated or understood.[167] The interest in going back to the established themes of the humanities arose within this context.[168] This interest in the place of the humanities and their relationship to culture as a whole continues the reaction expressed in the New Humanism and the Third Humanism against the materialism and positivism of the nineteenth and early twentieth centuries.

The intellectual concern about the socio-technological developments of the 1950s and 1960s supported an exploration of medicine through the humanities. There was a hope that through the humanities, which tie us to our cultural origins and to a tradition of reflection on the human enterprise and human values, there would be an intellectual reorientation to the fundamental values associated with humanitas.[169] The goal was to embed the enterprise of medicine in traditional concerns for human well-being, so as to avoid what appeared to be an incipient estrangement of medical technology and health care institutions from patients and the public.[170]

Against the background of these concerns and in terms of the rich ambiguities associated with humanism and being humane, one can better understand why a society established in 1968 to encourage research and teaching in the medical humanities was styled the Society for Health and Human Values. Out of context, the title is provocative. One might ask: what values are there except human values? Divine values? Since a significant proportion of the Society's members are men and women of religious conviction, an intended contrast with the *studia divinitatis* is not likely. What service, then, does the term "human" do? The answer is available only against the backdrop of the history just sketched. The term "human" indicates a direction and a focus. It indirectly lays claim to a tradition of learning and philanthropy. The unclarities are strategic. They invite men and women of quite different interests and convictions to join in mutually supporting and allied endeavors. As the term "human values" suggests both humane concerns as well as an appreciation of the values of human culture, the term contains all of the ambiguities that Gellius recognized in the Latin term *humanitas*.

The elision of ethics, human values, and the humanities in an account of the Society (published as part of a major report on the teaching of bioethics and the humanities in U.S. medical schools) demonstrates the magic of this conflation.

> The Society was formally established in 1968 to encourage research, teaching and public interest in questions of human values as they arise in health and medical care. Its members are drawn

> from a wide spectrum of educators, faculty members and health care practitioners who share a common interest in ethics, human values and the humanities in the health sciences.[171]

Though "ethics" is presumably one of the contemporary humanities, it is mentioned separately in a way that would be otiose, were it not to suggest broader intellectual vistas against which the reader should understand education in ethics.

The report also recognizes the rich nexus of ambiguities in the history of "humanism." "No program can possibly satisfy all the interpretations and expectations subsumed under such titles as 'human values,' 'humanism,' 'medical humanities,' or even 'medical ethics.'"[172] Moreover, it regards the humanities as properly incorporating a set of values, not just teaching them.

> The humanist must also be "authentic." The medical setting requires that the humanist incorporate the values he or she professes and the character traits that are embodiments of the liberal arts teachings, to be human if not humane . . . truly, the humanist must be "holier than thou."[173]

In addition, the study regards the humanities as morally transforming.

> So far as ethics and the humanities go, they undoubtedly raise the sensitivity of students and faculty to ethical and values questions . . . Almost everywhere, as a result, patients are better apprised of their part in clinical decisions, and of the value and moral issues woven into their relationships with the physician. This is a result to be desired in a society that is democratic, educated and pluralistic in its value systems. Whatever personalizes and particularizes healing will make it more humane.[174]

Teaching the history of medicine and bioethics is thus considered not just the communication of knowledge but a means for moral change.

A key figure in the development of medical humanities has been Edmund D. Pellegrino (1920–). Pellegrino argues that medicine constitutes a unique bridge between the sciences and the humanities: "Medicine is the most humane of sciences, the most empiric of arts, and the most scientific of humanities."[175] Pellegrino's perceptive and rhetorically well-directed remark has broad and radical force. It builds on the observation that the human condition and human well-being are the objects par excellence of medicine.

Medicine and the biomedical sciences are now able to respond to the frailties of human nature and thus reshape the conditions of birth, well-being, illness, and death. Medicine has become the paradigm response to human suffering. But beyond that, through the promises of genetic engineering, there is the likelihood that medicine in the end may reshape and redirect human nature itself and thus fundamentally recast the notions of human well-being and suffering. But to what ends and within what limits? It is impossible to conceive of medicine whole and complete without sketching its goals, purposes, and directions. And such goals, purposes, and directions can only be given a full account against an exegesis of *humanitas,* of human excellence. In this sense, medicine is "the most humane of the sciences:" it is directed to the human condition through and on behalf of human values and images of well-being. Moreover, its study of man and the human condition is empirical, a circumstance that makes at least plausible the claim that medicine is the most scientific of the humanities.

Pellegrino correctly diagnoses the great ambiguities, the potential influence, and the inflated hopes associated with the humanities. Humanism is regarded as a panacea.

> Medical humanism has achieved the status of a salvation theme, which can absolve the perceived "sins" of modern medicine. The list of those sins is long, varied, and often contradictory: overspecialization; technicism; overprofessionalization; insensitivity to personal and sociocultural values; too narrow a construal of the doctor's role; too much "curing" rather than "caring;" not enough emphasis on prevention, patient participation, and patient education; too much science; not enough liberal arts; not enough behavioral science; too much economic incentive; a "trade school" mentality; insensitivity to the poor and socially disadvantaged; overmedicalization of everyday life; inhumane treatment of medical students; overwork by house staff; deficiencies in verbal and nonverbal communication.[176]

This extensive catalogue of ills compasses intellectual, moral, and affective shortcomings. It includes failures of demeanor and style. In short, the list of things gone wrong is the obverse of the list of values and goals compassed by the wide range of meanings associated with *humanitas* and its cognates (e.g., humane, any humanitarian).

Interest in the medical humanities recruited energies from both the humanities and medicine. Just as thinkers in health care education recognized that health care ran the danger of being separated from the broader interests of the culture, so, too, humanities scholars recognized that the humanities ran the danger of being absorbed by technical rather than substantial questions. They resisted separating the humanities from the central and enduring preoccupations of civilization. Just as physicians and other health care professionals sought to regain from the humanities a sense of purpose, moral place, and proportion, the humanists sought to recapture from medicine a sense of engagement, relevance, and cultural importance. The medical humanities came to be regarded as a bridge or point of dialectical interaction between the biomedical sciences and scholarship in the humanities. It is not just that this dialectic offered to dissolve the isolation of medicine and the humanities from the perennial intellectual questions concerning human nature and human power. Medicine gave content to the humanities, and the humanities direction to medicine. The life-and-death questions of medicine could be moved from a merely technological context and recaptured within the moral, philosophical, historical, and literary reflections that sustain the enlightened life and whose threatened attenuation occasioned the birth of the Third Humanism.[177] The foundational questions of bioethics legitimated the metaphysical hunger (e.g., "what man is, why man exists"), which the medical humanities offered to satisfy.[178]

The American interest in teaching bioethics, which developed in the latter part of the 1960s, was conceived out of the rich ambiguity of *humanitas*, which associates cultivation of the mind, study of the humane arts, and the development of humane dispositions.[179] Were it not for its persistence and for its classical roots, one might conclude that this ambiguity, which involves conflicting intellectual and moral virtues, is no more than a clever means for creating a coalition of educational forces in order to effect changes in the medical curriculum. However, the perennial interweaving of this cluster of notions suggests that it is motivated by a complex, unavoidable, recurring question: what is the well-being of humans? The historical collage of the terms that cluster around the word "human" (e.g., humane, *humanitas*, humanness, humanist, humanism, humanity, etc.) discloses an answer: human well-being is intellectual and moral, derived from native capacities as well as from the results of cultivation and technological interventions. And, as one might expect, this ambiguity characterizes many if not most programs in the "medical humanities."[180] This ambiguity underlies interest in bioethics as a source of intellectual direction and moral motivation. Though bioethics as a scholarly discipline can *in sensu stricto* offer only intellectual insights, it is also regarded as effecting moral improvement. Concerns with theory and praxis have been tightly interwoven in bioethics, reflecting the complex history of humanism.

IV Competing Foundations for Bioethics and Health Care Policy[1]

1. The Two Secular Humanisms

In the twentieth century an account of "humanism" is complicated by the development of a cluster of philosophical schools, which at times have taken on the character of social movements.[2] As the New Humanism was focusing on developing a style of life and scholarship marked by a particular vision of *humanitas*, other humanists sought to meet the moral and political difficulties of the twentieth century. They were heirs of the progressive era. They addressed Abraham Flexner's concerns and undertook the Third Humanism's task of providing a living response to the challenges of the times. But, unlike many associated with the Third Humanists, these did not turn back to antiquity. Instead, they saw humanism as providing a basis for moral and political action in the future, though recognizing historical roots and sources of inspiration. Theirs is not primarily an endeavor of scholarship, nor an attempt to nurture a genteel or refined style of living. Their goals are much more sociopolitical.

The various interventionist philosophies that have called themselves humanisms in this century contrast with the traditional sense of humanism, as much of bioethics contrasts with the medical humanities generally. Though bioethics is a scholarly endeavor, it is nurtured by and directed towards actual moral and political controversies. The medical humanities, in contrast, have seen their prime task as providing an intellectual context and breadth of vision for health care. They attempt to place health care within the context of enduring human values and perennial human concerns so that health care can have proper ends and purposes. The final focus of the humanities in this sense is on understanding what makes the human endeavor worthwhile. In this way, the humanities remain in their core as forms of philosophical knowledge, ends in themselves. In contrast, the partisans of the various interventionist humanisms have sought a moral vision that can translate theory into practice and transform the world. Humanists in this latter sense have often seen themselves as providing an alternative religion or, as an alternative to religion.

These various humanist movements of the twentieth century were anticipated by the Rationalists of the seventeenth, eighteenth, and nineteenth centuries, as well as by Free Thinkers, who criticized the established churches. But unlike most contemporary Evolutionary, Naturalistic, Scientific, Secular, and even Religious Humanists, the majority of Rationalists affirmed the existence of God. For their part, the Free Thinkers were associated with much of the development of deism. Important works reflecting this view were Anthony Collins' (1676–1729) *A Discourse of Free Thought* (1713), and Thomas Paine's (1737–1809) *The Age of Reason* (1794–96). Denying any link to atheism, Collins claimed, "If there is any such rare Monster as an Atheist, David has given us his Character in these words, The Fool hath said in his heart, there is no God; that is, no one denies the Existence of a God but some idle, unthinking, shallow Fellow."[3] But by the mid-nineteenth century, many Free Thinkers were atheists, as shown by the association of the London Atheistical Society with the Freethought movement.[4] Freethought was also associated with Holyoake's secularism and his Secular Guild, which anticipated the twentieth-century phenomenon of secular humanism.

The humanist movements have been characterized as naturalistic in denying the supernatural and holding that nature is everything and that there is no stark discontinuity between man and nature.[5] Charles Hartshorne (1897–), who has defended the rational demonstrability of God's existence and affirmed man's continuity with nature, writes:

> Humanism, so conceived, amounts to two claims. First, it implies that, except for the animals and for the speculative possibility of inhabitants upon other heavenly bodies, man is evidently alone in the universe, dependent for friendship upon his own kind. Second, it maintains that the recognition of this loneliness will aid rather than hinder the good life here upon earth. In naturalism, as opposed to supernaturalism, the humanist finds not only truth, but the truth that makes us free and strengthens and enlightens us for the tasks of living.[6]

But the humanist movements are complex and no one characterization has been found congenial. Some humanists have termed themselves religious humanists and regarded humanism as a new faith: "Humanism is faith in the supreme value and self-perfectibility of human personality."[7] Humanism as a religion has provided a community for the faithful with social structures similar to traditional religious congregations. It has sought to cultivate a sense of personal consecration and devotion to ideals. Others, who have rejected religious appurtenances, have styled themselves Secular Humanists. However, even some Secular Humanists have styled themselves religious.[8] The term Evolutionary Humanist has also been employed to emphasize what is tantamount to a continuation of the nineteenth century progressive faith in improvement.[9] The term Scientific Humanism has been used as well and appears to have anticipated much that is captured by the term Evolutionary Humanism.[10] Still others have spoken of a Democratic Humanism.[11]

Unlike the New Humanists and Third Humanists who anticipated the contemporary interest in the medical humanities, one finds in these various interventionist humanisms interest in (1) foundationalism in the sense of grounding a philosophy or worldview with a view to making (2) socio-cultural changes. In particular, they wish to counter supernaturalism as well as religious intolerance through realizing a largely liberal political agenda. For instance, for over fifty years proponents of religious humanism have generally evidenced an interest in bioethical issues such as the legalization of easy access to birth control.[12] In political sympathies, these humanists contrast with the conservative sentiments of many of the New Humanists and their heirs. But, the proponents of naturalist, religious, secular, scientific, evolutionary, and democratic humanism share with the New Humanists (1) a judgment that civilization faces a significant challenge which is to be met (2) by developing a commitment to authentic human values.

This sense of cultural urgency found expression in the first Humanist Manifesto (1933). There was a background of religious interests: among the thirty-four signatories there was a significant representation by members or former members of the Unitarian Church.[13] Also, John Dewey (1859–1952), the pragmatist *bête noire* of the New Humanists, joined as one of the signers.[14] The Manifesto stated, among other things, that

> Religious humanism maintains that all associations and institutions exist for the fulfillment of human life. The intelligent evaluation, transformation, control, and direction of such associ-

> ations and institutions with a view to the enhancement of human life is the purpose and program of humanism. Certainly religious institutions, their ritualistic forms, ecclesiastical methods, and communal activities must be reconstituted as rapidly as experience allows, in order to function effectively in the modern world.[15]

The first Manifesto also endorsed "a socialized and cooperative economic order."[16] The last point was modified or clarified in the Humanist Manifesto II published in 1973. It recognizes that there are not only dangers from transcendently oriented religions, but that other ideologies also impede human advance. Some forms of political doctrine, for instance, function religiously, reflecting the worst features of orthodoxy and authoritarianism, especially when they sacrifice individuals on the altar of Utopian promises. Purely economic and political viewpoints, whether capitalist or communist, often function as religious and ideological dogma.[17] Both manifestos share the goal of not just gaining the intellectual allegiance of those who already concur with these philosophical statements, but of influencing public opinion.

Against this background, secular humanism takes on at least two meanings. First, secular humanism can be seen in contrast to Christian humanism. That is, secular humanism begins from and develops within the *studia humanitatis* in contrast with, but not necessarily in rejection of, the *studia divinitatis*. This is the traditional contrast rooted in the development of humanism in the late fifteenth and early sixteenth centuries.[18] More generally, secular humanism contrasts with all religious humanisms and special ideological humanisms (e.g., Marxist humanism). Secular humanism in this sense is a humanism that attempts to understand the normatively human and to ground a vision of moral and political theory without reference to, but without rejection of, the supernatural, transcendent, or metaphysical. Second, Secular Humanism contrasts with Religious Humanism, in that each is a particular sectarian movement. Here, Secular Humanism identifies a particular, informally organized intellectual movement with announced socio-cultural ambitions, in loose association with publications such as the *Secular Humanist Bulletin*. Here one might contrast Secular Humanism with secular humanism, as one distinguishes Catholic from catholic.

The seemingly organized character of Secular Humanism has led to serious attempts to construe it as a religion. In 1961, for example, the Supreme Court acknowledged that there are religions that do not involve belief in the existence of God, including "Buddhism, Taoism, Ethical Culture, Secular Humanism and others."[19] This acknowledgment of secular humanism as a religion was further developed in Smith v. Board of School Commissioners of Mobile County, when on March 4, 1987, Chief Justice Hand of the United States District Court of the Southern District of Alabama held that secular humanism constituted a religion for purposes of the First Amendment.[20] The controversy involved public-school textbooks, which allegedly gave deficient attention to the role of the Judeo-Christian religious tradition in American life, and which in addition allegedly taught that moral values were a matter of personal choice. The plaintiffs argued that the use of such textbooks involved adopting a particular religious viewpoint, and that as a consequence such books should be removed from the public school system. The court accepted the testimony of Russell Kirk (1918–), an individual influenced by the New Humanist movement.[21]

> According to Dr. Kirk, Humanist Manifesto I, Humanist Manifesto II and the Declaration of Secular Humanism are three documents which form a creed or body of doctrine for secular humanism. Dr. Kirk says that Christians immanentize symbols of transcendence by claiming that one enters upon immortality through perfection in grace in death. Secularists immanentize this by bringing the issue down to this world, and he says instead of salvation through grace in death, the secularists achieve the perfection of society here in this world. The equivalent of death to the secularists is passing through a form of revolution to a new order of a perfect kind. The role model for this secularist thinking, Dr. Kirk says, is the Marxist theory: revolution and then eternal changelessness here on earth, in a condition of perfect equality. This is an example of immanentizing of the eschaton — the eschaton being the essential belief, the representation of enduring reality.[22]

The Court appears to have relied on Kirk's arguments in holding that secular humanism is a religion from the point of view of the First Amendment.

The Court agreed that the use of textbooks that promoted secular humanist ideas violated the First Amendment prohibition against the establishment of a religion.

> This highly relativistic and individualistic approach constitutes the promotion of a fundamental faith claim opposed to other

> religious faiths. Such a relativistic claim can only be made on the basis of a faith assumption. This faith assumes that self-actualization is the goal of every human being, that man has no supernatural attributes or components, that there are only temporal and physical consequences for man's actions, and that these results, alone, determine the morality of an action. This belief strikes at the heart of many theistic religions' beliefs that certain actions are in and of themselves immoral, *whatever the consequences*, and that, in addition, actions will have extra-temporal consequences.[23]

In consequence, the Court required the removal from the public school system of a list of books held to promote secular humanism. This opinion was reversed by the United States Court of Appeals, Eleventh District on 26 August 1987. The Appeals Court found that a secular purpose supported the use of the textbooks, not an interest in establishing "secular humanism."[24]

The Court of Appeals raised the difficult problem of distinguishing between secular philosophy, that is, a philosophy that does not depend on a particular, established religious or metaphysical viewpoint, and the doctrines of a particular philosophical school or group, such as that of the Secular Humanists. On the one hand, pluralist societies tend to seek a neutral moral language through which their various constitutive moral communities can cooperate peaceably in political life, including the provision of health care. On the other hand, the very pursuit of that neutral language itself invites contending schools of thought regarding its nature and the nature of human well-being. Moreover, these schools of thought often take on the character of parties or factions.

For example, interest in supporting "humanistic" values and social structures has led to the formation of a number of groups, such as the Ethical Humanists, the International Humanist and Ethical Union, the American Humanist Association, and the British Humanist Association, which have been organized to encourage an appreciation of humanism.[25] The 1986 Encyclopedia of Associations provides the following characterization of the American Humanist Association:

> Persons who are devoted to Humanism as a way of life. "Humanism presupposes human's sole dependence on natural and social resources and acknowledges no supernatural power. Humanists believe that morality is based on the knowledge that humans are interdependent and, therefore, responsible to one

> another." Seeks to spread and promote Humanism through discussion groups, educational programs, television, radio and print.[26]

As with the Society for Health and Human Values, the meaning of humanism is strategically complex. It weaves together interests in both moral and intellectual virtues.

These groups have analogies to religious movements, only without belief in a transcendent God or supernatural forces. Some have explicitly regarded humanism as a religion, following the *Humanist Manifesto*, which itself has served as a quasi-religious statement.[27] Indeed, there are a number of groups that are humanist religious congregations.

> If one counts the total number of Ethical Culture societies and fellowships and then adds the Unitarian Universalist churches and societies that are explicitly or predominantly Humanist in orientation and practice, plus the various congregations of the Society for Humanistic Judaism — all existing examples of Humanist religious organization in the United States and Canada — the sum of such congregations would be in the hundreds. To that number must be added the members-at-large of the Fellowship of Religious Humanists and the considerable body of religious Humanists within the American Humanist Association, an "umbrella" organization that includes both the religious and the nonreligious . . . So while the religion of Humanism in North America is small when compared to other religious movements, it can hardly be dismissed as a myth created by its enemies![28]

As the passage shows, these groups endorse a set of moral values and afford a form of fellowship that has many analogies with traditional theistic religions.

> The societies also provide pastoral services, conduct weddings, funerals, or memorial services, do personal counseling, and organize social and cultural events for adults and young people. Their professionally trained leaders serve a role fully comparable to that of rabbis and ministers and are authorized under federal and state statutes to function as ministers of religion — a right that has been duly sustained in the courts. In every sense of the word an Ethical Culture leader is a minister of Humanist religion.[29]

The societies also resemble public interest groups or lobbies in supporting particular societal reforms or attitudes (e.g., tolerance), such that their social purpose and focus can be distinguished from the professional societies to which humanists might belong as scholars (e.g., the American Philosophical Association).

The various interventional humanisms have produced a specialized, popular philosophical literature. It contains various accounts of humanism, including analyses of human well-being, of justified health care policy, and of other bioethical issues. In these contexts, an account of Secular Humanist health care policy or bioethics can be provided, as one can provide an account of health care policy or bioethics in the Lutheran traditions. Organized communities exist which could in principle publish official analyses of bioethical issues.

Because of the accent on the value of individual liberty, one generally finds, as one would expect, a permissive attitude towards abortion and an endorsement of the right to refuse treatment. The arguments usually proceed from a concrete, content-full understanding of the values that should shape the treatment of patients. Thus, one finds in a recent book on the ethics of humanism arguments supporting a right to adequate medical treatment and a right to informed consent prior to treatment.[30] Also offered are arguments in favor of rights to privacy, including the right to use birth control, to have abortions and to have access to voluntary euthanasia when terminal and in the imminence of death.[31]

These claims are based on human interests and the consequences of actions for human interests.

> Though one may deceive others about the ontological status of rights, their content is still thoroughly *human*, which does not make them any the less morally obligatory. They are still clothed and sustained by all of the intensity of feeling and ardor that ideals can arouse in human conduct.
>
> If this is how human ideals, ethical principles, and human rights emerge, how are they to be tested? This is another matter, for as I have already suggested about other ethical norms, they are reinforced by the degree of fidelity and loyalty we attach to them. Also, and most appropriately, they are to be tested by their consequences. To say that there is a human right is simply to say (1) there are claims that we make as humans, and (2) if they are truly to be considered equitable and just, then we have an *a fortiori* obligation to respect and fulfill them. Why? Primarily, I

> think, because of the demonstrated negative effects of violating them. The test is consequential, for rights lay down effective rules for governing society.[32]

The moral underpinnings of a Secular Humanist bioethics developed within this framework are thus teleological. The goal is to identify sustainable moral claims in terms of their consequences for the achievement of immanent human ideals and concerns.

Organizations like the American Humanist Association, with publications such as *The Humanist*, can nurture a semi-popular literature in bioethics. They can influence law and public policy, at least indirectly. Examples are provided by a recent set of articles in *Free Inquiry* (the publication of the Council for Democratic and Secular Humanism) supporting voluntary euthanasia.[33] This bioethics literature has at times an almost sectarian cast, though its arguments tend to be put in general philosophical terms and without the transcendent foundations of most bioethics positions developed within particular faith traditions. The similarities to, and differences from, other contexts for scholarship make traditional characterizations difficult because this humanist literature is often produced by writers who usually eschew transcendent beliefs but at times still embrace religious sentiments.

The contrast between the *studia humanitatis* and the *studia divinitatis* is recast. It is no longer understood in the sense of a study of the human versus the divine, but rather in terms of an earnest striving for the things of humans rather than the transcendent things of God.

Kurtz (1925–) makes this opposition quite clear.

> Some of the classical religious models, I submit, are in a profound sense antihuman, and the source of deep-seated misery and unhappiness. I am referring to those systems of morality that preach withdrawal from this world, such as some forms of Buddhism, which advocate the extinction of desire in order to achieve a state of quiescent nirvana, or some aspects of Christianity, which emphasize salvation in the next life.[34]

Secular Humanism, and Secular Humanist bioethics, when so understood, involve not merely eschewing reference to the transcendent and the divine, but rejecting a life grounded in transcendent, otherworldly concerns.

One of the best summaries of Secular Humanist moral commitments is "A Secular Humanist Declaration," published in 1980.[35] The Declaration presents ten ideals that the signatories hold will be endorsed not only by democratic secular humanists, but many religious believers as well. The list includes some goals likely to be shared by moral strangers who engage in peaceable negotiation concerning common endeavors. Other goals reflect a particular view of the good life and of human well-being; they are likely to separate rather than to bind moral strangers.[36]

1. Free inquiry. This ideal is surely a presupposition in the encounter of moral strangers.

2. Separation of church and state. The signers suggest removing the tax-exempt status of church properties.

3. The ideal of freedom. The signers include the right both to organize free trade unions and to own property — likely claims when moral strangers meet.

4. Ethics based on critical intelligence. Though the signatories reject an "absolutist morality," they nevertheless hold that ethical values and principles can be discovered.

5. Moral education. Though the signers emphasize that children should be given an appreciation of moral values, they consider it improper to baptize or indoctrinate individuals before the age of consent.

6. Moral skepticism. Under this rubric the signatories deny that religious experience has anything to do with the supernatural and specifically reject the Divinity of Jesus and the Divine Mission of Moses.

7. Reason. The commitment to reasoning and testing claims is likely to be important under most circumstances to moral strangers.

8. Science and technology. Under this canon the Declaration endorses science and technology as the ways in which humans master reality. It also underscores the need to balance science and technology with art, music, and literature. Here the accent is similar to that of the Third Humanism.

9. Evolution. Evolution is endorsed as the account of the origin of life against fundamentalist attempts to deny its truth.

10. Education. The discussion under this title includes an assertion that television directors have an obligation to compensate for the large amount of programming purchased by "preachers, faith healers, and religious hucksters."

The Secular Humanist Declaration weaves together moral commitments that can be shared by moral strangers with those that are likely to be endorsed only by individuals who already possess a common, well-established vision of the good life, including common understandings of the nature of reality and the proper ranking of values.

A Secular Humanist bioethics in the sense of a bioethics articulated within the context of Secular Humanism is not just (1) this-worldly, but (2) incompatible with transcendent religious concerns. For example, arguments that euthanasia and suicide must be condemned out of interests in saving one's soul from eternal damnation would not merely be outside of the scope of a Secular Humanist bioethics, but in conflict with it. Such a Secular Humanism not only eschews but also rejects transcendent claims. It requires a moral perspective in principle unacceptable to the believer who makes health care choices with a view towards eternal salvation. The believer is asked not just to refrain from imposing religious convictions on moral strangers. Transcendent or supernatural considerations are to be abandoned even in areas outside the sphere of common action with moral strangers.

To justify a rejection of private transcendent beliefs, Secular Humanist bioethics is obliged to establish the non-existence of God and the unjustifiability of transcendent supernatural goals. It is not enough to show that proofs for the existence of God and justifications of transcendent supernatural goals are not possible via conclusive discursive arguments in terms of premises that should have a rational claim upon moral strangers. One might contrast an atheist and an agnostic secular humanist bioethics. The first requires more than general secular reasoning can accomplish, since such reasoning must limit itself to what is available to human understanding and experience and cannot prove or disprove claims about the transcendent.[37] Agnostic secular bioethics does not reject transcendent claims, it simply eschews or ignores them in order to focus on what men and women share even as moral strangers.

Secular humanism as a neutral moral framework for moral strangers and Secular Humanism as a particular moral movement differ not just in terms of their metaphysical claims (the one agnostic, the other atheist), but in terms of their social structures and their tolerance for a parallel dimension of moral discourse. Atheist Secular Humanism and other interventionist humanist movements are often characterized by particular social structures that have analogies to the social structures of organized religions. Secular Humanism has spawned proposals for "Secular Humanist Centers" or "Friendship Centers" organized to provide fellowship and educational services.[38] Though many members of humanist movements, especially religious humanists, are agnostic, not atheist,[39] the groups still have a social particularity. Some even possess quasi-official texts such as manifestoes, which serve as moral exemplars and provide a concrete, content-full moral viewpoint with bioethical implications. In this way, Secular Humanism is a movement in competition with other organizations which attempt to define and realize a particular view of the moral life whether agnostic or theistic. However, what is needed in a secular pluralist society is a viewpoint that can be shared by moral strangers, individuals who meet as members of diverse moral communities, but who can also understand themselves as participating in a general moral perspective or standpoint.

Such a viewpoint, and the social structure it entails, is not at first real. It is only virtual, existing insofar as individuals endorse the project of resolving controversies with moral strangers without recourse to force. Such a community of moral strangers can function somewhat as Kant's *mundus intelligibilis*.[40] Moral strangers interested in sharing a common world and resolving issues in health care policy can see themselves as part of a kingdom of strangers bound by a moral fabric. The question is whether such a moral standpoint or community can be specified without arbitrarily importing one out of many possible axiologies. Can such a moral perspective be specified (i.e., as a secular humanism) so that a bioethics can be intellectually justified without that moral perspective becoming just one more among many possible moral visions of human well-being (i.e., just another particular understanding of Secular Humanism), leading to the failure to justify a bioethics in general secular terms?

2. The Particular, the Parochial, and the Universal: Competing Visions of Human Well-being

Humanism and its family of allied terms (e.g., humanitarian concerns, the humanities, etc.) emerge from a two-and-a-half-millennium exploration of the meanings of human excellence and well-being. This exploration has provided numerous different but remarkably mutually supporting portrayals of special aesthetic, moral, and intellectual ideals and virtues. The aesthetic virtues include grace of action, eloquence of expression, and cultivation of manners. The intellectual virtues include knowledge of the classics, an understanding of their meaning, and a wisdom drawn from their analysis. The moral virtues include beneficence, altruism, and *philanthropia*. In addition, and especially against the backdrop of the

Middle Ages, tolerance and respect of individual choice and liberties became a special mark of humanist aspirations. The result has been a bundle of interwoven traditions that are overlapping, largely mutually reinforcing, and remarkably heuristic, despite or perhaps because of their ambiguities. The attempt to justify a humanist vision of the good life, to make sense of that vision, to understand its force and power, has also produced various humanisms as philosophical doctrines concerned with establishing often inchoate claims about the nature of the humanities, the character of the humanities, and the essential goals or ideals of humans.

The possibility of a humanist philosophy has been a source of intellectual hope. This aspiration comes from the Greeks and the origins of humanism. If one could only disclose the concerns that are integrally tied to the nature and excellence of being human, then perhaps one could justify a morality that can bind our different races, nations, and cultures. Given the long human history of war, aggressive genocide, immoral human experimentation, and the impending threat of total annihilation and the need to control and properly use new biomedical technologies (e.g., genetic engineering), these reflections are not merely theoretical. They have special urgency.

However, the intellectual question remains: can one philosophically justify a morality, an understanding of human well-being, in particular a bioethics, for moral strangers, based only on what we share as humans? The answer is the key to understanding the possibility for global cooperation, the avoidance of global destruction, and the use of medical technologies that can change the human condition.

A principal difficulty lies in the fact that, even if people agreed to a short list of important human goals and ideals, it is unlikely they would all agree to, or could justify, a particular canonical ranking or a particular algorithm for coordinating or weighting these goals or ideals. For example, until one knows how to rank, relate or coordinate interests in liberty, equality, and security, one will not know which particular possible society or health care system to endorse or what moral content to affirm for a world-wide peaceable community of humans or for the delivery of health care. Each and every articulation of the human vision appears to have an unavoidable particularity, idiosyncrasy, or parochial character. It is your humanism over against my humanism, it is their understanding of the proper goals and aspirations of humans versus ours, it is your bioethics over against mine. There is no reason to believe there cannot be as many humanist sects as there have been religious sects, with as many understandings of human well-being and bioethics. Nor (as we will see in greater detail in the next chapter) will an appeal to consequences help to resolve such controversies. To be able to assess consequences, one must know how to weight outcomes, and that is not possible without a canonical ranking of values or a canonical algorithm for coordinating the pursuit of values.

The twentieth century, with Fascism, National Socialism, and Communism, has provided us with sufficient examples of how atheists who considered themselves true humanists killed and wrought destruction on previously unparalleled numbers of humans and created medical establishments that used persons as means merely. Indeed, in absolute numbers, the millions who died at the hands of the People's Republic of China, the Soviet Union, and Nazi Germany would appear to equal if not far exceed the deaths due to religious intolerance over the last two millennia. Nor has religious fanaticism supported the large-scale use of humans in medical experiments against their will. The difficulty is not simply this vast carnage of lives, which was not avoided by a humanist deliverance from religious intolerance. The difficulty is justifying the condemnation of that carnage in a way that should lay claim to the convictions of moral strangers, since many rational individuals, some with an education in the humanities, found the carnage perfectly justifiable. The point is that, if one cannot establish a canonical hierarchy of values, one cannot show when the slaughtering of millions on the altar of history or the use of unwilling human experimental subjects is justifiable or abominable. Although one may attempt to convert others to one's particular vision of man and of the ideal human condition, the intellectual question remains: can one justify any particular vision in general rational terms on the basis of what we share as humans? As emotionally difficult as it may be, one must recognize that undoubtedly at least some who engaged in the Stalinist purges and the Nazi experimentations (subsequently condemned by the Nüremberg Code[41]) saw themselves as acting with moral rectitude and justification. They were sure that, in the end, history and a future humanism would understand and forgive, if not praise, their actions.[42] Paul Kurtz' recollection of his conversations with polite, considerate, and probably erudite SS officers raises this difficulty.[43]

But, the problem is not simply that individuals with a good education in the humanities can do things we find to be inhumane. The central problem in ethics is to establish a canonical hierarchy or rational account of values. It is only if such can be established that we can determine what is correct to do in health care on the basis of more than an appeal to particular, culturally determined intuitions. In short, is an objective grounding possible for morality in general and bioethics in particular? If one is not to be left with only the device of comparing and exploring competing visions of history, human excellence, and bioethics, in the hope that one side or the other will convert, then one must ask whether a humanist vision, or any vision, is in some sense generally and uniquely justifiable. However, *miserable factu*, as long as particular understandings of humanism remain in principle parochial, there appears to be no way by appeal to human nature and the human condition to justify a universal morality, a morality for moral strangers, a morality through which individuals with different views of human excellence and human community can speak to each other, lay claim to a common moral fabric, and justify intellectually a common understanding of bioethics. Are we left, as the Sophists told us more than two thousand years ago, free to argue either side of any serious moral issue with the same force and apparent success?

V A Secular Health Care Policy: Of This World but not Opposed to the Other

1. The Secular and the Religious

The distinction between secular and religious bioethics rests on a distinction between what can be demonstrated by natural reason and what can be known by reason aided by grace, revelation, and faith. St. Thomas Aquinas (1225–1274) employed this distinction when he argued that it was ". . . necessary that, besides the philosophical disciplines investigated by reason, there should be a sacred doctrine by way of revelation."[1] The latter, he argued, is more complete in its account of human well-being. However, because the second depends on special premises that cannot be secured by reason alone, it cannot without grace be shared with others. The philosophical disciplines, by contrast, are secular by being in principle open to all persons without special religious or cultural commitment. Natural reason, or spiritually unaided reason, came to be contrasted with reason aided by grace, faith, or the instruction of a particular faith tradition, as much to indicate a common basis for discourse as to protect a place for religion despite the interests of reason. Moreover, many faith traditions, especially those with Abraham as their patriarch (i.e., the Jewish, Christian, and Islamic faiths), contrast with the secular by regarding themselves as developing out of a special gift of divine grace. Faith traditions are regarded by their committed adherents as more surely true, not simply more content-rich, than what reason alone can supply.

It is very difficult to identify truly secular arguments (i.e., arguments that do not crucially depend on special faith claims or special traditions of moral thought). One of the difficulties is that religiously embedded arguments are often advanced as if they were secular. For example, there is frequently a reliance within particular faith traditions on philosophical or, more particularly, metaphysical arguments, which purport to establish the existence or nature of God and of divine moral requirements. Many may even be convinced that these arguments demonstrate the existence of God.[2] Or for that matter, as with Roman Catholic bioethics, one may hold that one can prove through reason alone that abortion and contraception are morally wrong. Indeed, the core of bioethical and health care policy claims within the Roman Catholic tradition, ranging from issues of social justice to euthanasia and suicide, is frequently justified in terms of natural law.[3] Though from outside this tradition the claims are seen to be strongly, if not decisively, influenced by the Roman Catholic faith, such has not been the standard perception from within. Instead, the core bioethical arguments within the Roman Catholic tradition have been regarded as based on reason, not on faith or grace. The same can be said with respect to claims made by Marxists, or for that matter with regard to many working within particular secular traditions of moral philosophy.[4] As a result, rather than discovering a single secular tradition that contrasts with the faith traditions, one is again confronted by an embarrassment of riches. Ranging from natural law claims proffered by Roman Catholics and scientific ethical claims made by Marxists to arguments voiced by secular philosophers, including secular humanists, there does not appear to be a single common moral structure in which and through which moral strangers can meet and frame health care policies. One encounters, instead, numerous religious and secular accounts that address what reason can establish without faith. The accounts differ due to substantial disagreements regarding both first principles and canonical intuitions. We are thus faced with the question: is there a philosophically justifiable foundation for a bioethics that can be shared by all persons?

In an attempt to answer this question, we return, then, against the background of two and a half millennia of humanistic reflections, to the question raised in the first chapter: can we come to terms with the conflicting claims of the various religious and secular ethics? How can one rationally choose among the traditions of moral reflection within which bioethical analyses are undertaken and health care policy framed? One might seek a minimalist ethic or an ethic of the least-common-denominator, hoping that there is in fact enough to share so that a rationally justified moral discourse is possible among moral strangers. Or one might seek to show that there are moral commitments that obtain simply in virtue of one's being a human or a person. If we cannot secure as an intellectual possibility a moral foundation that people share as moral strangers, then a definitive rationally justified resolution of controversies regarding euthanasia, abortion, suicide, and the just distribution of health care resources will not be feasible. In short, the question is whether one can secure a secular ethic (in particular, a secular bioethics) in the special sense of an ethic not beholden to any particular faith or moral tradition, but grounded in the very requirements of a rational ethic or in the nature of man or reality itself. Such a grounding has been the goal of philosophical reflection since antiquity. The hope has been that one can objectively establish canonical lineaments for proper conduct, which are independent of particular faith commitments or moral traditions.

The question is how to accomplish this task. Controversies can be rationally resolved either by indicating an internal contradiction in the positions of all but one of those participating in the controversy and/or by showing that all but one make false claims about the world. But this strategy does not appear to offer hope for bioethics in particular, or ethics in general. Appeals to the formal character of reason will not provide moral content. One will not be able to show what one ought to do, only how one should reason about what one ought to do, if one has true premises. Moreover, as philosophers from David Hume[5] (1711–1776) to G. E. Moore[6] (1873–1958) have shown, it is not possible to argue from facts to values. From what is the case, one cannot establish what ought to be done. From the fact that all people on earth are likely to die if event X occurs, and that most individuals are appalled by this prospect, though a few are not, nothing logically follows as to whether it would be morally good or bad if all people died, given event X. Perhaps there are causes worth the death of all mankind? Perhaps their death is followed by a more than compensatory afterlife? To derive ought statements from mere factual statements, one must have already interpreted the facts within a particular moral or faith tradition. The facts must already be value-infected. For example, diseases are usually, all else being equal, disvalued.[7]

To judge that some outcomes are better or worse than others, or to judge what people ought to do, one first must rank the major goals of, or moral constraints on, human conduct or devise an algorithm for coordinating or weighting them. In order to justify establishing a particular health care system, one will need to decide many matters of policy which presuppose such rankings and algorithms. For example, to decide whether abortions are morally permissible, as well as what amount of money should be invested with what probability to save a life, one will need to know how to balance the wishes of the mother against the possible interests of the fetus and how to compare expenditures for luxuries with expenditures to save lives. The difficulty is to justify a particular canonical ranking or account of values. Depending on the priority one assigns to liberty, equality, prosperity, security, and other goals, one will be obliged to endorse radically different social systems, including radically different systems for the distribution of health care resources. One can only discover the morally correct social system if one can identify a canonical moral ranking, account, algorithm, or moral sense. Moreover, one cannot appeal solely to consequences to establish a morally canonical social order, because in order authoritatively to assess consequences, one must know how to weight them. And in order to weight them, one needs a canonical ranking of goals or goods. But to identify a canonical ranking, one will need a canonical moral sense. The problem is then how to choose the correct moral sense. One cannot secure it by appealing to a higher level moral sense, *ad infinitum*.

The Enlightenment attempt to ground a content-full secular morality by appeal to reason alone is doomed to failure, thus justifying post-modern skepticism regarding the weakness of humanism. This failure warrants the contemporary concern about the post-modern age lacking a way to mediate the conflicting claims of diverse ideologies and religions. The hope to move from a religiously justified content-full morality to a secular morality that can be justified in general rational terms does not appear feasible. The grounds for this failure can be summarized under six rubrics, under which, somewhat procrusteanly, all attempts to discover the content for a secular bioethics and health care policy can be gathered.[8]

A. *Why hypothetical choice theories fail*

Hypothetical choice theories are invoked in order to show what a rational individual or disinterested observer would affirm as being morally correct. The idea is that, if an account of a disinterested observer can be developed, which possesses the general lineaments of a rational decision-maker, then all who act in accord with the prescriptions and proscriptions of such a disinterested observer or ideal decision-maker will be acting rationally, and those who do not will be acting irrationally, so that they will not have rational grounds to protest, should rational individuals condemn them. Moreover, if the decisions of a rational person or decision-maker are imposed on non-conforming persons, the behavior imposed is not alien to their nature (i.e., as rational beings).

The difficulty is in justifying such an account. For example, one might mount an argument that a rational decision-maker would choose a social welfare system that guaranteed a decent minimum level of health care for all, even if this policy had an adverse impact on the prosperity of the society as a whole. However, the success of such an argument depends on the weight given to security with respect to a possible need for health care versus the desire for greater prosperity. As is illustrated by the fact that many individuals knowingly risk disease or disability in order to achieve financial success, it is not possible to establish a proper ranking of risks to health versus risks to financial success without begging the very question at issue. One must first endorse a particular ranking or account of risks and benefits.

The difficulty is that, if a hypothetical decision-maker or disinterested observer is fully disinterested and truly a partisan of no particular moral position, then that hypothetical decision-maker or disinterested observer will have no moral sense whatsoever. For example, a fully disinterested observer will not be able to determine whether it is better to provide equal health care or a decent minimum level of health care for all. One gains generality at the price of moral content, thus rendering the ideal observer or hypothetical rational decision-maker useless. On the other hand, to impute any particular moral sense or thin theory of the good to the ideal observer or the hypothetical decision-maker is already arbitrarily to choose a particular moral sense, vision, or perspective, and thus beg the central question at issue. The hypothetical decision-maker or ideal observer is either useless or partisan.

B. Why hypothetical contractor theories cannot succeed

Accounts of ethics or of the grounding of political authority on the basis of appeals to the decisions of hypothetical contractors fail for the same reason that appeals to hypothetical rational decision-makers or ideal observers fail. One must impute to the contractors some thin theory of the good, some moral sense, some canonical moral intuitions, or one will not be able to show why one health care system is the morally preferable choice over others. To rephrase the maxim from computer information theory: values in, values out. Hypothetical contractor theories can justify a particular moral perspective only insofar as the bases for the moral perspective of the contractors are already accepted as premises in order to constrain the choices of the contractors.

C. *Why appeals to rationality or to a concrete concept of morality are flawed*

Just as hypothetical decision theories cannot ground a particular moral perspective without begging the question, so, too, appeals to the character of moral reasoning will fail as well. One must first have built into one's account of reason or morality a particular moral understanding, perspective, or sense. For example, in order to argue that it is wrong to hire women to work as surrogate mothers, one will need to establish that there are certain things to which women may not rationally or morally consent. That is, the concept of moral action must be so elaborated or described so that it excludes certain free choices, such as the choice to work as a surrogate mother. But the moral exclusion of such actions depends on a particular view of rationality or morality. Just as plausibly, one could regard the decision to work as a surrogate mother as a valuable expression of human liberty. One will not know which moral understanding, perspective, or sense to endorse without appealing to a higher moral understanding, perspective, or sense, and so on *ad infinitum*. Either one will be doomed to an infinite regress, or one will need arbitrarily to endorse a particular ranking of values or algorithm for weighting values.

Of course, proponents of this genre of argument do not conceive of themselves as endorsing a particular ranking of values. Instead, they regard themselves as discovering moral content through, or within, reason. A classical example of such argumentation is provided by Kant in his *Grundlegung zur Metaphysik der Sitten* (*Foundations of the Metaphysics of Morals*). There Kant appeals to a contradiction in will in order to ground obligations of charity, because he realizes that such obligations cannot be demonstrated by showing that their denial would involve a logical contradiction.[9] But what for Kant is a contradiction in will is for the skeptic a lack of imagination. What appears to Kant as a contradiction in will is a contradiction only within a particular moral perspective. The contradiction disappears once the moral perspective is changed.

D. *Why appeals to consequences also fail*

For the purposes of argument, one might agree that individuals generally seek through social structures to achieve and protect liberty, equality, prosperity, and security. However, even if one grants this communality of goals, one will not know which social structure to endorse unless one knows how one ought to rank these desiderata. This is as true for consequentialists, including utilitarians, as it is for hypothetical choice theorists. In order to compare the consequences of different social systems or societal structures (or of rules or actions), one will need to compare liberty consequences, equality consequences, security consequences, and prosperity consequences. But of course, that again is the key moral question at issue. One cannot appeal to consequences in order to determine how to rank consequences.

To illustrate the difficulty, consider a consequentialist argument about voluntary euthanasia. On the one hand, one can argue that the value of respecting the freedom of individuals and allowing them to avoid pain and indignity is outweighed by the risk of slipping down a slope to where severely senile or mentally retarded individuals will be euthanatized, given their diminished competence, without valid consent (i.e., the risk of non-voluntary as opposed to involuntary euthanasia). On the other hand, proponents of voluntary euthanasia could acknowledge the same likelihood of abuse but discount its significance because of a lesser weight given to the moral significance of non-voluntary euthanasia. There will be no way to decide which consequences are worse unless one already has a way of ranking consequences.

Appeals to preferences will not resolve the issue, either. One will need a moral theory to determine how to compare various intensities and refinements of preference. Is a well-thought-out preference to be given the same, greater, or lesser weight than a passionate, immediate preference? For example, should a rationally developed preference for the rule of law outweigh the preference of the majority expressed in a mob pursuing a quick and pleasant lynching? The character of preferences is rich and diverse, and one needs a basis for deciding how to compare and rank them. Among other things, one must know how one should compare and weigh present versus future preferences. For example, how does one weigh the preference of a severely injured person to die, when an experienced physician believes that the individual can be saved and will in the future very likely be pleased to have been saved? Definitive moral comparisons can be made only if one has a canonical hierarchy or account to which one can appeal in order to rank or weigh present versus likely future preferences, passionate impulsive preferences versus well-considered preferences.

This means that there is no way to appeal to consequences in order to choose among social systems on the basis of which "works" without first knowing the criteria of "working." Does the social system of Albania work better or worse than that of Switzerland? That depends on the criteria one uses to measure success. But there does not appear a way to discover the correct canonical hierarchy or account. As a result, it follows that one cannot discover the correct way to weigh consequences. Appeals to consequences fail to provide a way out of moral nihilism or unconstrained moral relativism.

E. Why appeals to nature or to what is natural are useless in secular moral controversies

An appeal to what is natural or to nature would be morally decisive if one could show in general secular terms that there are in nature lineaments for human conduct. It is unclear, though, how one could derive normative content from nature. For example, how do we find in nature implicit moral guidelines for genetic engineering or technologically-assisted reproduction? One may even acknowledge a creator God and still hold that nature, including human nature, is given as a challenge for persons to transform according to their own judgment or according to moral canons given by God. Such claims will be decidable only if (1) one has an intuitive power to recognize a morally constraining design in nature or (2) one has a revelation from God about how one should recognize design in nature and how such design should be morally constraining. The first will not resolve controversies between competing hypotheses by appealing to criteria of either consistency or falsifiability. The matter is not one of logical validity or of empirical claims that are falsifiable without already accepting a particular value-infected interpretation of nature. For any one interpretation endorsed by some, a different one may be endorsed by others without their being contradictory or falsified by the facts of the matter. From the bare fact that something is the case, it does not follow that anything else in particular should be done. A bare fact becomes a circumstance rich with implications as it is embedded in a nexus of considerations and facts. Only then can it be interpreted.

For nature to have a moral claim on our conduct, other than through shaping the consequences of our actions, one must have already endorsed a particular normative account or interpretation of nature. But how will one know which normative account or interpretation of nature to endorse? One will need some higher-level account that allows one to choose with moral warrant among the competing accounts of the moral implications of nature. One is thus returned to some other foundation for morality. After all, within a secular perspective, human nature and nature in general are merely the products of physical processes and can have no moral significance outside a context of moral interpretation. Human nature within a purely secular perspective is, depending on the circumstances, an opportunity, a hindrance, or a benefit for persons. For example, high fertility is either a bane or a blessing depending on how many children one wants. Manipulating fertility will be either good or bad depending on considerations other than a mere appeal to nature unless one can establish a canonical normative account or interpretation of nature. In the absence of the possibility of an appeal to a decisive normative account or interpretation of nature, one cannot determine whether nature should be protected, manipulated, or transformed (e.g., through genetic engineering).

F. *Appeals to intuitions or to the outcomes of a reflective equilibrium among one's moral principles and intuitions will also not be decisive*

For any moral intuition, opponents can proffer contrary intuitions. Some individuals, for example, find the sale of human organs for transplantation (i.e., regarding human organs as commodities) as *ipso facto* immoral, and the solicitation of individuals to sell their organs as *prima facie* a misuse of persons. Yet others, to the contrary, will regard such purchases as a reasonable and morally permissible (or indeed praiseworthy) way of procuring desired organs. Unless there is a criterion outside particular moral intuitions, there will be no way to settle such disputes. Nor for fundamental disputes will it help to bring intuitions into a system, if the disputants embrace different systems of intuitions. Insofar as moral strangers adopt different moral visions, they will have different understandings about how appropriately to mediate between moral principles and moral intuitions. They will not have an independent rational basis for agreeing on the proper outcome of a reflective equilibrium between principles and moral intuitions. Moreover, unless some arguments have succeeded on other bases, it will not be possible to establish which moral principles should be compared with which moral intuitions.

G. *A summary: why nihilism and relativism appear unavoidable*

It is not possible rationally to discover a canonical, moral account with content. Appealing within moral reason to moral intuitions fails; appealing outside moral reason to consequences or to nature fails as well. Nor is it possible to appeal to the structure or character of reason in order to secure content for the moral life. It becomes impossible to establish any act or condition as intrinsically wrong by appeal to generally available secular considerations. Against this failure of the Enlightenment project to provide a secular grounding for morality, it is not feasible to establish a secular humanist bioethics as one might have hoped. It does not seem feasible to provide a moral basis that moral strangers should share while fashioning health care policies. Therefore, a concrete bioethics or health care policy seems justifiable only in terms of a particular religion, faith tradition, or ideology.

With the collapse of the universalistic aspirations of secular humanism,[10] secular humanism becomes simply one ideology or tradition among many others. Rather than providing a neutral or common perspective, secular humanism then adds to the confusing cacophony of moral visions. Indeed, it would seem that secular humanism leads dialectically to its own destruction. The attempt to ground a general morality brings the entire project of morality into question, so that one is confronted with the choice of either becoming a committed believer (e.g., converting to a particular religion) or abandoning morality in favor of realizing through force (including through a particular public policy) the advantages of a particular group, class, or moral community.

2. The Death of God, the Death of Man, and the Death of Nature

The death of God is a metaphor for the beginning of the modern secular age, the age in which appeals to religion fail convincingly to resolve moral controversies. Analogously, the death of man can be taken as a metaphor for the post-modern age, when appeals to human nature fail as well. The modern age was the interlude between medieval times (which were characterized by the grounding of morality in faith and reason) and the post-modern age in which morality has shattered into moralities, each defended by a particular partisan group. The post-modern age brings into question the very project of humanism and any hope of a univocal, canonical, humanistic account of health and medicine. In this age: (1) humane sentiments have become particular psychological inclinations without a generally justifiable moral warrant or interpretative context; (2) the literary and intellectual tradition of Western humanism has become one among many literary and intellectual traditions without any special moral claim on those outside the tradition; and (3) the philosophical attempt to ground morality in human nature or rationality has failed to provide an intellectually justified common moral basis for the cooperation of moral strangers. This circumstance has profound implications for the development of secular health care policies.

A. The loss of teleology: the relativity of well-being and of the meaning of sexuality

If one cannot read off from nature in general or human nature in particular canonical normative goals, then the correct definitions of health and disease cannot simply be discovered. One cannot by examining humans or other animals, without presupposing a particular vision of human or biological excellence, discover whether a human or an animal is healthy or ill. Instead, health or well-being becomes understood in terms of the realization of aesthetic, functional, or other goals within a particular environment. This is because successful adaptation cannot be defined except with respect to a particular environment and with respect to the goals by which success is to be measured. In particular, though from the perspective of evolution one might regard health or successful adaptation as that which maximizes inclusive fitness, many persons may have non-reproductively oriented views of success. Even though sickle-cell trait may contribute to the inclusive fitness of humans in environments where *falsiparum malaria* is endemic (in the absence of effective prophylaxis or treatment), those who carry the trait or who develop sickle-cell disease may still not regard themselves as possessing a marker of health.[11] In fact, in many environments having an IQ over 140 may not contribute to either individual or inclusive fitness, but may still be regarded as not constituting a defect, disability, or illness. In short, health and disease are relativized because there is no unambiguous, canonical goal for adaptation.

The meaning of the term "disease" is generally set by its usual role within health care. As such, "disease" identifies a state of affairs which is, all things being equal, disvalued. For a disvalued state to be a disease, it cannot be one under direct personal control (e.g., non-tissue destructive pain due to torture) because the focus is on what medicine can ameliorate, not what law, religion, or morality should address. Further, the state of affairs must be considered to be embedded in a causal framework amenable in principle to medical explanation and manipulation (e.g., not a state of possession by the devil) so as to make engaging the institutions of health care appropriate. Thus, states of affairs are identified as states of disease insofar as they (1) make it difficult (or are likely to make it difficult) for individuals to perform functions considered to be appropriate for individuals of a particular age and sex; (2) involve pain or distress considered under the circumstances to be inappropriate; (3) cause disfigurements or a lack of grace; or (4) cause premature death, all insofar as these states of affairs are not directly under the volitional control of the individual involved, and are explainable in patho-physiological, -anatomical, or -psychological terms.[12] The identification of a state of disease or health involves an appeal to ideals of function, ideals of freedom from pain and distress, ideals of human form and grace, or ideals of appropriate longevity. Since such ideals involve particular rankings of human goals, understandings of them and appeals to them will be culture-influenced and relative, and determined by the circumstances and choices of each individual.

This relativity can be illustrated by the phenomenon color blindness. Though color-blind individuals cannot easily identify differences in hues, they have an advantage in spotting camouflage, because camouflage cannot easily be matched with the environment both for hue and for shades between black and white.[13] Since one can very well imagine environments in which being able to identify camouflage would be useful for personal survival, as well as for survival of a group, one can envisage circumstances in which colorblindness would maximize both individual and inclusive fitness. Again, whether a trait is considered to be a defect or an advantage depends on context and goals.

Because many diseases (e.g., cancer of the lung or coronary artery disease) are identified as such because they tend to impede whatever goals humans might have, they will appear as diseases, illnesses, deformities, or disabilities across cultures. In fact, they depend on different sets of culturally influenced and individually accepted human ideals for significance as a disvalued state of affairs. In nearly every, but not necessarily all, context such states of affairs will foreclose the realization of important human goals, whatever those might be. It is the particular goals of particular individuals, endorsed by health care systems established by particular groups, in particular contexts, that makes a particular state of affairs stand out as a disease state.[14]

Such culturally dependent understandings of health and disease have been defended by Humanists.[15] For example, Joseph Margolis, one of the signers of the "Humanist Manifesto II,"[16] has argued in favor of the cultural relativity of concepts of disease.[17] Here one finds an instance where arguments within secular humanism as well as Secular Humanism lead to the same conclusion. Understood in general secular humanist terms, there is no unique way to understand health and disease because there is no canonical interpretation of nature. Nature exists as the result of physical processes. Within a secular humanist perspective, persons must give meaning to nature. Nature cannot declare its meaning to persons. Moreover, *if* there is no single canonical account of values, then concepts of health and disease are human cultural constructs fashioned to serve human purposes within particular human contexts. The meanings of health and disease are human social fabrications.

If there are no intrinsic moral constraints given in nature, and if there are no actions that are intrinsically right or wrong, then human nature and nature generally are available for human manipulation. Within such a secular perspective, individuals will manipulate human nature to meet the needs of persons.

Contraception is a prime example of an area where freedom for manipulation is supported by Secular Humanists, and condemned by some religions.[18] From a secular perspective, there is nothing one can say about the purposes and moral meaning of sexuality. Sexuality in the range of its biological and psychological expressions represents only an opportunity for individual and group choice. There is nothing content-full that can be said about its moral significance a priori. Like all natural characteristics of humans it must be judged in terms of the goals and purposes of persons.

Indeed, within a consistent secular humanist vision, the fields of assisted reproduction and genetic manipulation cannot be placed within moral restraints other than those set by prudential considerations and the concerns of the persons involved. Arguments in this vein have been made, for example, by Joseph Fletcher, the author of *Situation Ethics*[19] and a signer of the "Humanist Manifesto II,"[20] as well as of the "Secular Humanist Declaration."[21] In supporting the manipulation and assistance of human reproduction,[22] including human genetics,[23] he has elaborated an understanding of bioethics founded on the premise that "right and wrong are humanly perceived, not religiously revealed. In a word, ethics is humanist."[24] Reality, including human nature, is given meaning by being humanized, manipulated to serve the purposes of humans. Here, the conclusions of secular humanism and Secular Humanism coincide.

B. The loss of moral content: the emergence of a permissive bioethics

The impossibility of establishing a single canonical ordering or account of values has influenced secular humanist reflections, explicitly and implicitly. The difficulty of giving a straightforward answer to most content-full moral questions of right and wrong is recognized indirectly in an appreciation of the pluralism that unavoidably characterizes large-scale non-authoritarian secular states. As a consequence of the unavailability in many, if not most, areas of rationally definitive answers to questions about what is good and what is bad, reflections within secular humanist bioethics have tended to focus on the consent of participants in health care and on the provision of refuseable welfare rights. Again, this is as one would expect in the absence of a canonical account of values. For example, in the absence of special religious or moral premises, it is impossible categorically to forbid aiding and abetting suicide or euthanasia. As one might expect, one of the more nuanced sets of studies from a secular humanist perspective concerning euthanasia and infanticide has been produced by an individual who signed both the "Humanist Manifesto II" and the "Secular Humanist Declaration," Marvin Kohl.[25] The analysis does not set moral limits beyond those that follow from respecting the wishes and interests of actual persons. Insofar as the accent falls on the wishes of actual persons, the conclusions of secular humanism and Secular Humanism will tend to coincide.

Also, without special metaphysical principles, one cannot establish that fetuses have the same moral status as adult persons. As a result, the choice of whether to have an abortion, from a Secular Humanist perspective, has generally been seen as one belonging to the woman, since she is the person bearing the immediate consequences of gestation.[26] This conclusion would also be supported in general secular humanist terms: the major accent is on the free and informed consent of the person primarily involved. Secular bioethics quite easily becomes a bioethics where everything is allowed, as long as it is done between consenting, competent adults. In the next section of this chapter the theoretical foundation for this characteristic will become clearer. Here the point can be put in somewhat sociological terms. Even if people cannot agree about when treatment should terminate, about whether they should practice euthanasia, or about whether and under what circumstances it would be appropriate to seek an abortion, they can at least agree that they will not subject persons to medical treatment, euthanasia, or abortion without their consent, and will not stop those who competently choose to make use of such modalities.

A secular humanist bioethics thus contrasts with most religious bioethics in not possessing content-full moral canons that exclude the use of procedures such as artificial insemination from a donor, abortion, euthanasia, or *in vitro* fertilization and embryo transplant. Secular Humanism has difficulty (to say the least) showing that any medical intervention is intrinsically wrong. Rather, wrongness when it is recognized tends to be grounded in the violation of the requirement that individuals must permit a procedure (or restraint) before it is applied to them. To say that a secular humanistic bioethics is permissive is thus a *double entendre*: a secular humanist bioethics (1) tends to permit those interventions to which the participants have given consent, and (2) makes the permission of participants a cardinal element of bioethics.

C. *The loss of a transcendent focus: the purposelessness of suffering and death*

Most religious world-views provide an account of the meaning of suffering and death. They give an ultimate significance to the major passages of human existence from birth to death. They indirectly place health care within a framework that transcends the life and death of particular individuals. In addition, religious visions of reality often construe death not as the end of life, but as the realization of one's final destiny. As a result, the death of the faithful true believer can properly be taken as much as an occasion for joy as for sorrow. Many religious viewpoints also convey a meaning to suffering by explaining its occurrence in terms of past failings. Others see suffering as a way in this life of discharging the temporal punishment due to sin that would otherwise need to be faced after death.[27] In such an interpretation, suffering becomes valuable. In many religious accounts, God's hidden purposes can be presumed, such that the circumstances of one's suffering and death are not surd and accidental, but a part of divine providence. Suffering and death can be redeemed by being placed within a transcendent understanding of the human condition.

Such transcendental accounts are false from the usual Secular Humanist perspective and beyond the scope of secular humanism. For the Secular Humanist, death is final. Rather than being regarded as a step to a better life, death is a loss of all goods, pleasures, and personal contacts. The Secular Humanist is, as a result, critical of belief in immortality, regarding it as reluctance to face reality.

> A humanist views this as a failure to face the finality of death and an inability to see life for what it really is. This attitude has all the hallmarks of pathology, for one is out of touch with cognitive reality. It is an immature and unhealthy attitude, a form of wish fulfillment. It exacerbates an illusion in order to soothe the heart aching over the loss of a loved one or avoid accepting one's own impending end. Death is a source of profound dread. There is an unwillingness to let go. It is the tenacious refusal to confront the brute finitude of existence, the contingent and precarious, often tragic, character of human life.[28]

The Secular Humanist attempts to accept with courage the finitude of human existence. Suffering and anxiety, apart from offering an opportunity for the development of courage and strong character, have no transcendent significance. Unless their mastery is understood within some special secular Spartan vision of the disciplined person, they will be seen within a secular context only as experiences to be avoided. Thus, while the flagellants of the late Middle Ages sought through suffering to discipline the flesh,[29] the denizens of the post-modern secular world must seek deliverance from pain and anxiety through analgesics and tranquilizers.

For many believers, however, death is not final. For example, the devout Roman Catholic should regard staying alive as a concern subordinate to many others, particularly that of eternal salvation. As a consequence, there is no obligation to use other than ordinary means to maintain life.[30] However, the non-believer may not face such choices with the same canonical clarity. As a consequence, there is a difficulty both for private choices and public policy in the shadow of death. If this is the only life, how much money should be expended to preserve it? What amount of resources should be invested to pursue what chance of saving someone's life (e.g., should $100,000 be expended by a patient, by a patient's family or a patient's society for treatment if there is only one chance in a hundred of surviving, making the cost per life saved $10,000,000)? Without a canonical account of values, no correct answer can be discovered.

3. The Will to Morality: Coming to Terms with Nihilism and Relativism in the Post-Modern Era

If the attempt to establish a content-full moral vision fails, more is lost than natural teleology or grounds for proscribing voluntary euthanasia or abortion on request. The grounds for respecting persons (or acknowledging the dignity of persons) are brought into question as well. Why should regard for persons be greater than concerns with security or prosperity? If a conclusive solution to this difficulty cannot be secured, the secular humanist (not to mention the Secular Humanist) will have no generally articulatable bases for protesting in principle against the most all-encompassing state tyranny or exploitative slavery. If the general attempt to establish a morality for moral strangers and the particular attempt to establish the concrete morality of Secular Humanism go aground, one can justify neither respect of persons nor the value of liberty. If all becomes relative, and neither a canonical ordering of values nor moral constraints on human actions can be established, then the entire project of a secular morality collapses. Individuals will either assert the truth of their own moral intuitions and impose them with force, or use force without any pretense of religious or ideological justification. If a general morality for moral strangers cannot be established, then from a general secular perspective neither of these uninviting alternatives can be condemned.

The implications for bioethics and health care would be dramatic. There would be no general justification for condemning the imposition of a particular religious viewpoint on all health care systems (e.g., the criminalization of contraception and abortion), nor would there be general moral grounds for condemning Nazi experimentation on unconsenting subjects. Unless something can be saved of the Enlightenment endeavor, one will simply have intuition confronting intuition, tradition confronting tradition, ideology confronting ideology, religion confronting religion, and emotion confronting emotion.

This would mean the collapse of a central assumption of Western culture — the notion that reason can resolve moral controversies and justify a moral viewpoint. The death of humanism (metaphorically, the death of man) would mean more than the collapse of the possibility of justifying a secular moral framework or a Secular Humanism. It would mean more than the loss of the possibility of grounding a morality that can bind moral strangers, that is, a morality grounded in what is shared by us as humans or persons. It would mean the abandonment of the central adjudicative function of rational argument.

The project of secular morality must be fundamentally reconceived if a generally justifiable moral failure is to be secured for moral strangers. Instead of seeking a canonical account of values, or a content-infected algorithm for coordinating values, one must look to the very notion of resolving moral controversies: ethics as the commitment to resolving controversies between moral strangers without primary recourse to force but with common moral authority. If individuals are interested in resolving controversies without direct appeal to force, and if God remains silent (e.g., those participating in the controversy do not share a common faith tradition or ideology), and if reason fails (e.g., those participating in the controversy do not share sufficient values and descriptions of situations in common so that a moral controversy can be reduced to a manageable logical or empirical controversy), then the only way to resolve controversies with common authority will be by peaceable negotiation. Which is to say, if one cannot discover who is *in* authority or *a* moral authority by appeal to God or reason, then authority will need to be derived from the consent of those participating in an endeavor.

Thus, even if God is silent and the project of discovering a content-full ethics fails, insofar as one is interested in engaging in ethics, that is, in resolving controversies without foundational recourse to force, one can still participate in a common moral world with moral strangers. The necessary condition for participating in that world is mutual respect, the non-use of others without their consent. This side constraint is not grounded in a value given to autonomy, liberty, or to persons, but is integral to the grammar of controversy resolution when God, facts, and reason do not provide bases for peaceably resolving a dispute.[31] Mutual respect is accepted because it is the one way to ground a common moral world for moral strangers without arbitrarily endorsing a particular ranking of values.

Accepting this ground for secular ethics is equivalent to accepting the moral point of view which requires the fewest assumptions: an interest in having common moral authority for collaborative endeavors when God is silent and reason impotent. It is intellectually the least costly way of establishing a common moral world. All others require the intellectual cost of accepting particular values, a particular ranking of values, a particular content infected algorithm for coordinating values, or a particular metaphysical viewpoint. To have a morality for moral strangers, one need only refrain from using them without their consent and acknowledge them as entities that can agree or refuse to negotiate (i.e., because the failure of such an acknowledgment is tantamount to rejecting a morality for moral strangers).[32]

Mutual respect allows one to recognize other moral strangers who are willing to act ethically, that is, who are willing to resolve controversies other than through foundational appeal to force: they negotiate peaceably and use force only in defense or in punishment for unconsented-to actions against them. Appeal to mutual respect also allows one to recognize those moral strangers who are unwilling to act ethically, that is, who insist on resolving moral controversies by the use of force (even if they appeal to what should from a general secular perspective appear as a pseudo-justification, as, for example, would be the case with a claim that they are authorized by God or by a rational argument). Such aggressors cannot complain in ways that are justifiable to moral strangers when the aggressors are subject to defensive or punitive force. They have set themselves outside of, made themselves outlaws with respect to, the morality that binds moral strangers. That is, if one subjects peaceable moral strangers to coercion on grounds that cannot in principle be justified to moral strangers, one loses all general rational grounds for protest when one is subjected to defensive and punitive force. One has become a moral outlaw.

One can still step outside of any particular, content-full moral perspective and have a moral language through which moral strangers can communicate. Though reason fails to discover a content-full *ius naturale* or a common content-full morality for moral strangers, a common morality can come into existence through a common will. It is the will to morality that can set nihilism aside. The will to morality has a rational focus: the creation of a world of meaning within which morally justified respect and punishment are possible. This account of a secular morality provides a rationale for moral actions, without any content-full moral assumptions and without any metaphysical assumptions. As such, it is not just one moral vision alongside others, one moral proposal among many others. Quite to the contrary, it is the only way in which one can justify a general basis for the mutual cooperation of moral strangers without begging the question by presuming a particular moral view, a particular thin theory of the good, or a particular moral sense. In addition, it provides an account of the actions of those who reject it in terms that disable them from giving a coherent general rejoinder. It also provides a limit to relativism: the requirement not to use others without their permission. Thus, involuntary euthanasia, the use of human subjects in research without their consent, and the treatment of patients without their permission are all immoral. In addition, explicit agreements gain moral status (e.g., a contract to work as a surrogate mother). Moreover, by negotiation (including certain democratic processes), procedures with secular moral authority can be established to determine how to use common goods for joint purposes such as the provision of a "decent" amount of health care for all. It is only through decisions made in terms of such established procedures that one can determine with secular moral authority whether health care will be chosen for societal support and what will count as a "decent" or "adequate" amount of health care.

This constitution of morality is similar to the constitution of empirical science. Following Immanuel Kant (1724–1804), one need not hold that empirical science allows one to know truly the world as it is in itself. It is enough that one understand that empirical science provides the grammar for the intersubjective resolution of disputes regarding facts about the world without appeal to intuitions, God, or force. The metaphor of grammar is borrowed from Ludwig Wittgenstein (1889–1951) and Immanuel Kant. Wittgenstein remarked that "Essence is expressed by grammar."[33] In this he followed Kant and took the search for categories as the search for the "elements of a grammar."[34] Both Wittgenstein and Kant can be understood as identifying or defining integral constraints on cardinal human practices. Knowledge about those constraints is not empirical knowledge. It is rather grammatical, categorial, or transcendental knowledge.[35] It discloses the fundamental structure of a basic human practice.

In this sense, neither empirical science nor morality is grounded in particular value assumptions or metaphysical claims. Each is rather a possibility for persons. If accepted, each opens up a major sphere of meaning that can be shared with moral strangers. If one lives an extraordinarily truncated life, one need not engage in the practices of empirical science or secular morality. But if one does so engage, one implicitly accepts their rules. Each sphere of meaning depends simply on the participants' interest in resolving a particular genre of disputes in a way other than through force. In that force provides no intellectual satisfaction, and in that the worlds of secular morality and of empirical science allow one commonly to address a wide range of phenomena regarding which most individuals have some interest, there is therefore in each case an intellectual merit in willing its existence. But one need not claim that either world has a transcendent or ultimate justification. The rewards of entering the worlds of secular morality and of empirical science are found in those worlds themselves. This secular humanist account thus rests on no metaphysical or value assumptions. Nor does it suffice to provide a general justification for a Secular Humanist morality insofar as this involves concrete moral claims. It is, rather, a necessary condition for the possibility of articulating a secular humanist morality binding moral strangers. Secular humanist ethics is an intellectual possibility available to be willed by individuals whenever they meet as moral strangers and wish to resolve controversies peaceably and with common moral authority.

Though social structures are created that embody the secular humanist vision, *per definitionem* they should not be regarded as organs of a moral or political movement competing with other concrete, content-full moral or ideological visions (e.g., religious). Secular humanist undertakings and concrete moral undertakings (e.g., Secular Humanism) exist at different moral levels. Secular humanist undertakings should make no claims as to how members of moral communities should understand themselves and consensually cooperate with each other — or how they may peaceably approve of or condemn others (e.g., over the use of abortion, euthanasia, or third-party-assisted reproduction). As long as partisans of particular moral visions attempt to convert moral strangers by witness without coercion, secular humanism as a morality for moral strangers is satisfied. However, insofar as secular societal organs (e.g., the police) attempt to enforce a particular content-full view of proper human conduct, they become analogous to the organ of an established religion (e.g., forbidding competent Jehovah's Witnesses to refuse life-saving transfusions).

From a secular perspective, it is the will to morality that distinguishes moral individuals from immoral individuals and creates a common language for moral strangers. The will to morality does not involve any particular moral content. One will know *a priori* that one must keep promises in order to be moral (i.e., deceiving others by not keeping promises would count as an instance of using them without their permission). However, only within particular contexts will it become clear what promises ought to be made (e.g., what agreements one may make as a surrogate mother). Actions will be constrained by the requirement of mutual respect, including prior agreements. Within and through that constraint, moral strangers can fashion common moral undertakings, such as health care systems. Insofar as they agree on a content for that system, they will have created a common moral world. The difficulty will be to determine when such agreement occurs and the extent to which individuals have exempted themselves from common endeavors.

A. Two levels of moral discourse

The secular humanist vision just elaborated provides a moral framework for moral strangers. It allows individuals who do not share a common view of the good life to collaborate in joint ventures, such as the formation of health care policies. It permits individuals from divergent communities to work together, though they do not share a common content-full understanding of morality. This is the secular morality that properly holds together large-scale states which compass a plurality of moral communities. This secular morality is exemplified in state institutions such as the post office, which provides services to citizens irrespective of their moral viewpoints. A post office of a non-authoritarian secular pluralist society will mail both religious literature and anti-religious literature, racist tracts and anti-racist tracts, socialist propaganda and the publications of the John Birch Society. It asks only that the customers pay sufficient postage. As long as the endeavors are peaceable, no judgment is made regarding the moral content of the literature.

Secular humanism thus provides the morality for G. W. F. Hegel's (1770–1831) universal class, the civil servants.[36] It supplies the undergirding for what Hegel referred to as a mature liberal state, which compasses in toleration numerous and divergent sects.[37] In this Hegel finally corrected a central error of Western thought, which modeled its view of the state on Aristotle's account of the polis. Western political philosophy has endeavored to apply the model for a city-state of no more than 100,000 citizens to large-scale modern states. However, this is impossible. Aristotle assumed near homogeneity of values, while modern nations are fragmented into diverse communities of belief and moral commitment. Aristotle's model was probably not appropriate even for the city-states of his own time.[38]

As the individuals from divergent moral communities stand in line at the post office, each will understand the right to use the post office, though the members of some communities will be condemning the members of other competing groups. Those who support pornography will regard as narrow-minded those about to mail anti-pornography leaflets, while the authors of the leaflets will be convinced that the pornographers stand before the brink of hell. Insofar as the members of these divergent groups are willing to live peaceably and to convert others through witness, not coerce their acquiescence through force, they will understand that individuals have a secular right to use the post office, though what they are doing is morally wrong.

A situation similar to the post-office scenario obtains in the use of secular health care systems. Individuals who oppose contraception will understand that those using contraception will have a secular right to do so (in the sense that in a secular society coercive force may not be justified against such individuals), though their actions will be understood to be immoral. Repeatedly, in the context of health care, one will be able to maintain that "X has a moral right to do A, but it is wrong." The seeming contradiction is the result of a bifurcation in the moral life. On the one hand, individuals live their lives within particular concrete, content-full moral visions. Within such contexts, they understand whether and under what circumstances contraception may be used. On the other hand, insofar as they live in a tolerant, secular pluralist society, they will recognize that many do not understand the true character of concrete morality. In the impoverished moral sphere where moral strangers meet, much must be tolerated that one deeply abhors and condemns. Religious physicians will have as patients individuals who have had abortions, or who have diseases as a result of their sinful lives. As long as the moral and cultural opinions remain private, a secular health care system (e.g., Veterans Administration Hospitals) can function.

Secular humanism as has just been elaborated is itself not a way of life but a moral vision one assumes when one meets moral strangers. It contrasts with Secular Humanism which is a particular, content-full philosophical movement. Such content-full moral visions provide the moral context within which most individuals grow up, make friends, choose spouses, become ill, understand their illnesses, seek health care, receive medical treatment, and fashion the fabric of their life projects. The full, complete significance of their lives can only be explained to moral friends, to those who understand, to those with whom one shares a tradition and concrete moral vision. With moral strangers, such sharing is not possible, though a world of cooperation is still feasible.

The contrast between these two levels of the moral life (i.e., that of (1) one's concrete moral community, and (2) the language of moral strangers) will not seem at all stark for cosmopolitans. They, after all, specialize in freeing themselves from divisive moral traditions in order to cooperate easily with individuals throughout the world. For them to understand the contrast, they should imagine what would be involved in an Orthodox Jew, a devout Sunni Muslim, and a born-again Southern Baptist meeting in Dallas to establish a multi-national health care venture.

B. Three senses of secular humanism

For some, Secular Humanism is a concrete moral vision. It is instantiated in particular moral communities that regard themselves in competition with religious sects. Secular Humanists in this sense can share with each other a concrete moral understanding of health and medicine. By contrast, "secular humanism" identifies those elements of the Western philosophical, moral, and literary traditions that, without reference to religious or particular ideological viewpoints, have attempted to delineate a concrete morality that humans can share as humans (see Chapter III). Secular humanism in this sense, as we have seen in this chapter, must be restated in terms of a much more restricted moral vision and language. This third sense of secular humanism (i.e., the second sense revised, a revision which is the result of the reflections in this and the previous chapter) is the grounding of the moral language of moral strangers. As has been seen, this sense of humanism focuses not on *humanitas*, but on what one might term *personitas*: the nature of persons as constituting a practice of peaceable negotiation that sustains a moral language for moral strangers.[39] It is this language that holds together tolerant, peaceable, secular pluralist societies. In particular, it is this perspective that must provide the ethos for the provision of medical care in large-scale states. Those who provide health care on behalf of large-scale states must be like post office clerks in protecting the rights of moral strangers. A secular health-care system must articulate a moral context for the provision of medical care that will allow individuals of divergent moral perspectives to collaborate as patients, physicians, and health care workers. Unlike many forms of Secular Humanism, this understanding does not discount transcendent beliefs or commitments. It insists only that they cannot be imposed on moral strangers without their consent.

4. Health and Medicine in a Secular Humanist Perspective

A. Free and informed consent: the conveyance of the authority to treat

Free and informed consent is integral to the language within which health professionals and patients can meet as moral strangers and still decide together on plans of treatment. On the other hand, the accent on free and informed consent has a lineage that can be traced back to pagan, Anglo-Saxon, and Germanic understandings of the law. These pagan perspectives tended to portray rights more as limits on the authority of others than as powers (*potestates*, as the Latin has it). This is best illustrated by the right not to be touched without one's consent, the right against battery.[40] For this reason torture, which was widespread in the Roman empire, was nearly unknown among the pagan Germans. One had rights against such governmental actions, for the authority of governments did not extend to battery against individuals.[41] There was an accent on individual consent,[42] and on freedom of the individual expressed in a reluctance to be submissive to others.[43]

These attitudes became enshrined in Anglo-Saxon common law and its protection of individual persons and their property.[44] All of this can be seen as foreshadowing, if not influencing through Anglo-Saxon customary law and later folk remembrances of the rights of Englishmen, a view of the law as based in a fundamental agreement among individuals.[45] Thus, one finds an American court holding that:

> Anglo-American law starts with the premise of thorough-going self determination. It follows that each man is considered to be master of his own body, and he may, if he be of sound mind, expressly prohibit the performance of life-saving surgery, or other medical treatment.[46]

This historically embedded understanding of rights and authority is very close to that which is justifiable in general secular terms. Religious obligations or the rationality of a treatment are not sufficient to justify treating an unconsenting competent person (in the absence of special obligations to third parties: for example, being a voluntary member of the armed forces). Consent is cardinal because it is a source of authority. The appeal to consent requires neither an appeal to God nor a convincing rational argument about the best course of action. The treatment chosen for a patient is not the *authorized* treatment because it is the best form of treatment, but because it is the treatment chosen by the patient and the physician.

The result is a secular humanist basis for cooperation among moral strangers. No presupposition regarding an orthodox view of health or of the goals of medicine need be made. Instead, a secular framework of consent between patient and care-giver can establish a web of moral authority. Without any assumptions regarding the best interests of moral strangers, a general policy can be established for the cooperation of moral strangers in health care.

B. *Rights to privacy: abstentions from the common moral project*

American constitutional law offers some paradigmatic moral frameworks for the collaboration of individuals who are members of diverse religious, moral, and ethnic groups. To compass the moral diversity of its citizens, a government must provide a secular structure through which individuals from divergent moral communities can work together without imposing through law their own concrete moral perspectives on unconsenting others. Though American constitutional law has achieved this moral neutrality only in some areas (and is in fact in retreat from its achievement in the area of abortion rights),[47] it still provides a model for many spheres of public policy, and for health care policy in particular.

This constitutional perspective is not born of the twentieth century. It was present at the inception of the American government, which was in many respects a secularizing event (e.g., involving a complete separation from any relation to the established Church of England).[48] Rather than the central government being regarded as incorporating a content-full moral vision, it was seen as a *res publica* constituted out of a limited delegation of authority.[49] The government did not need to be construed as deriving its authority either from God or from rationally defensible content-full views of justice. The American Constitution was secular from its beginnings. Moreover, it was understood to be a morally limited instrument. Thus, the second American Compact, the American Constitution (written in 1787, put into effect in 1789, and fully valid among all thirteen states in 1790), followed the Articles of Confederation (adopted in 1777 but put into full force only in 1781) by not addressing the justice or morality of hereditary slavery.[50] It did not make slavery a matter of central governmental legislative authority. Slavery was left a "peculiar institution," peculiar to some of the states, left to their own moral address.[51]

Though the immorality of hereditary slavery cannot be disputed from a general secular moral point of view, still the American constitutional restraint in this case is morally instructive in presenting a constitution and government created by contract, not on the basis of a concrete view of positive human rights.

American constitutional foundations contrast dramatically with subsequent European constitutional history, which focuses on concrete, material rights and duties.[52] The American Constitution was not established to articulate and protect concrete positive rights, but rather to allow for better cooperation among the states.[53] The peculiar American emphasis on rights to privacy, as rights to be let alone by the government, can be seen in this light, that is, as developing out of a limited delegation of authority.[54] Whether it is moral or immoral to use contraception or to provide abortions prior to viability was ruled in the 1960s and 1970s to be beyond the scope of legitimate government authority in the absence of a special compelling state interest.[55] In this fashion, a whole range of bioethical issues relating to the generation of human life can be regarded as involving both legal and moral rights to privacy. Whatever the future of American constitutional law might hold in store (e.g., a complete reversal of its protection of access to abortion as a right to privacy), the legal concept of a right to privacy illustrates a number of the important conclusions of secular humanist reflection.

Constitutional rights to privacy are implicit in amendments such as the Ninth, and frame a limited notion of the government ("the enumeration in the Constitution of certain rights shall not be construed to deny or disparage others retained by the people"). Through the Fourteenth Amendment, the constraints set by rights to privacy have been applied to the States.[56]

> There is no clause in the Constitution, except the Ninth Amendment, which makes a declaration of the sovereignty and dignity of the individual . . .
>
> The Ninth Amendment announces and acknowledges in a single sentence that (1) the individual, and not the State, is the source and basis of our social compact and that sovereignty now resides and has always resided in the individual; (2) that our Government exists through the surrender by the individual of a portion of his naturally endowed and inherent rights; (3) that everyone of the people of the United States owns a residue of individual rights and liberties which have never been, and which

are never to be surrendered to the State, but which are still to be recognized, protected and secured; and (4) that individual liberty and rights are inherent, and that such rights are not derived from the Constitution, but belong to the individual by natural endowment.[57]

This reflection on constitutional law introduces a basic point in secular moral theory: rights to privacy as moral rights against governments are not grounded in a particular constitution but rather in the fundamental limits of governmental authority. Moral rights to privacy disclose those areas of conduct regarding which one cannot assume that individuals have delegated authority to a society or state.

These constitutional reflections bear on the moral justification of coercive state power in a secular context. When there is an intellectually irresolvable plurality of moral viewpoints (for which one dissident will suffice), there will not be a common basis for coercive constraints justified uncontroversially in a particular common concrete view of the good life. For example, the immorality of hereditary slavery is integral to ethics itself (i.e., to a commitment to resolving issues peaceably without recourse to force when no concrete generally justifiable rational warrant for force can be established).[58] The immorality of hereditary slavery thus does not depend on a particular view of the good life.[59] However, the proscription of indentured servitude, the sale of human organs, or surrogate motherhood for profit are so dependent insofar as they involve only consenting collaborators. Therefore their legal prohibition should always be under moral suspicion in a secular pluralist society. This secular moral understanding of rights and of governmental moral authority grounded in the consent of those involved has significant implications for a wide range of issues in bioethics, from rights to abortion and contraception to rights to refuse life-saving treatment.

This grounding provides rights to privacy with a negative, not a positive, foundation: rights to privacy are grounded in the incapacity of governments morally to justify certain intrusions upon the actions of individuals. The context for the post-modern examination of health and medicine is set by fragmentation of belief and moral commitment and by skepticism whether there is an intellectual or moral foundation that can unite people around concrete moral commitments. Though this circumstance is at root an intellectual problem, it has profound social implications.

The authoritative resolution of controversies through coercive state force is brought into moral question unless one can establish:

(1) what is correct to do,
(2) that one has the moral authority to impose the findings of (1) on the unconsenting, and
(3) that (2) will lead to more benefits than harms.

For example, do the United States have the moral authority to forbid the sale of contraceptives? How could one establish a moral claim to the use of such governmental coercive force? The challenge is intellectual: to establish public policy with moral authority following the disintegration of the Christian intellectual hegemony and the abandonment of the Enlightenment hope to ground a content-full morality in reason. Against this challenge, rights to privacy have the significance of fundamental rights to forbearance. In this light one can understand why, unlike the Americans, the Texans made their Bill of Rights irrevocable.[60] Fundamental rights involve areas of individual prerogative that individuals cannot reasonably be presumed to have delegated to others without actually being asked. Rights of individuals to self-determination become salient, not because the rights are valued, but because communal authority is brought into question. Rights to refuse treatment are, thus, withdrawals or suspensions of authority for continued joint collaboration. This secular understanding gains a generality that is founded on the ubiquity of skepticism and the dubiousness of sweeping claims on behalf of group authority.

Secular humanism provides by default an account of fundamental rights. Individuals may freely choose where there is no authority for others to intervene. The account is secular by spanning in a neutral fashion a myriad of possible, content-full moral understandings of health and medicine. It is humanist in being grounded in what we share as persons: the project of the peaceable resolution of moral disputes with moral strangers. It accomplishes this task by privatizing much of the morality and value judgments involved in health care.

C. Health care entitlements as provisions of a secular insurance policy

It does not follow from the failure to discover a content-full view of proper moral conduct with moral strangers that individuals from disparate moral communities cannot fashion health care systems or welfare programs. With the goods they share in common, moral strangers can create projects to provide for health care. It is simply that they cannot discover *a priori* what they ought to do (only what they ought not to do; e.g., interfere with a competent person's acting as a surrogate mother for profit). There will be no hypothetical choice theory or consequentialist analysis that will deliver *the* correct answer to disputes regarding the proper fashioning of health care systems. Instead, various groups, acting in terms of their own visions of health and proper medical care, will support particular health care systems as the most reasonable, the most efficient, and the most likely to achieve the goals of prudent men and women. Insofar as their goals are shared with others, such arguments will be persuasive. So, too, and for similar reasons, will consequentialist arguments. However, from the standpoint of a political system established (*inter alia*) to administer the common resources of a secular pluralist society, there is no vision of the proper support of health care services that is correct *a priori*. The correct vision is the one endorsed by the established political procedures. Though one cannot discover what is correct to do, one can convey authority on a commonly-endorsed plan of action and determine how one will calculate the balance of benefits and harms.

Without any appeal to concrete theories of justice or rights to health care, health care systems can be fashioned as ways of insuring individuals against losses at the natural and social lotteries. That is, health care systems can be constructed and supported through common funds in order to aid individuals in adapting their minds and bodies to the achievement of a wide range of human goals, the realization of which might be undermined by the vicissitudes of nature (i.e., by losses at the natural lottery), which may occasion the need for health care expenses, the costs of which can be prohibitive (i.e., if the same individuals have also lost the social lottery). Thus a society must determine what will count as an "adequate" or "decent" amount of health care. Each society through its commonly established procedures regarding the use of common funds must determine the line between those non-provisions of treatment, which may be regarded as unfair (i.e., failures to provide governmentally guaranteed treatment), versus those that are simply unfortunate.

In the process of framing such societal decisions, different groups will use different moral arguments in the attempt to convert others to their understanding of a just health care system or the proper compass of rights to health care. What will count as intellectual moral arguments for one group will appear as propaganda from outside the group, or as exercises in the persuasive or emotive use of language. But from the perspective of secular humanist bioethics, there will be no canonical content-full understanding of a just health care or of the rights to health care. Instead, particular understandings of justice and charity are transformed through a common political process into a political commitment to a particular health care system. A just health care system is what the participants in a society freely choose and support through common funds. It will, however, be important to ensure that all participate in the ways established by the society's compact for the distribution of common resources.[61]

The limits of reason and human vision which underlie the limits of secular human authority along with the limits of human resources predestine any health care system to being partial and incomplete. A secular health care system cannot and may not morally try to accomplish all the things that individuals could hope from it. The tragedy of being human is that we have the aspirations of gods and goddesses but only the intellectual capacity, moral authority, and purses of finite men and women. Every health care system will therefore be a compromise. It will represent what individuals can agree to support (to will) with their common goods. In a secular society, such support may only occur in the presence of rights to privacy, as well as the right to use private resources to fashion one's own understanding of proper health care. Because of the moral limitations of a secular vision, there should always be inequalities and multiple systems of health care.

No secular society is likely to have the resources or moral authority required to achieve equal health care for all. To achieve equal health care for all, one must either (1) provide all health care that can possibly benefit anyone (i.e., including everything from cosmetic surgery to expensive intensive-care unit treatment likely to extend life only minimally), or (2) restrict the freedom of individuals who have private resources from purchasing more health care than that provided out of common funds. The first is unlikely to be practically possible. The second is immoral in a secular society, for it involves coercively establishing a particular lexical ordering of equality over liberty and other societal goals. Nor is it permissible to claim all private resources for common public endeavors, for one cannot plausibly hold that all resources are public.[62] It is as impossible to show that all property is communal as it is to show that all property is private.[63] This leads unavoidably to acquiescing in a mixed system (i.e., both public and private) of health care provision. The conclusion that resources are both common and private results from recognizing the finitude of human moral arguments. One must always be tolerant of collateral, competing, or supplementary health care systems, supported from private funds in pursuit of particular understandings of health or proper health care.

D. Fashioning joint endeavors in health care

Though it is morally impermissible to forbid consenting peaceable competent individuals from engaging in joint health care ventures with their own funds, it will be quite another thing to support morally controversial undertakings out of common resources. As a result, in secular pluralist societies, compromises such as have occurred in the United States will be inescapable. For instance, though one will not have the moral authority to forbid abortion, in most areas one does not have the moral agreement to provide elective abortions through public funds. The rights of consenting competent individuals are thus harmonized with the rights of citizens to withhold communal support from what most hold to be immoral.

This harmonization is also implicit in much of the bureaucratic ethic which guides the use of common funds. Federal rules concerning research on human subjects provide a good illustration. There are few federal laws governing experimentation on human subjects. But there are extensive regulations governing research involving human subjects when supported by federal funds. These regulations resulted primarily from the recommendations of the National Commission for the Protection of Human Subjects of Biomedical and Behavioral Research.[64] The Commission appealed to three ethical principles (i.e., (1) respect for persons, (2) beneficence, and (3) justice[65]), elaborated within a particular moral perspective, and which can be justified (save for an element of the principle of respect for persons) only in terms of a particular moral sense or ranking of values. However, in a truly secular society, the endorsement of such a bureaucratic ethic will not be problematic as long as (1) it is not regarded as expressing generally binding moral obligations, but rather (2) a set of general rules created for the administration of common funds.

All such bureaucratic ethics (ethics required in a secular pluralist society for the administration of common funds) should be grounded in a general procedural ethic. This procedural ethic has been characterized as the new civil religion of the United States, a civil religion appropriate to secular pluralist societies, which must compass divergent moral perspectives.[66] This procedural ethic must in turn be understood in terms of the authority conveying (and limiting) character of peaceable negotiation among individuals, which is the core of secular humanism in the post-modern world.

E. Why market solutions are so unproblematic in secular humanist bioethics

The market has a justification similar to that of democratic communal endeavors. It is justified by the authority of each and all who participate. When one seeks the authority of any transaction (presuming that the traders own what they trade and are not deceiving or coercing each other), the immediate answer is that the market derives its authority from the choices of the participants. The market is the outcome of numerous consensual actions among individuals. Its outcomes are justified by the consent of the participants. As a result, the market offers a form of pure procedural justice where in the absence of fraud and coercion each gets exactly what has been agreed.[67] Because the market presupposes no concrete theory of justice nor a concrete view of proper correct outcomes, the market can reach out across and ignore every and all political, religious, and ideological divisions. Protestants, Catholics, Jews, Muslims, and Hindus may bitterly dispute about the character of the after-life, the meaning of suffering, the allowability of artificial insemination, and the morality of abortion. However, they all are able to trade together in the markets of the world (e.g., buying and selling antibiotics); the market by itself is free of ideologies and religions.

The market functions without any presuppositions about the ultimate purposes and goals of its participants. The market is the ultimate means, the consummate meeting of instrumentalities. By requiring only peaceable, non-coerced, non-fraudulent exchanges, the market can allow strangers to transfer goods for services without the endorsement of a particular morality. A pure market in health care services and products (including health care insurance contracts) requires only respect of (i.e., non-coercion of) the participants by other participants. It does not require the endorsement of a particular hierarchy of values. If there are goods or services that some are morally opposed to buying or selling, they will be absent from the market, insofar as the suppliers of the goods and services agree not to enter the market (e.g., the sale of organs for transplantation). Otherwise, those who oppose the sales, insofar as the market goes, must content themselves with not buying or selling (e.g., those who wish to hire surrogate mothers will, and those morally opposed will not). Insofar as individuals enter the market, the market usually (i.e., in the absence of some desire to manipulate the market for "moral" purposes) excludes any content-full moral judgments. It records only the interest and ability to make a trade. The market is a way of creating answers where proper answers cannot be discovered.

Because the market is the creature of mutually consenting persons, it will always have a presumed moral authority. Hence the moral difficulty, as we have seen, of forbidding a second private tier of health care. Because a free market in health care requires no particular content-full rationally justified vision of proper health care policy, only the consent of the participants, the market will always have an intellectual advantage over egalitarian health care systems that depend on a particular content-full vision of proper health care distributions. But the market involves unavoidable moral untidiness because the patterns of health care distribution are the outcome of numerous free choices, not central planning. Which is to say, the variety of goods for sale will tend to be greater when the market plays a central role.

F. *Individuals*

Because secular humanism is not a tradition but a way of reaching across traditions, it regards individuals outside their embeddedness in particular moral communities. This does not mean that they cannot belong to moral communities or that a sense of community should cease — far from it. It is just that moral strangers as such do not share in a common concrete moral community. Secular humanism cannot supply a content-full account of individuals that places them within a particular moral context. Thus, for secular humanism, individuals are salient and central. It is individuals who meet as moral strangers. It is individuals who exist before moral theories are articulated or common endeavors created. Since common moral endeavors are, from a secular humanist perspective, the work of actual individuals in actual contexts, the accent is on individual responsibility. It is individuals who will to engage in empirical science and secular morality and thus sustain general practices that have no *a priori* content beyond the sparse grammar that governs this function. It is individuals who through secular social structures create the fabric and focus of common endeavors. In all of this, individuals are not given precedence because they are valued. Within the sparse morality of moral strangers, one cannot talk about persons as being valued or as having moral worth. They, and their consent, are simply necessary for a morality of moral strangers (only in a particular moral community can a person have moral value and worth). As moral strangers, individuals are respected, not because they are valuable, but because such respect is integral to a morality for moral strangers. Secular humanism does not involve a value commitment to individualism. Individuals are salient by default. Since one cannot discover a general, morally authoritative social nexus ontologically prior to individuals, individuals hold center stage when moral strangers meet.

G. Creating the meaning of health and giving a direction to medicine: a summary of the constructive task of secular humanism

Secular humanism, understood not as a concrete vision or movement but as the fulfillment of the general humanist aspiration to establish a common secular basis for men and women to collaborate, shows how individuals can create content and establish authority, not how they can discover it. There is no univocal way in general secular terms to discover *a priori* the meaning of health, suffering, illness, death, or the purposes of medicine. Such meaning must from a secular perspective be fashioned by actual communities and individuals in real circumstances.

1. *Creation of authority and content at the micro-level: free and informed consent*

The process of free and informed consent between patient and physician establishes content for their common action and authority for their joint undertakings. That is, the patient and the physician must jointly decide what will be the concrete focus of their therapeutic contract (i.e., what treatment will be provided and under what circumstances).

2. *Moral limits to the creation of authority and content at the macro-level: rights to privacy*

Since individuals cannot be presumed to have conveyed to the community authority over all areas of their lives, large spheres of human interaction lie beyond the authority of the state. They remain as possibilities for the creation of common endeavors outside of the moral authority of the state. It is here that most morally contested medical moral choices occur. Moreover, it is especially in areas of radical disagreement that individuals cannot be presumed to have ceded to the state authority over themselves.

3. *Creation of authority and content at the macro-level: the fashioning of common enterprises*

From communal resources with common consent, joint endeavors can be undertaken, such as (1) research with human subjects and (2) the establishment of a public health care system.[68] Decisions about how to allocate scarce public medical resources or limit the public support of treatment because of costs involve proper choices among alternative possible communal definitions of "decent" or "adequate" health care.

4. *Physicians, patients, and the social fabric*

This volume describes, it does not propose. Against brief sketches of the history of secularity and humanism, the possibility of a secular humanist philosophy has been explored. There have been two reasons for this undertaking: first, to see if it is at all possible to justify a moral perspective bridging the numerous moral communities that define the pluralism of the post-modern condition; second, to determine the implications such a view has for health and medicine. The answer to the first is in the affirmative. The answer to the second is without moral content. A justified secular humanism allows us to secure a general moral framework via a commitment to peaceable negotiation. Moral authority comes from those who collaborate. Moral content is established by common agreement. Moral authority has limits set because of its source, because it is derived from consent.

There is nothing one can say *a priori* about the meaning of well-being, the content of the good life, of the meaning of sickness, illness, and death. Such meanings must be framed by actual individuals in particular moral communities. The same can be said about the meaning of sexuality and the proper purposes of procreation. The meaning of the passages and endeavors of human life from birth to copulation to death are not to be discovered *a priori* from a secular humanist perspective. One cannot even determine *a priori* what human life is worth. There is no way to speak concretely of the dignity of persons. It is the case that one is constrained from using persons without their permission. One knows that all peaceable entities that can participate in a moral controversy have a right to mutual forbearance. This right will include particular rights to forbearance such as the right to refuse life-saving treatment. But as to concrete content-full questions, no *a priori* answers will be forthcoming. One will need through particular agreements to decide who heals, when and how, and who pays for the healing. The meaning of care will likewise be derived in particular contexts. And finally, there will be no way to speak of any ultimate meaning of suffering and death. The answers to such important questions will be available only within particular concrete moral visions.

Imagine, for example, an atheist patient asking a Catholic physician for euthanasia within a secular social fabric that does not overstep the limits of its authority. If the Catholic physician has prudently informed the patient in advance of the physician's moral commitments, the matter will be quite straightforward. The physician will simply say, "Remember that my moral commitments forbid me from either helping you or suggesting how you can secure help. That you must see to on your own. Remember also that, although there are many euthanasia societies that may assist you, and though the state will not interfere, all costs will have to be privately borne. Moreover, for the sake of your eternal salvation, I sincerely suggest you reconsider the matter." As the example shows us, there is much that society must tolerate, given the limits of secular reason. The limits of secular reason do not undermine moral commitments. However, such commitments will often require disclosure to others so that they are not hindered by an avoidable false impression from making alternative plans.

To find our way through the complexity and fragmentation of a post-modern world, physician and patients will need carefully to explore the implications for a physician-patient relationship of their different moral commitments.

5. Secular Humanism After the Death of Man

Secular humanism is the attempt to justify and elaborate a common moral framework grounded in what we share as persons. It stands against the centrifugal forces of post-modern fragmentation. As Enlightenment assumptions about the capacity of reason weaken, sects abound which need no longer contend with a central content-full governing moral focus. Moreover, communication technology now allows individuals of like moral viewpoint to associate without direct physical contact. Individuals scattered across the world can create a community. Alvin Toffler in *Future Shock* has described this as "a surfeit of subcults." He has predicted that "the human race, far from being flattened into monotonous conformity, will become far more diverse socially than it ever was before. The new society, the super-industrial society now beginning to take form, will encourage a crazy-quilt pattern of evanescent life styles."[69] Secular humanism offers a way of converting this fragmentation of humanity into a pluralism understood within a common moral language that can span and tolerate contrary assertions about the meaning of human life, health, illness, and death. Secular humanism contrasts with Secular Humanism, which presumes it can discover the content of the good life. Because Secular Humanism holds it can discover the truth, it opposes itself to the pluralism of religious cults and subcults as a kind of rationalist orthodoxy. However, secular humanism requires tolerance and restraint over against the possible intolerance of some subcultures, the despair of others, and the insouciance of the cosmopolitans.

Secular humanism provides both the moral language of moral strangers, and a reflective statement of the lived philosophy of many cosmopolitans. The role of secular humanism is amphibious. Secular humanism secures the moral framework in terms of which individuals from intact moral communities with divergent understandings of the meaning of life, health, medicine, and death can cooperate. Such individuals do not live their lives primarily in terms of secular humanism. Rather, secular humanism provides them with a moral framework when they step outside of their content-full lives to meet and work with strangers. On the other hand, cosmopolitans are men and women who have shed intensely held, content-full understandings of life, health, medicine, and death that focus on moral ultimates. Their lives are constructed around instrumental goods, not ultimate moral commitments. For them, secular humanism can provide a way of giving coherent statement to their way of life.

Secular humanism humanizes by introducing a sense of sophrosyne and a sense of human finitude. This has traditionally been an office of the humanities: to be an antidote to hubris. In terms of the limitations of human reason and human authority, secular humanism can provide a peaceable mediation of the divergent views that humans have regarding life in general, and health and medicine in particular. It can bring the wide scope of human aspirations within a single lens and let human experience be seen from a perspective that stands outside of particular content-full moral visions. On the other hand, it can help those whom the modern world has despoiled of a content-full moral life to see their own condition as embodying a moral asceticism which eschews moral content in the service of peaceable cooperation. It may seem odd to regard cosmopolitans (yuppies!) as the monks and nuns of the post-modern age. Yet their foregoing marriages with moral ultimates (their cloistering themselves from transcendent moral goals) allow them to span many moral communities and stand outside content-full moral controversies.

In a very humble and restricted way, secular humanism can give an account of *humanitas*. It can show how divergent notions of philanthropy can be harnessed to support common endeavors in health care. It can embed reflections on what is commonly shared by humans in the larger question of what can be shared by persons, thus realizing the classical aspiration to a *ius naturale*. Despite the failure of the Enlightenment to discover or rationally justify canonical moral content for the moral life, secular humanism provides a general justification for a moral enterprise that is universal in scope and able to withstand the onslaughts of nihilism. Still, secular humanism cannot insure, or perhaps even motivate, moral deportment in general or a just health care policy in particular.[70] The service is intellectual.

Even this modest success has its price. By providing a moral standpoint for moral strangers, secular humanism sets itself free from its historical roots and deprives itself of its traditional content. The higher truth of *humanitas* is *personitas*, what we share as persons.[71] We are left with a moral perspective within which not only gender, race, and culture become morally irrelevant, but species membership itself.[72] All that remains to ground a general secular morality, and then a secular health care policy, is the possible bond of mutual respect among persons. The focus is on persons as such because they are the only beings who pose moral questions and attempt to answer them. Still, it is the particular concerns of persons that provide the flesh and blood of actual traditions and communities, and of human life itself. Content is particular, the particular is parochial, and the parochial has moral substance.[73] In the ruins of modern moral philosophy's hopes, a common morality is still possible.[74] But, moral content must be found amidst the post-modern pluralism of moral visions.[75]

Notes

I. Secular Humanism, Bioethics, and the Post-Modern World

1. Bob Sutton, "Humanism: Man as Master," in *Secular Humanism* (Mobile, Ala.: Integrity Publications, 1979), p. 42.
2. R. J. Rushdoony, "The World's Second Oldest Religion," in *Secular Humanism*, p. 11.
3. Howard Carter, "The Conflict of the Ages," in *Secular Humanism*, p. 65.
4. Rushdoony, "The World's Second Oldest Religion," p. 21.
5. Ibid., p. 19.
6. Marlin Maddoux, *America Betrayed!* (Lafayette, La.: Huntingdon Press, 1984), p. 29.
7. David Ehrenfeld, *The Arrogance of Humanism* (New York: Oxford University Press, 1978), p. 3.
8. Ibid., pp. 45–47.
9. Ibid., pp. 5–6. Ehrenfeld lists as the false certitudes of humanism the view that (1) "all problems are soluble," (2) "all problems are soluble by people," (3) "many problems are soluble by technology," (4) "those problems that are not soluble by technology, or by technology alone, have solutions in the social world (of politics, economics, etc.)." (5) "When the chips are down, we will apply ourselves and work together for a solution before it is too late." (6) "Some resources are infinite; all finite or all finite or limited resources have substitutes." (7) "Human civilization will survive" (pp. 16–17).
10. Paul Kurtz, *In Defense of Secular Humanism* (Buffalo, N.Y.: Prometheus Books, 1983), p. 189. Groups outside the United States such as the British Humanist Association and the Indian Radical Humanist Association do not appear to involve very large numbers either.
11. The Declaration appeared in the first issue of *Free Inquiry*, published by the Council for Democratic and Secular Humanism. "A Secular Humanist Declaration," *Free Inquiry* 1 (Winter 1980–81), 3–7.
12. David L. Edwards, *Religion and Change* (London: Hodder and Stoughton, 1969), p. 16. Larry Shiner identifies five key concepts of secularization: "1. Secularization is conceived as the decline of religion . . . 2. Secularization is conceived as conformity with the world . . . 3. Secularization is conceived as the desacralization of the world . . . 4. Secularization is conceived as the disengagement of society from religion . . . 5. Secularization is conceived of as the transposition of beliefs and patterns of behavior from the 'religious' to the 'secular' sphere." "The Meanings of Secularization," in *Secularization and the Protestant Prospect*, ed. James Childress and David Harned (Philadelphia: Westminster Press, 1970), pp. 31, 33, 35, 37, 38. See also David Martin, *A General Theory of Secularization* (Oxford: Basil Blackwell, 1978).
13. Edward Schillebeeckx, "Silence and Speaking About God in a Secularized World," in *Christian Secularity*, ed. Albert Schlitzer (Notre Dame, Ind.: University of Notre Dame Press, 1969), p. 156.

14. Peter L. Berger, *The Social Reality of Religion* (London: Penguin, 1969), p. 130.

15. It is interesting to note that the total number of pilgrims and tourists going to Lourdes increased from 1951 through 1971, though 65% of the pilgrims were not practicing Catholics. See René Laurentin, "The Persistence of Popular Piety," in *The Persistence of Religion*, ed. Andrew Greeley and Gregory Baum (New York: Herder and Herder, 1973), pp. 144–156.

16. One of the striking milestones of secularization has been the collapse of the Roman Catholic Church. In the seven years following the replacement of the Tridentine Mass by the Novus Ordo Mass in 1969, the number of priests in the world declined from about 410,000 to about 245,000. The period was also one of a major loss of communicants. For example, in the period from 1965 to 1974, weekly Church attendance among Canadian Protestants dropped 19% but among Canadian Catholics 29%. *Index to International Public Opinion, 1978–1979* (Westport, Conn.: Greenwood Press, 1980). To give another example, over the last sixteen years, the number of churchgoers in the diocese of Amsterdam has decreased from 45,000 to 10,000, necessitating a drop in the number of active churches from 65 to 45, of which half will be closed in the next six years. Siggi Weidemann, "Altäre unter dem Hammer," *Süddeutsche Zeitung* (18 April 1989). As these losses in church attendance occurred, there developed a significant hostility on the part of much of the hierarchy to the traditional Tridentine Latin Mass. As a consequence, one of the major defenders of the traditional Mass and its pieties, Archbishop Marcel Lefebvre, has found himself excommunicated, though his seminaries are of the few in the West with increasing numbers of young men willing and eager to become celibate priests. The thoroughgoing secularization of the Roman Catholic Church has led to the defenders of its traditional rites and understandings being regarded as members of a sect.

But of course there are those who deny the very phenomenon of secularization or the weakening of traditional religious influence. Yet they are faced with the problem of accounting for the "'one shot' decline in church practice in the late sixties and the early seventies" (Andrew M. Greeley, *The Catholic Myth* [New York: Scribner's Sons, 1990]), which occurred as traditional social structures and traditional forms of religious piety weakened. During this period, for instance, the incidence of divorce in the United States increased from 2.2 per thousand in 1960 to 4.8 per thousand in 1975. There was a major departure from the traditional social mores of the West. Mark S. Hoffman (ed.), *The World Almanac* (New York: Ballantine, 1988), p. 809.

For an interesting study of the secularization of post-Vatican II Roman Catholicism, see Louis Bouyer, *Der Verfall des Katholizismus* (Munich: Kösel, 1970). The volume first appeared in French with the title *La Décomposition du Catholicisme*.

17. Alan D. Gilbert, *The Making of Post-Christian Britain* (London: Longman, 1980), p. ix. T. S. Eliot recognized the secularization of Britain in the 1930s and addressed the problem in a collection of essays written during the late 1930s and early 1940s published under the title, *The Idea of a Christian Society* (London: Faber and Faber, 1982). In the closing essay of the volume (originally written in 1937) he remarks: "We must remember also that the choice between Christianity and secularism is not simply presented to the innocent mind, *anima semplicetta*, as to an impartial judge capable of choosing the best when the causes have both been fully pleaded. The whole tendency of education (in the widest sense — the influences playing on the common mind in the forms of 'enlightenment') has been for a very long time to form minds more and more

adapted to secularism, less and less equipped to apprehend the doctrine of revelation and its consequences. Even in works of Christian apologetic, the assumption is sometimes that of the secular mind" (p. 190).

18. Daniel Lerner, *The Passing of Traditional Society* (Glencoe, Ill.: Free Press of Glencoe, 1962). Harvey Cox also argues that "urbanization means a structure of common life in which the diversity and the disintegration of tradition are paramount." *The Secular City* (New York: Macmillan and London: SCM Press, 1966), p. 4.

19. Granville C. Henry, Jr., *Logos: Mathematics and Christian Theology* (Lewisburg: Bucknell University Press, 1976), p. 29.

20. Richard Rorty, "Habermas and Lyotard on Postmodernity," in *Habermas and Modernity*, ed. Richard J. Bernstein (Oxford: Polity Press, 1985), p. 161–175.

21. Jean-François Lyotard, *The Postmodern Condition*, trans. G. Bennington and B. Massumi (Manchester: Manchester University Press, 1984), p. 37.

22. Flavio Biondo can probably be credited with first viewing as a whole the period we have come to call the Middle Ages. Though he himself did not use the term (e.g., *medium aevum*), in his *Historiarum ab inclinatione Romanorum imperii decades*, written between 1439 and 1453, he provided a historical portrayal of the period as a millennium set off from the ancient world. In the 32-volume work (some have alleged originally only 31; see Alfred Masius, *Flavio Biondo, Sein Leben und seine Werke* [Leipzig: B. G. Teubner, 1879], especially p. 37), he covered the period between A.D. 410 and A.D. 1442, giving a scope to the time interval, which became established as the conventional portrayal (i.e., the Middle Ages has been considered to be that period extending more or less from A.D. 325 or 476 to about A.D. 1453). For a study of Biondo, see Denys Hay, "Flavio Biondo and the Middle Ages," *Proceedings of the British Academy* (London: Oxford, 1960), pp. 97–125.

Only later does an explicit treatment of the concept of the *media tempestas* (1469), the *media aetas* (1518), and *medium aevum* (1604) develop. Otto Brunner, Werner Conze, Reinhart Koselleck (eds.), *Geschichtliche Grundbegriffe* (Stuttgart: Klett-Cotta, 1978), vol. 4, p. 98. With the Renaissance, the Middle Ages came to be regarded as a period of darkness between the light of the ancient world and that of modern times. The three-fold division of history appears full-blown in Christoph Cellarius, *Historia Universalis, breviter ac perspicue exposita*, in *Antiquam et Medii Aevi ac Novam divisa* (1685). One also finds Thomas James in his *Treatise of the Corruptions of Scripture, Councils, and Fathers* speaking of "auncient, middle-aged, or moderne writers." Nathan Edelman, "The Early Uses of Medium Aevum, Moyen Age, Middle Ages," *The Romanic Review* 29 (February 1938), 7. But as these works show and as Edelman points out, it took quite a while before the term middle ages came unambiguously to identify the period of time that had been the focus of Biondo's history. Cellarius identifies different periods as *antiquus* or as *medium aevum*. See also Nathan Edelman, "Other Early Uses of *Moyen âge* and *Moyen temps*," *The Romanic Review* 30 (December 1939), 327–330.

What is new and important is the concept of the middle ages. The distinction between modern and ancient times had already existed since Cassiodorus (c. A.D. 480–575) contrasted *modernus* with *antiquus*. Franz Overbeck, *Christentum und Kultur* (Basel: Schwabe, 1919), ed. C. A. Bernoulli, p. 243. It is clear that by his time the term *modernus* had become well established. In fact, it was already used by Gelasius I, who as Pope (492–496) used the term *modernus* without further explanation in a letter written in 494/495. Walter Freund, *Modernus und andere Zeitbegriffe des Mittelalters* (Cologne: Böhlau, 1957), p. 4.

Cassiodorus regards the ancient world somewhat as would the scholars of the Renaissance: *"nostris temporibus videatur antiquitas decentius innovata,"* p. 28. Also, *"antiquorum diligentissimus imitator, modernorum nobilissimus institutor"* and *"modernis saeculis moribus ornabantur antiquis,"* p. 32. For further explorations of the concepts modern and modernity, see "Modern, Modernität, Moderne," in O. Brunner, W. Conze, R. Koselleck (eds.), *Geschichtliche Grundbegriffe* (Stuttgart: Klett-Cotta, 1978), vol. 4, pp. 93–98. See also Ernst Robert Curtius, *Europäische Literatur und lateinisches Mittelalter* (Bern: Francke, 1954), pp. 256–261.

23. The Renaissance was a complex movement that included the rebirth of secular art in the style of the ancients, a reaction against the clericism and pieties of the Middle Ages, the development of national understandings of culture and purpose, interest in progress in science, as well as the Reformation. See Herbert Weisinger, "The Renaissance Theory of the Reaction Against the Middle Ages as a Cause of the Renaissance," *Speculum* 20 (October 1945), 461–467. The concept of the Renaissance was in part developed within a cyclic understanding of history that portrayed the Renaissance as a new period of enlightenment similar to that of the ancient world, separated from the latter by a period of darkness, the Middle Ages. See Herbert Weisinger, "Renaissance Theories of the Revival of the Fine Arts," *Italica* 2 (1943), 163–170; and Jochen Schlobach, *Zyklentheorie und Epochenmetaphorik* (Munich: Wilhelm Fink, 1980), especially p. 167.

24. Lionel Trilling, *Beyond Culture* (London: Secker & Warburg, 1966), p. xiii.

25. Octavio Paz, *Children of the Mire*, trans. Rachel Phillips (Cambridge, Mass.: Harvard University Press, 1974), p. 27.

26. Lionel Trilling argued that "Between the end of the first quarter of this century and the present time there has grown up a populous group whose members take for granted the idea of the adversary culture." *Beyond Culture*, p. xiii. He fails to recognize that the Renaissance, the Age of Reason, the Enlightenment, have all been adversary cultures, cultures opposed to the traditional Christian culture of the West, which for more than a millennium held cultural and political hegemony over Europe.

27. "As early as the eighteenth century, the word 'modern' acquired something of the ring of a war cry, but then only as an antithesis of 'ancient' – implying contrast with classical antiquity." Carl E. Schorske, *Fin-de-Siècle Vienna* (New York: Alfred Knopf, 1985), p. xvii. The definition of modernity over against the literature and science of the ancients has been captured in the jargon term "the *querelle*." The *querelle* or quarrel was whether the literature and culture of the moderns was not better than that of the ancients. The modern notion of cultural and scientific progress with its face to the future contrasted with the first period of the modern age, the Renaissance, with its face to the past. See Hans Baron, "The *Querelle* of the Ancients and the Moderns as a Problem for Renaissance Scholarship," *Journal of the History of Ideas* 20 (January 1959), 3–22; and J. W. Lorimer, "A Neglected Aspect of the 'Querelle des anciens et des modernes'," *The Modern Language Review* 51 (April 1956), 179–185.

28. "In the last one hundred years, however, 'modern' has come to distinguish our perception of our lives and times from all that has gone before, from history as a whole, as such. Modern architecture, modern music, modern philosophy, modern science — all these define themselves not *out* of the past, indeed scarcely *against* the past, but in independence of the past." Carl E. Schorske, *Fin-de-Siècle Vienna* (New York: Alfred Knopf, 1985), p. xvii.

29. Marshall Berman, *All That Is Solid Melts Into Air* (New York: Simon and Schuster, 1982), p. 30.

30. The term modernity has consanguinities with the term modernism in Catholic moral reflections. The heresies of Modernism (an attempt to secularize Catholicism and to understand its significance in terms of the modern age, rather than through its traditional transcendent commitments) and Americanism (the desire on the part of some members of the American hierarchy not to make reference to traditional Catholic dogma that might make adaptation in the modern world difficult) were condemned by Pope Pius X on July 3, 1907, in his encyclical *Lamentabili*. See Franz Heiner, *Der neue Syllabus Pius X* (Mainz: von Kirchheim, 1907). For a study of Modernism, see Joseph Schnitzer, *Der katholische Modernismus* (Berlin: Protestantischer Schriftenvertrieb, 1912). It is out of this history that traditionalist Catholics have regarded Vatican II as the triumph of Modernism. Moreover, with Pius X's condemnation of Modernism, one can understand the appropriateness of the traditionalist Archbishop Marcel Lefebvre naming his society of priests the Fraternité sacerdotale St-Pie X.

31. The official traditional religious control of society collapsed. This can be seen in the liberalization of laws on such issues as abortion, divorce, and homosexual conduct. This collapse is a part of the secularizing developments of the contemporary age, even if one holds that the amount of true believers has remained constant.

32. There have been other developments that have intensified the character of the debate and interaction between humanism and Christianity. In particular, a tension developed between the rationalized and instrumentalized life of technological industrial society on the one hand and the subjective experience of the self on the other. "Modernity in the broadest sense, as it has asserted itself historically, is reflected in the irreconcilable opposition between the sets of values corresponding to (1) the objectified, socially measurable time of capitalist civilization (time as a more or less precious commodity, bought and sold on the market), and (2) the personal, subjective, imaginative *durée*, the private time created by the unfolding of the 'self.' The latter identity of *time* and *self* constitutes the foundation of modernist culture. Seen from this vantage point, aesthetic modernity uncovers some of the reasons for its profound sense of crisis and for its alienation from the other modernity, which, for all its objectivity and rationality, has lacked, after the demise of religion, any compelling moral or metaphysical justification. But, being produced by the isolated self, partly as a reaction against the desacralized — and therefore dehumanized — time of social activity, the time consciousness reflected in modernist culture also lacks such justifications. The end result of both modernities seems to be the same unbounded relativism." Matei Calinescu, *Faces of Modernity: Avant-Garde, Decadence, Kitsch* (Bloomington: Indiana University Press, 1977), p. 5.

33. Here one might acknowledge the putative coinage of the "post-modern period" by Arnold Toynbee to indicate a period of reflection on the modern age. See Harry Levin, *Refractions* (New York: Oxford University Press, 1966), p. 277. However, one must note that the use of post-modern is part of a fad to preface important words with "post." Thus, one finds references to "post-capitalist society", as by Ralf Dahrendorf, *Class and Class Conflict in an Industrial Society* (London: Routledge & Kegan Paul, 1959). Others, such as George Lichtheim, refer to the "post-bourgeoise society." As Lichtheim observes, "there cannot be a bourgeoisie without a proletariat, and if the one is fading out, so is the other, and for the same reason: Modern industrial society does

not require either for its operation" (George Lichtheim, *The New Europe: Today and Tomorrow* [New York: Praeger, 1963], p. 194). So, too, one finds the phrase "post-industrial society." "The concept 'post-industrial society' emphasizes the centrality of theoretical knowledge as the axis around which new technology, economic growth and the stratification of society will be organized" (Daniel Bell, *The Coming of Post-Industrial Society* [New York: Basic Books, 1973], p. 112). These characterizations identify synergistic changes in societal structure and technological capacity. The passing in Europe of a true proletariat, so that there is no longer a true bourgeoisie, fundamentally altering the social structures that emerged with the Renaissance, is also tied to the emergence of a new technology of communication. "The advent of the post-modern period has been marked by the rapid rise of a new technology of knowledge, which serves data collection and analysis, simulation, and systems analysis. It has been said that the computer is to the production of knowledge what the steam engine was to production of materials" (Amitai Etzioni, *The Active Society* [New York, 1968], p. 9). Etzioni argues that the post-modern age began in 1945 because of developments in the technology of production and information transfer and social phenomena they influence. These social and technological changes underlie, or at least have taken place in parallel with, many of the recent cultural developments analysed in this volume.

The post-modern age, like the modern age, must look to its antecedents and to the future. The modern age looked back in criticism and forward in confidence. The post-modern age, though it looks backward in criticism, looks to the future with disorientation. There is no unique, morally content-full point of focus. In abandoning the unifying perspective of critical reason, and in the absence of a new authoritarian orthodoxy, either the life of values loses its intensity and ultimate significance (so that the cardinal values are now instrumental values, values of a technological society, which cannot define its ultimate aims), or one is left with no guidance except grace or the accidents of history as to which of the possible orthodoxies one should affirm as one's own.

34. Peter Bürger, *Theorie der Avantgarde* (Frankfurt: Suhrkamp, 1974). The alienation of art from society is in part a consequence of art no longer serving an established societal function, as it once did for the Church, and no longer receiving special patronage, as it once did through its contribution to the life of the aristocracy. The Church and the court integrated artistic styles within the culture and mitigated against the fragmentation of artistic traditions into different communities of experience and style, which communities now constitute barriers against a general understanding of art. On the one hand, the reproductions of old masterpieces allow the traditional art of the past to appear as art achieved in the appropriate and canonical fashion (e.g., prints of Rembrandt hang in the houses of the middle class and over 90% of the music played by symphony orchestras is not by contemporary composers). On the other hand, works of art developed within particular contemporary understandings of art are likely to appear opaque, not understandable, and produced only for other artists. This is especially the case with modern electronic music, which is dependent on particular technological choices from a rapidly developing technology. Luca Lombardi, "Die Schöne im Fischteich," colloquium given June 13, 1989, at the Wissenschaftskolleg zu Berlin. Just as there no longer appears to be one religion or canonical sense of reason or justice, there is no one sense of good art.

35. "We might say that the history of reason or enlightenment from its beginnings in Greece down to the present has led to a state of affairs in which even the word reason is suspected of connoting some mythological entity.

Reason has liquidated itself as an agency of ethical, moral, and religious insight." Max Horkheimer, *Eclipse of Reason* (New York: Continuum, 1974), p. 18. See also Max Horkheimer and Theodor W. Adorno, *Dialektik der Aufklärung* (Frankfurt/Main: Suhrkamp, 1984; 1st ed. 1944) for a study of some of the contradictions ingredient in the Enlightenment. For a study of the interaction of the technology and culture in the post-modern era, see Peter Koslowski, *Die postmoderne Kultur* (Munich: C. H. Beck, 1987).

36. Ihab Hassan, *Paracriticisms* (Urbana, Ill.: University of Illinois Press, 1975), p. xiii.

37. Walker Percy, *The Message in the Bottle* (New York: Farrar, Straus and Giroux, 1987), p. 27. The post-World War I period provided many indications of the rejection of the core assumptions of the modern age, including reason itself. Dada is a good example. The Vietnam War also evoked rejections of rationality. Consider, for example, Charles Reich's account of what he describes as reactions to "bad examples of reason, including the intellectual justifications of the Cold War and the Vietnam War." In response, reason is experienced as leaving out "too many factors and values — especially those which cannot readily be put into words and categories." *The Greening of America* (New York: Random House, 1970), p. 257.

38. Mainline Christianity in its accommodation with the world contrasts with the Church of ancient times. There is not one exhortation to liberation theology in all of the New Testament, nor is biblical Christianity supportive of many of the elements of feminism. Indeed, St. Paul enjoins that "everyone must submit himself to the governing authorities" (Romans 13:1), "if a woman does not cover her head, she should have her hair cut off" (I Cor. 11:6), "women should remain silent in the churches" (I Cor. 14:34), and "wives, submit to your husbands as to the Lord" (Eph. 5:22). In addition, contemporary mainline Christianity appears largely bereft of the asceticism once thought central to the Christian life. "The Christian ought not to be a slave to wine, nor fond of meat, nor in general to find pleasure in food or drink; for 'everyone that striveth for the mastery refraineth himself from all things' [I Cor. 9:25] . . . The Christian should not grumble, either at the scarcity of his necessities or at the labour of his tasks, for those charged with authority in these matters have final decision over each thing . . . The Christian should not be ostentatious in clothing or sandals, for all this is idle boasting." St. Basil, Letter XXII, "On the Perfection of the Monastic Life" (c. A.D. 364), *The Letters*, trans. Roy J. Deferrari (Cambridge, Mass.: Harvard University Press, 1972), pp. 133–135.

39. In fact, secular humanism as a rational system itself seems suspect, as do all rational accounts. "In reality the contents of both philosophy and religion have been deeply affected by this seemingly peaceful settlement of their original conflict. The philosophers of the Enlightenment attacked religion in the name of reason; in the end what they killed was not the church but metaphysics and the objective concept of reason itself, the source of power of their own efforts. Reason as an organ for perceiving the true nature of reality and determining the guiding principles of our lives has come to be regarded as obsolete. Speculation is synonymous with metaphysics, and metaphysics with mythology and superstition." Horkheimer, *Eclipse of Reason*, pp. 17–18.

40. Alan D. Gilbert, *The Making of Post-Christian Britain*, pp. 38–39.

41. Harold Rosenberg, *The Tradition of the New* (London: Thames and Hudson, 1962). The de-Europeanization of European culture has extended to the traditional religions of the West. Consider as an example the following critique: "Conservative Catholics in the more secularized parts of Europe are deeply attached to a certain refined form of culture that is threatened by

present developments: their religion is connected with a certain 'Europeanism', not quite as unabashed as Hilaire Belloc's, but just as inveterate." Gregory Baum, "The Survival of the Sacred," in *The Persistence of Religion*, ed. Andrew Greeley and Gregory Baum (New York: Herder and Herder, 1973), p. 15.

42. Marshall Berman, *All That Is Solid Melts Into Air*, p. 17.

43. Facts are always placed within theoretical frameworks that allow us to recognize information and disregard noise. Theories tell us what to see, what it means, and what we may ignore. It is in terms of theories, social values, and social contexts that facts are engendered and developed. In short, there are no "naked" facts. We see data in terms of contexts or paradigms.

Employing the term "paradigm" to designate a network of conceptual, theoretical, instrumental, and methodological commitments, Thomas Kuhn showed that scientists usually do not bring their basic scientific assumptions into question (Thomas Kuhn, *The Structure of Scientific Revolutions* [Chicago: University of Chicago Press, 1962, [2]1970]). Instead, scientists usually engage in what he termed "normal science;" they work within their basic fundamental (paradigmatic) assumptions without challenging them. Paradigms are the core of traditions. A suggestion from Margaret Masterman about Kuhn's work is helpful. Though Kuhn uses the word "paradigm" in some twenty-one different ways, they may all be reduced to three basic groups: metaphysical paradigms, construct paradigms, and sociological paradigms. "The Nature of a Paradigm," in *Criticism and the Growth of Knowledge*, eds. Imre Lakatos and Alan Musgrave (London: Cambridge University Press, 1970), pp. 59–89. The character of the ultimate structure or furniture of reality is given by ontological or metaphysical paradigms or the ontological or metaphysical dimension of paradigms. Construct paradigms (or the construct dimension of a paradigm) provide examples of good understandings or construals of reality. Finally, the community with which one ought seriously to discuss and argue matters, and which is the bearer of metaphysical and construct paradigms, is identified by sociological paradigms or the sociological dimension of a paradigm.

These distinctions can be applied to the role of tradition both scientific and cultural. For example, one can notice similarities between scientific and religious traditions. Both scientific and religious traditions describe the basic structure or furniture of reality. Both include a component of theory. Traditions in both science and religion provide us with instructive examples of knowing and believing correctly (i.e., they provide construct paradigms). In science, construct paradigms include textbooks, tools, instrumentation, or instructive analogies. Religious traditions provide religious textbooks and creeds. Scientific and religious traditions also depend on particular social structures: traditions inform us who are the true scientists as well as the true believers. Each of these kinds of analyses identifies a dimension of a tradition. The first identifies the basic structures of what is experienced, the second includes short-hand images of reality that guide day-to-day encounters, and the last provides the social structures within which experiencers are brought to their encounter with reality.

Kuhn applies "paradigm" primarily to the natural sciences, rather than to such applied sciences as medicine. In this he differs from Ludwig Fleck (*Entstehung und Entwicklung einer wissenschaftlichen Tatsache* [Basel: Benno Schwabe, 1935]; *Genesis and Development of a Scientific Fact*, ed. T. J. Trenn and R. K. Merton, trans. F. Bradley and T. J. Trenn [Chicago: University of Chicago Press, 1979]). Moreover, Kuhn's notion of a paradigm is tied to a particular account of scientific revolutions. However, the idea of a guiding framework is so attractive that it is applied to many major societal endeavors. Such a notion can be used to disclose fundamental structures and commitments not only in science, but also in medicine, law, and religion. Hans Küng, for example, has applied the notion of paradigm to religion. See *Theology for the Third Millennium: An Ecumenical View,* trans. Peter Heinegg (New York: Doubleday, 1988). One needs a term that identifies something like a "thought-style," "thought-community," or "paradigm" and that indicates the frameworks that account for reality, provide exemplars of knowing, valuing, and doing, and disclose social structures through which men and women see themselves and realize themselves as participants in a common endeavor. In particular, the term should be able to identify the value traditions within which health care is provided. Such a broader notion has been suggested recently by Thomas Sowell, using the metaphor of "vision."

Sowell employs "vision" to identify a "'pre-analytic cognitive act.' It is what we sense or feel *before* we have constructed any systematic reasoning that could be called a theory, much less deduced any specific consequences as hypotheses to be tested against evidence. Visions are the foundations on which theories are built" (*A Conflict of Vision* [New York: William Morrow, 1987], p. 14). Sowell is at pains to distinguish his notion of *vision* from Kuhn's notion of *paradigm*, and to an extent he succeeds in so doing. I shall use what is helpful in Sowell's notion of vision, recast for my own purposes. The metaphor of "vision" stresses an important Kantian point: appearance gains its final structure in our apprehension (vision) of it.

To examine a moral tradition or vision and the health care policies and bioethics it supports, one must attend to its ontological (or metaphysical), axiological, and social structures. It is also necessary to analyse the exemplars of knowledge and recipes for action that direct it. The complex relationship among these factors can be portrayed in a five-dimensional space in which one plots on five axes the elements of a tradition or vision. Different traditions will differ by their ontological and axiological commitments. Insofar as traditions or visions are really different, they will tend to have different social structures which support and define them. Finally, members of different traditions will be guided by different exemplars of knowledge and recipes for coming to terms with reality and achieving value commitments.

44. H. T. Engelhardt, *The Foundations of Bioethics* (New York: Oxford University Press, 1986).

45. Generally, when not using the term bioethics simpliciter to refer to secular humanist bioethics, I will qualify it as Jewish bioethics, Islamic bioethics, Catholic bioethics, etc.

46. For a study of the difficulties of meeting the human needs of individuals through a welfare system, see Michael Ignatieff, *The Needs of Strangers* (New York: Viking Penguin, 1985).

47. As we shall see, it is persons as entities who can understand the possibility of mutual respect, not humans as members of a particular biological species, who constitute the foundations of the moral enterprise. It is what we can share as persons, as entities capable of mutual respect, that will constitute the basis of a morality for moral strangers. See H. T. Engelhardt, Jr., *The Foundations of Bioethics* (New York: Oxford, 1986).

48. The reader will note the embeddedness of the author in particular moral communities. This rootedness is often exhibited to remind the reader of the compatibility of secular humanism with continued commitment to, and life within, traditional communities. For example, I sing my religious convictions as taught by Basil of Caesarea and John of Antioch. Though I

reject the rationalist excesses (and other errors) of the Roman patriarchate, as a Catholic, albeit a sinner, I accept the teachings and disciplines of the Fathers.

49. Given the general disestablishment of religion, the marginalization of belief, and the secularity of the age, all religions are reduced to sects, in that few can claim special priority as *the* religion or *the* church of a society. Pluralism has in significant measure been the product of secularization, which has allowed numerous sects to develop and flourish without state interference, and individuals somewhat freely to move from one religion to another. Consider the following observation by Franklin Littell. "The late Roman Catholic bishop of Salt Lake was raised in a fine Methodist family, and chose as an adult the faith and career which he served with distinction. The present Protestant Episcopal bishop of California grew up a Catholic and consciously chose the Episcopal church and ministry. An American can choose, without loss of legal rights or privileges, to join any religious body or none at all. Such a situation is new in human history." *From State Church to Pluralism* (Chicago: Aldine, 1962), p. xi. This secularization has allowed not only numerous faith traditions to live and compete side by side, but also the emergence of various ideological groups, which contend for acceptance as the secular equivalent of religious communities (e.g., Secular Humanists or the members of the American Humanist Association). As Peter Berger and Thomas Luckmann have noted, "the global historical force producing pluralism is rather secularization, by which we mean the progressive autonomization of societal sectors from the domination of religious meanings and institutions." "Secularization and Pluralism," in *Sociology of Religion: Theoretical Perspectives* (Cologne: Westdeutscher Verlag, 1966), p. 74.

In discussing pluralism in this volume, I will follow Berger and Luckmann's definition of pluralism as "a situation in which there is competition in the institutional ordering of comprehensive meanings for everyday life" (ibid., p. 73). In a condition of moral pluralism, there is a competition "between bureaucratically organized religious cartels, engaged in continuous 'deals' with each other and with the state, marketing a number of religious commodities to an increasingly selective population of consumers" (p. 78). See also Gerhard Lenski, "Religious Pluralism in Theoretical Perspective," in *Religious Pluralism and Social Structure* (Cologne: Westdeutscher Verlag, 1965), pp. 25–42.

Finally, the interplay of secularity and pluralism must be underscored. On the one hand, a plurality of moral perspectives and communities can flourish openly only when the state is secular in the sense of being morally neutral regarding the peaceable choice of a particular concrete moral perspective and community. On the other hand, when there is a plurality of peaceable moral communities, it will be to their advantage to maintain the secularity or moral neutrality of the state. "A secular society is in practice a pluralist society, in so far as it is truly secular. Societies which enforce, whether by State coercion, or by social pressures, a uniform attitude of behaviour in important matters of human behaviour and values, whether or not these are regarded as religions, are in effect sacral societies of the traditional form, and not secular societies." D. L. Munby, *The Idea of a Secular Society* (London: Oxford University Press, 1963), p. 17.

50. By good life I do not mean *la dolce vita*. Instead, I identify that which meets the moral and aesthetic canons within a particular value tradition for proper deportment and for judging that a life is or has been lived well. Within certain value traditions, this may be equivalent to *la dolce vita*.

51. The Roman Catholic position excludes all direct abortions, but the Orthodox Jewish requires an abortion in order to save the life of the mother. See *Babylonian Talmud*, Obolot 7:6, and I. Jakobovits, *Jewish Medical Ethics: A Comparative and Historical Study of the Jewish Religious Attitude to Medicine and its Practice* (New York: Bloch, 1975), especially pp. 182–191.

52. The distinction was between positive law (*dikaion nomikon*) and natural law (*dikaion physikon*). See Francis de Zulueta, *The Institutes of Gaius* (Oxford: Clarendon Press, 1976), vol. 2, p. 13.

53. "*Jus naturale est, quod natura omnia animalia docuit.*" "The law of nature is that law which nature teaches to all animals." Lib. I, Tit. II. Thomas C. Sandars (ed. & trans.), *The Institutes of Justinian* (Westport, Conn.: Greenwood Press, 1970), p. 7. The Institutes of Justinian were published A.D. 533. For a study of their development see Tony Honore, *Tribonian* (Ithaca, N.Y.: Cornell University Press, 1978).

54. ". . . *quod vero naturalis artio inter omnes homines constituit, id apud omnes populos peraeque custoditur vocaturque jus gentium, quasi quo jure omnes gentes utuntur.*" "But the law which natural reason appoints for all mankind obtains equally among all nations, and is called the law of nations, because all nations make use of it." *Justinian*, Lib. I, Tit. II, 1. Ibid., p. 8.

55. ". . . *quod uero naturalis ratio inter omnes homines constituit, id apud omnes populos peraeque custoditur uocaturque ius gentium, quasi quo iure omnes gentes utuntur.*" Liber I, 1. Francis de Zulueta (ed. & trans.), *The Institutes of Gaius* (Oxford: Clarendon Press, 1976), vol. 1, p. 3. Gaius wrote between A.D. 130 and 180.

56. For the development of a Southern tradition for blacks and whites alike, see Anne Norton, *Alternative Americas* (Chicago: University of Chicago Press, 1986).

57. Tristram Engelhardt, Jr., with Edmund L. Erde, "Philosophy of Medicine," in *A Guide to the Culture of Science, Technology, and Medicine*, ed. Paul T. Durbin (New York: Free Press, 1984), pp. 364–461.

58. Patricia D. White, "The Concept of Person, the Law, and the Use of the Fetus in Biomedicine," in William B. Bondeson et al. (eds.), *Abortion and the Status of the Fetus* (Dordrecht: D. Reidel, 1983), pp. 119–157.

59. President's Commission for the Study of Ethical Problems in Medicine and Biomedical and Behavioral Research, *Securing Access to Health Care* (Washington, D.C.: U.S. Government Printing Office, 1983).

60. National Commission for the Protection of Human Subjects of Biomedical and Behavioral Research, *The Belmont Report* (Washington, D.C.: U.S. Government Printing Office, 1978).

61. More precisely, secular health care policy has tolerated the right of competent adults to refuse treatment or otherwise exempt themselves from involvement in health care, even if grounds for the refusal appear from a secular point of view incredible (e.g., that it would be morally improper to use contraceptives or blood products). To some extent, particular moral communities have been tolerated in their attempts to establish their own special approaches to health care problems (e.g., natural family planning clinics). However, it has not allowed the use of special criteria for the definition of death (e.g., whole-body definitions to meet the doctrinal needs of many orthodox Jews).

62. The distinction between what can be known through revelation versus that which can be known by natural reason unaided by grace or special revelation is already well articulated by St. Thomas Aquinas. See *Summa Theologica* I, Art. 1.

63. For example, Norman Daniels in *Just Health Care* (Cambridge: Cam-

bridge University Press, 1985) applies the arguments that Rawls develops in *A Theory of Justice* (Cambridge, Mass.: Harvard University Press, 1971) to the question of secular health care policy.

64. To understand this claim about a dialectical relation, one might think of the relationship that Hegel develops in *Philosophy of Right* between abstract right and morality on the one hand, and the family and civil society on the other. In "Abstract Right" and "Morality" Hegel shows that one can in general establish that promises should be kept and that one should do the good, but not what promises one ought to make nor how the good is concretely to be understood. One can understand the answer to such questions only within concrete moral circumstances such as one finds in the family and civil society.

II. The Secular as a Neutral Framework

1. The *Saeculares Ludi* (*Ludi Terentini*) were first celebrated in 249 B.C. in honor of Dis and Proserpina, as prescribed by the Sibylline books. They were next held in 146 B.C. and then in 17 B.C., at the direction of Augustus Caesar. The term secular was also used to refer to the secular song or hymn (*carmen saeculare*) composed by Horace at the command of Augustus and first sung in A.U.C. 737 (i.e., 17 B.C.) in both Greek and Latin. For a discussion of the time period of the *saeculum*, see Theodor Mommsen, *Die römische Chronologie* (Berlin: Weidmannsche, 1858), especially pp. 168–189. See also Ernst Robert Curtius, *Europäische Literatur und lateinisches Mittelalter* (Bern: Francke, 1954).

2. The *Oxford Latin Dictionary* gives the following definitions of *saeculum*: "1. the body of individuals born at a particular time, generation; a generation within a single family; (pl.) the succession of generations; 2. a breed, race; 3. the present time, the contemporary generation, the age; 4. the period of time corresponding to the lifetime of a particular person or persons, age; 5. a human lifetime, generation; 6. a period of one hundred years, a century; 7. one of the imaginary divisions or ages (golden, silver, etc.) of human history; 8. (pl.) future ages, posterity; 9. (pl.) throughout the ages, for ever; the course of human affairs; 10. human life, the world."

3. *Prudentius*, "A Reply to the Address of Symmachus (*Contra Orationem Symmachi*)," trans. H. J. Thomson (Cambridge, Mass.: Harvard University Press, 1953), II, 53, 55, 57.

4. "A dreadful rumor came from the West. Rome had been besieged and its citizens had been forced to buy their lives with gold. Then thus despoiled they had been besieged again so as to lose not their substance only but their lives. My voice sticks in my throat; and, as I dictate, sobs choke my utterance. The City which had taken the whole world was itself taken." Jerome's Letter 127, 12. "To Principia" [written ca. A.D. 412], *A Select Library of Nicene and Post-Nicene Fathers of the Christian Church*. Sec. series, VI (New York, 1893), p. 257. Quoted in A. Vasiliev, "Medieval Ideas of the End of the World: West and East," *Byzantion* XVI (1942–43), 462–463. In his preface to Ezekiel, Jerome wrote: "I was so stupefied and dismayed that day and night I could think of nothing but the welfare of the Roman community . . . But when I heard that the bright light of all the world was quenched, or rather that the Roman Empire had lost its head and that the whole universe had perished in one city: then indeed, 'I became dumb and humbled myself and kept silence from good words.'" *Select Letters of St. Jerome*, trans. F. A. Wright (Cambridge, Mass.: Harvard University Press, 1980), p. x. It is interesting to note that, though Jerome was overwhelmed by the news of Rome's fall, he had in some sense clearly anticipated it. "The Roman world is falling, and yet we hold our heads

erect instead of bowing our necks." Letter XV, "To Heliodorus," p. 303. This letter was written in approximately A.D. 396. Jerome's reference to "holding our heads erect" was a condemnation of the Romans for failing to pray.

5. *"Et ecce ego vobiscum sum omnibus diebus usque ad consummationem saeculi"* [And surely I am with you always, to the very end of the age] Matthew 28:20. The Latin translation uses the term *"saeculi"* for the Greek *"aionos,"* which is rendered in English as "of the age." The Greek term *"aion,"* like *"saeculum,"* indicated the lifespan of an individual or a generation. It also was used to identify an age or a long period of time, often a thousand years. Georg Stadtmüller, "Aion," *Saeculum* 2 (1951), 315–320. See also John of Damascus, *Orthodox Faith*, II. 1. In the passage from Matthew, *"saeculum"* and *"aion"* indicate a long period of time, an age. The *"saeculum,"* the "age" of which the Vulgate speaks, is the span of time that extends until the end of this world. The structures of this world are the secular structures.

6. For instance, St. Augustine of Hippo argues in *The City of God* that, had the Fall not occurred, men and women would not be moved by lust. Nor would humans in the non-fallen state have required secular political structures, for natural social structures (e.g., the family) would have sufficed. See, for example, Book XV, chap. 1. Had there not been the Fall, life without the state would not have been "solitary, poore, nasty, brutish and short." Thomas Hobbes, *Leviathan, or the Matter, Forms, & Power of a Commonwealth Ecclesiastical and Civill* (London: Andrew Crooke, 1651), part 1, chap. 13, p. 62. One would not have needed political structures in order to coordinate disordered social structures.

7. The papal constitution of secular authority through the coronation of Charles the Great created a secular realm that was theoretically dependent on the earthly representative of the city of God, the Pope. The coronation shaped Europe until the secularization of 1803 and the end of the Empire with the abdication of Emperor Franz II on August 6, 1806. Karl Beumer, *Geschichte der Deutschen Reichsverfassung* (Tübingen: Mohr, 1913).

Relying on his claims to authority (and in fact to shore up his precarious situation at the time), Pope Leo III at the third Mass on Christmas Day, 800, crowned Charles the Great sixty-eighth emperor of Rome, considering the imperial throne to be vacant because of Constantine VI's (780–797) removal by his mother Irene (797–802). As the *Annales Laureshamenses* state, Charles was made emperor "because the name of emperor had ceased to exist in the land of the Greeks . . ." Donald A. Bullough, *The Age of Charlemagne* (London: Paul Elek, 1973), pp. 167. For an account of the coronation, see also François Ganshof, *The Imperial Coronation of Charlemagne* (Glasgow: Jackson, 1949), and Robert Folz, *Le couronnement impérial de Charlemagne* (Paris: Gallimard, 1964), p. 166. The old rite of acclamation of the emperor by the people followed the coronation by the pope: "most pious Augustus, crowned by God, the great and peace-giving Emperor." *Liber pontificalis*, quoted in Bullough, p. 183. In so doing, the pope "transferred" the Empire back from Constantinople to Rome, or at least revived the Empire in the West. There is some evidence to suggest that Irene had in fact supported the coronation. J. B. Bury, "Charles the Great and Irene," *Hermathena* 8, 17 (1891), 17-37. Whatever the antecedents, the coronation, at least in the opinion of some, changed the character of history. "The coronation of Charles is not only the central event of the Middle Ages, it is also one of those very few events of which, taking them singly, it may be said that if they had not happened, the history of the world would have been different." James Bryce, "The Coronation as a Revival of the Roman Empire in the West," in *The Coronation of Charlemagne*, ed. Richard E. Sullivan (Boston:

D. C. Heath, 1959), p. 41. Among other things, the coronation was an important step in the fashioning of Western European civilization, on the basis of which the Renaissance and its interest in humanism would later develop. Christopher Dawson, "The Coronation as Evidence of the Birth of a New Civilization," in *The Coronation of Charlemagne*, p. 50. The coronation also set a precedent followed by Pope John XII when he crowned Otto the Great in 962. The theory of papal supremacy in temporal matters developed over time and found one of its classical articulations in Boniface VIII's Bull, *Unam Sanctam* (18 November 1302).

8. *Concilium Lateranense* IV, *Constitutiones* 3, *De haereticis*, and 25, *Quod electio facta per saecularem potestatem non valeat*.

9. Hans-Wolfgang Strätz, "Der kanonistische und staatskirchenrechtliche Begriff," in *Geschichtliche Grundbegriffe*, ed. O. Brunner, W. Conze, R. Koselleck (Stuttgart: Klett-Cotta, 1984), vol. 5, p. 796.

10. Though American law was generally tolerant of all religions, including Judaism, the Supreme Court for most of the history of America regarded the Christian faith (without the endorsement of any particular sect) as a part of American custom and law. Thus, in an 1844 decision the Supreme Court held that "It is also said, and truly, that the Christian religion is a part of the common law of Pennsylvania." Vidal v. Girard's Executors 43 U.S. 2 How. 127, 198 [11:205, 234] (1844). This opinion was quoted with approval in the Church of the Holy Trinity v. United States 143 U.S. 457 (1926).

11. The American Constitution of 1787 provided in Article 6, Section 3, that "no religious test shall ever be required as a qualification to any office or public trust under the United States." In addition, the First Amendment to the Constitution provided that "Congress shall make no law respecting an establishment of religion, or prohibiting the free exercise thereof . . ." Some individual states continued into the early nineteenth century to maintain what was tantamount to an established religion, and religious tests for office (e.g., averring the existence of God) remained as qualifications for office into the twentieth century.

12. The reader will notice a significant accent on the Roman Catholic Church in the discussion of secularity. This is unavoidable, given the unique role of the Catholic Church in European history. First, for over a thousand years it was *the* established church of Europe. Second, even after the Reformation, it remained *the* major international European Christian church in the sense of transcending national politics and pursuing its own European diplomatic interests.

13. The third edition of the *Dictionnaire françois-allemand-latin* (1663) gives the following definition of *seculariser*: "*weltlich machen, Clericum religiosum ad seculares rescribere, clericum religiosum ad seculares clericos referre*." Quoted in *Geschichtliche Grundbegriffe*, ed. O. Brunner, W. Conze, R. Koselleck (Stuttgart: Klett-Cotta, 1984), vol. 5, p. 792. For a discussion of secularization after the Reformation and through the *Pax Westfalica*, see Fritz Dickmann, *Der westfälische Frieden* (Münster: Aschendorff, 1959), pp. 316–324.

14. Hans-Wolfgang Strätz, "Wegweiser zur Säkularisation in der kanonistischen Literatur," in *Säkularisierung und Säkularisation vor 1800*, ed. Anton Rauscher (Munich: Schöningh, 1976), p. 43–67, especially pp. 50–56.

15. Josef Höfer and Karl Rahner (eds.), *Lexikon für Theologie und Kirche* (Freiburg: Herder, 1964), vol. 9, pp. 248–254.

16. For a study of the secularization of church land in Germany during the Reformation, see Hans Lehnert, *Kirchengut und Reformation* (Erlangen: Palm & Enke, 1935).

17. Hans-Wolfgang Strätz, "Wegweiser zur Säkularisation in der kanonistischen Literatur," in *Säkularisierung und Säkularisation vor 1800*, ed. Anton Rauscher (Munich: Schöningh, 1976), p. 58–61.

18. Hans-Wolfgang Strätz, "Der kanonistische und staatskirchenrechtliche Begriff," in *Geschichtliche Grundbegriffe*, ed. O. Brunner, W. Conze, R. Koselleck (Stuttgart: Klett-Cotta, 1984), vol. 5, pp. 792–793.

19. Heribert Raab, "Geistige Entwicklungen und historische Ereignisse im Vorbild der Säkularisation," in *Säkularisierung und Säkularisation vor 1800*, ed. Anton Rauscher (Munich: Schöningh, 1976), pp. 15–17. See also Heribert Raab, "Landgraf Ernst von Hessen-Rheinfels und der Jansenismus," in *Archiv für mittelrheinische Kirchengeschichte*, ed. L. Lenhart and A. Brück (Speyer: Jaeger, 1967), pp. 41–60.

20. Albert Mathiez, *Les Origines des cultes révolutionnaires* (Geneva: Slatkine, 1977; 1st ed. 1904). See also André Latreille, *L'Église catholique et la révolution française* (Paris: Hachette, 1948), 2 vols.

21. "Der Reichsdeputationshauptschluss," in *Quellen zum Verfassungsorganismus des heiligen römischen Reiches deutscher Nation*, ed. H. H. Hofmann (Darmstadt: Wissenschaftliche Buchgesellschaft, 1976), pp. 329–358.

22. John Walsh, "Religion: Church and State in Europe and the Americas," in *The New Cambridge Modern History*, ed. C. W. Crawley (Cambridge: Cambridge University Press, 1965), vol. 9, p. 155.

23. The German writer Joseph Freiherr von Eichendorff lamented the consequences of secularization, which among other things replaced charity with oversight of the poor by the police. "Über die Folgen von der Aufhebung der Landeshoheit der Bischöfe und der Klöster in Deutschland," in Eichendorff, *Werke und Schriften* (Stuttgart: Cotta'sche, 1958), vol. 4, pp. 1133–1184.

24. Laicism (in German *Laizismus* or in French *laïcisme*) is allied historically with laicization, the process by which a cleric is rendered a layman or church property comes into lay control. Paul-Emile Littré's *Dictionnaire de la langue française* indicates that the term *laïcisme* is derived from a sixteenth-century English usage, which identified the passing of church property into the control of laymen. This origin would thus indicate its embeddedness in the changes that took place with the establishment of the Church of England. Laicism and its various equivalents in other European languages tend to indicate an opposition to the influence of the Church in culture, law, and politics.

25. Kurt Galling (ed.) *Die Religion in Geschichte und Gegenwart* (Tübingen: J. C. B. Mohr, 1959), vol. 4, p. 210. See also Maurice Reclus, *Jules Ferry* (Paris: Flammarion, 1947). See, in particular, pp. 91–222.

26. Josef Höfer and Karl Rahner (eds.), *Lexikon für Theologie und Kirche* (Freiburg: Herder, 1961), vol. 6, pp. 750–751.

27. For an overview of George Jacob Holyoake's life and writings, see Charles W. Goss, *A Descriptive Bibliography of the Writings of George Jacob Holyoake* (London: Crowther & Goodman, 1908).

28. Towards this end, Holyoake supported utilitarian analyses of morals and public policy. For example, he was the editor of the *Utilitarian Record*, which appeared weekly between 1846 and 1848. Charles W. Goss, *A Descriptive Bibliography of the Writings of George Jacob Holyoake* (London: Crowther & Goodman, 1908), p. 66.

29. The principles of Secularism were first stated in the *Reasoner* in 1847; see George Holyoake, *The Origin and Nature of Secularism* (London: Watts & Co., 1896), p. 51. The term Secularism was first used in print in *The Reasoner* on

December 10, 1851, on page 62 (see Holyoake, p. 52), though Holyoake employed it in a speech in 1850; see Goss, *A Descriptive Bibliography of the Writings of George Jacob Holyoake* (London: Crowther & Goodman, 1908), p. xli. It would appear that Charles Frederick Nicholls applied "Secularism" to the movement for the first time in a letter published in *Reasoner* with the title "The Future of Secularism" on February 4, 1852, p. 187 (Holyoake, p. 52). Secularism was understood as a movement that rejected "those parts of the Scriptures or Christianism, or of Acts of Parliament, as conflict with or obstruct ethical truth." "Nature of Secular Societies," *Reasoner* (August 18, 1852), 152 (Holyoake, p. 52).

30. George Jacob Holyoake, *The Principles of Secularism* (London: Austin and Co., 1871), 3rd ed., p. 11. Also, "Secularism is a code of duty pertaining to this life, founded on considerations purely human, and intended mainly for those who find theology indefinite or inadequate, unreliable or unbelievable. Its essential principles are three: — 1. The improvement of this life by material means. 2. That science is the available Providence of man. 3. That it is good to do good. Whether there be other good or not, the good of the present life is good, and it is good to seek that good." Holyoake, *The Origin and Nature of Secularism; Showing that Where Freethought Commonly Ends Secularism Begins* (London: Watts & Co., 1896), p. 41.

31. The extent to which Holyoake's Secularism is regarded as anti-religious and not a religion of its own depends on one's understanding of religion. Goss provides the following observations on Holyoake: "It is most difficult to follow the progress of Holyoake's mind and views, but whilst it was believed that he adhered to the old atheistic doctrine, he was devising a system of secular principles apart from atheism and theism, maintaining that wherever a moral end was sought, there was a secular as well as a religious part to it" (p. xl).

George Holyoake was arrested (3 June 1842), tried, and convicted for atheism, for which he served six months in prison. Holyoake, *The History of the Last Trial by Jury for Atheism in England* (London: James Watson, 1851). During a pretrial examination by a magistrate, one Bransby Cooper, Holyoake was told, "You cannot be an atheist . . . you don't look like one." To this Holyoake recalls responding, "Out of respect to my own conscience, I must say that I was an atheist" (p. 15). Prior to his arrest, Holyoake had had a congregation of which he describes himself as the "anti-priest" (p. 4); he served as a "Social Missionary." Despite his conviction for atheism, Holyoake did not regard Secularism as committed to atheism. "Though respecting the right of the Atheist and Theist to their theories of the origin of nature, the Secularist regards them as belonging to the debateable ground of speculation. Secularism neither asks nor gives any opinion upon them, confining itself to the entirely independent field of study — the order of the universe." Holyoake, *The Origin and Nature of Secularism*, p. 42.

32. Holyoake envisaged using the Secular Guild to establish a social structure that could award "Orders of Secularism". At times his sectarian interests are more than obvious: ". . . even in instances of towns where Secular Societies do exist, persons in direct relation to the Secular Guild would be able to furnish Secular direction where the tradition and usage of a Secular Society are unknown, or unfamiliar." *The Principles of Secularism*, p. 20.

33. For a discussion of the first (1872) application of "secularization" (i.e., by Graf Paul Yorck of Wartenburg) to the Church, not to church goods or clerics, see Hermann Lübbe, *Säkularisierung* (Freiburg: Karl Alber, 1965), p. 79. A more extensive account is provided by Hermann Zabel, "Zum Wortgebrauch von

'Verweltlichen/Säkularisieren' bei Paul York von Wartenburg und Richard Rothe," in *Archiv für Begriffsgeschichte*, ed. Karlfried Gründer (Bonn: Bouvier, 1970), vol. 14, pp. 69–85. The *Oxford English Dictionary* notes a use of secularization in 1863 relating to art, and in 1865 relating to the "general secularisation of the European intellect." It also gives an occurrence from 1711 about ministers being increasingly "secularized in their conversation" (vol. 9, p. 366).

34. Larry Shiner, "The Meanings of Secularization," *International Yearbook for the Sociology of Religion* (Cologne: Westdeutscher Verlag, 1967), pp. 52–57. For some reflections on Shiner's classification, see Arno Baruzzi, "Zum Begriff und Problem 'Säkularisierung'," in *Säkularisierung und Säkularisation vor 1800*, ed. Anton Rauscher (Munich: Schöningh, 1976), pp. 121–134. For a general treatment of secularization, see Georges de Lagarde, *La naissance de l'esprit laïque au déclin du moyen age* (Louvain: Nauwelaerts, 1962), 5 vols.; Hermann Lübbe, *Säkularisierung* (Freiburg: Karl Alber, 1965); Martin Stallmann, *Was ist Säkularisierung*? (Tübingen: Mohr, 1960); and Friedrich Delekat, *Über den Begriff der Säkularisation* (Heidelberg: Quelle & Meyer, 1958). There are of course individuals who deny the existence of the sociological phenomenon of secularization or at least wish robustly to qualify its significance. See, for example, Gregory Baum, "The Survival of the Sacred," in *The Persistence of Religion*, ed. A. Greeley and G. Baum (New York: Herder and Herder, 1973), pp. 11–22; and David Martin, *The Religious and the Secular* (London: Routledge & Kegan Paul, 1969). But, of course, it is one thing to find that a sort of feral religiosity survives in secular societies, expressed in interest in astrology, reincarnation, and new-age theology, and quite another to deny that the regnant religious structure of Western society for over a millennium and a half has decayed.

35. Harvey Cox, *The Secular City* (New York: Macmillan and London: SCM Press, 1965), p. 15.

36. Harvey Cox argues that "this disenchantment of the natural world provides an absolute precondition for the development of natural science. Since today's technical city would not have been possible without modern science, disenchantment is also an essential precondition for modern urbanization. Science is basically a point of view." Ibid., p. 21.

37. The initial steps in the secularization of the modern age, as Ernst Troeltsch observes, were quite complex. With the Reformation, he argues, Christian ethics was secularized, but also the saeculum was spiritualized. See especially "Das Verhältnis des Protestantismus zur Kultur" [1913], in *Aufsätze zur Geistesgeschichte und Religionssoziologie* (Aalen: Scientia, 1981), pp. 202–254, especially pp. 210f.

38. Friedrich Jodl, *Geschichte der Ethik in der neueren Philosophie* (Stuttgart: Cotta'schen, 1882), vol. 1, chap. 3, "Die Anfänge einer selbständigen Ethik in der neueren Philosophie," pp. 85–107. Jodl's work itself provides an example of the results of secularization in offering an introduction to a non-religious understanding of ethics.

39. One might think, for example, of the Deutsche Gesellschaft für ethische Kultur, which constituted a secular moral movement in Germany in the latter part of the nineteenth century. "Die ethische Bewegung in Deutschland" (Berlin: Verlag für ethische Kultur, 1926). This movement appeared in America under the title ethical culture. Horace L. Friess, *Felix Adler and Ethical Culture*, ed. Fannia Weingartner (New York: Columbia University Press, 1981).

40. "Urbanization means a structure of common life in which the diversity and the disintegration of tradition are paramount. It means an impersonality in

which functional relationships multiply. It means that a degree of tolerance and anonymity replace traditional moral sanctions and long-term acquaintanceships." Harvey Cox, *The Secular City*, p. 4.

41. In the nineteenth century, the changes were most marked in Protestantism, as von Hartmann noted. "Liberal Protestantism has necessarily become an irreligious phenomenon of history, because Protestantism has taken the interest of modern culture to be the criterion." Eduard von Hartmann, *Die Selbstzersetzung des Christenthums* (Berlin: Duncker's, 1874), p. 87.

42. Émile Durkheim, *The Elementary Forms of the Religious Life* (Glencoe, Ill.: Free Press, 1947; 1st ed., 1915), trans. Joseph Swain, p. 427.

43. Ibid.

44. See, for example, Max Weber, *Gesammelte Aufsätze zur Religionssoziologie* (Tübingen: Mohr, 1978; 1st ed., 1920), vol. 1., "Die protestantische Sekten und der Geist des Kapitalismus," pp. 207–236.

45. Eduard von Hartmann, *Die Selbstzersetzung des Christenthums* (Berlin: Duncker's, 1874). The secularization of nineteenth-century continental Christianity, in particular, Protestantism, was both described and influenced by Arthur Schopenhauer (1788–1860), David Strauss (1808–1874), and Ludwig Feuerbach (1804–1872).

46. Overbeck, for example, speaks of Christianity being rendered worldly, of its *Verweltlichung*. Franz Overbeck, *Christentum und Kultur* (Basel: Schwabe, 1919), p. 245.

47. Adalbert Klempt, *Die Säkularisierung der universalhistorischen Auffassung* (Göttingen: Musterschmidt, 1960).

48. Ernst Laas, *Idealistische und positivistische Ethik* (Berlin: Weidmannsche Buchhandlung, 1882), pp. 396–398.

49. Ibid., p. 27. Also, "secular instruction neither assails Christianity nor prejudices the learner against it . . . Secular instruction implies that the proper business of the school-teacher is to impart a knowledge of the duties of this world; and the proper business of chapel and church is to explain the duties relevant to another world . . .' Holyoake, *The Origin and Nature of Secularism*, p. 61.

50. As an indication of the once stark differences among certain religious hospitals, consider an instruction given by Father Edwin F. Healy, S.J., in a book that appeared with *imprimi potest, nihil obstat*, and *imprimatur*. Healy recommended that physicians should when possible baptize infants in serious danger of death, the wishes of the parents to the contrary notwithstanding, if this could be done discreetly so as not to cause ill-will that would hinder the Church. "Ordinarily speaking, then, every dying child who has not as yet achieved the use of reason should be baptized whether the parents are willing or not. In case it is foreseen that the parents would not consent to the baptism, the sacrament should be administered secretly." *Medical Ethics* (Chicago: Loyola University Press, 1956), p. 367.

51. Pope Boniface VIII, for example, in his bull *Unam sanctam* of 18 November 1302, states: "We are required to believe in one, holy, catholic and apostolic church, and we also believe and sincerely confess her to be such, outside which there is neither salvation nor remission of sins." Henricus Denzinger (ed.), *Enchiridion Symbolorum* (Freiburg: Herder, 1965), p. 279 [my translation]. Consider also, for example, "Whoever believes and is baptized will be saved, but whoever does not believe will be condemned" (Matthew 16:16) and "Jesus answers, 'I tell you the truth, no one can enter the kingdom of God unless he is born of water and the Spirit'" (John 3:5). This led to the development of the view that outside the sacraments provided by the Church there was no

salvation. "Unless we are reborn in water and the spirit, we are not able . . . to enter into the kingdom of heaven" (*Bulla unionis Armenorum*, the Council of Florence, 22 November 1439); Centro di Documentazione (ed.), *Conciliorum Oecumenicorum Decreta* [Freiburg: Herder, 1962], p. 518).

52. Allan Bloom, in his account of the intellectual innocence of students entering college, remarks concerning their religious vacuity. "As the respect for the Sacred—the latest fad—has soared, real religion and knowledge of the Bible have diminished to the vanishing point . . . The dreariness of the family's spiritual landscape passes belief. It is as monochrome and unrelated to those who pass through it as are the barren steppes frequented by nomads who take their mere subsistence and move on . . . Nobody is quite certain of what the religious institutions are supposed to do anymore . . ." *The Closing of the American Mind* (New York: Simon & Schuster, 1987), pp. 56, 57, 342.

53. Data indicate that at least 73% of Catholics approve of the use of artificial means of contraception. George Gallup, Jr., and Jim Castelli, *The American Catholic People* (Garden City, N.Y.: Doubleday, 1987), pp. 50–51.

54. Religious differences were once central to an individual's self-identity, and religious jokes tended in the past to reinforce group solidarity and commitment.

Patrick O'Reilly, who has left his small village in western Ireland to study in Dublin, returns after two years to visit his family. Rumors have circulated that he is no longer a practicing Catholic. As he gets off the train, he is met by the local priest, who confronts him straight off and asks, "Patrick, is it true that you've become a Protestant?" Patrick, aghast, retorts, "A Protestant! Oh, gosh, no Father. I've become an atheist." To which the priest responds, "It's a shame, my son, that you have lost your faith, but at least you haven't lost your reason."

55. Alasdair MacIntyre, *After Virtue* (London: Duckworth and Notre Dame, Ind.: University of Notre Dame Press, 1981), pp. 104–105.

56. Friedrich Nietzsche's account of the death of God is a subtle and sophisticated analysis of the consequences for European civilization of no longer taking the existence of God seriously. Nietzsche sees the development of modern European culture as having killed God, as having removed God from the central significance He once had for the West. In this, he completes a line of analysis already begun by Hegel when Hegel realized that it was ". . . the feeling that 'God himself is dead,' upon which the religion of more recent times rests . . ." (G. W. F. Hegel, *Faith & Knowledge or the Reflective Philosophy of Subjectivity in the complete range of its forms as Kantian, Jacobian, and Fichtean Philosophy* [1802], trans. Walter Cerf [Albany: State University of New York Press, 1977], p. 190). When Nietzsche asks what sacred games we will need to invent, now that we have killed God (*Die fröhliche Wissenschaft*, 1882, sec. 125), he challenges us to create moral foundations for our social structures now that their traditional grounding is gone. Which is to say, if God is dead, we will need to create morality where previously we received it from God.

57. The fanatical commitments of the 1920s and 1930s, which led to the slaughter of millions in order to realize history or to achieve the destiny of a people, can in part be seen as desperate and inhumane reactions against the general loss of belief that anticipated our post-modern era. These commitments produced strained philosophical exegeses. Consider, for example, the following excerpt from Martin Heidegger's lectures during the summer semester 1941: "'Workers' and 'soldiers' open the gates to reality. They bring about the refashioning of the fundamental structures of human creativity that were previously called 'culture'." *Grundbegriffe* (Frankfurt/Main: Klostermann, 1981), *Gesamtausgabe* vol. 51, pp. 57–58.

58. For cosmopolitans, establishing a moral outlook is somewhat analogous to developing an aesthetic sense. It involves fashioning the appropriate constellation of value commitments. Thus, moral reflection becomes value clarification. See, for example, Sidney B. Simon, Leland W. Howe, Howard Kirschenbaum, *Values Clarification* (New York: A & W Visual Library, 1978; 1st printing, 1972).

59. An excellent description of yuppies and their lifestyle is provided by *The Yuppie Handbook*, which among other things describes Yuppies as individuals who define their lives around a striving to achieve prestige, fame, social status, power, and money. Marissa Piesman and Marilee Hartley (New York: Simon and Schuster, 1985; 1st ed. 1984). As an index of the international character of the yuppie phenomena, see, for example, *Das Yuppie Handbuch: Einblicke in die Lebens- und Konsumgewohnheiten der Young Urban Professionals*, trans. Volker Schmiddem (Berlin: Sympathie-Verlag, 1987).

60. The last three decades have been marked by a number of religious and parapsychological movements, statements, and publications that suggest a coming affirmative transformation of mankind. "Contemporary mystical experiences from many individuals and many parts of the world have centered in recent years on a collective and intensifying vision, the sense of an impending transition in the human story: an evolution of consciousness as significant as any step in the long chain of our biological evolution. The consensual vision, whatever its variations, sees this transformation of consciousness as the moment anticipated by older prophecies in all the traditions of direct knowing — the death of one world and the birth of a new, an apocalypse, the 'end of days' period in the Kabbalah, the awakening of increasing numbers of human beings to their godlike potential." Marilyn Ferguson, *The Aquarian Conspiracy* (London: Routledge & Kegan Paul, 1980). One among many examples of the new religious literature is *The Urantia Book* (Chicago: Urantia Foundation, 1955), which purports to be dictated by an Orvonton Divine Counselor and introduces such novel theological terms as "Universe Power Directors." As of 1986, these scriptures of over 2097 pages had gone through at least nine printings. Another example is provided by the scriptures of Ramtha "channeled" through a young woman. Ramtha purports to be a "sovereign entity" who once lived on earth thirty-five thousand years ago and who traced half his ancestry from Atlantis. Ramtha explains, in a fashion reminiscent of Hinduism, that the reader is really God and in addition predicts the immanent arrival of the "Age of God." Steven Lee (ed.), *Ramtha* (Eastsound, Washington: Weinberg Sovereignty, 1986).

61. The image of the cosmopolitan is offered as a heuristic device by which to portray the widespread secularity of the age. The reader should not seek narrowly to find its embodiment in all the endeavors of a particular class or in all social structures that are secular.

62. Harvey Cox, *The Secular City* (New York: Macmillan and London: SCM Press, 1965), p. 2.

63. It should be noted that I depart from this international language of modernity by way of both illustration and confession when making reference to my faith as an orthodox Catholic, or to the singular world-historical significance of what Moses Austin (1761–1821) wrought.

64. Alasdair MacIntyre, *Whose Justice? Which Rationality?* (London: Duckworth and Notre Dame, Ind.: University of Notre Dame Press, 1988), p. 396.

65. Ibid., p. 388.

66. Marshall Berman, *All That Is Solid Melts Into Air* (New York: Simon and Schuster, 1982), p. 15.

67. To speak of the ethos of the cosmopolitans as an international civil religion is to use religion in Émile Durkheim's (1858–1917) sense. Unlike Jean Jacques Rousseau (1712–1778), who saw civil religion as an ethos to be fashioned and preserved by political leaders, Durkheim understood it as that which unites individuals into a single moral community. It is an emergent social property.

68. Leon Kass, *Toward a More Natural Science: Biology and Human Affairs* (New York: Free Press, 1985).

69. Edmund Pellegrino and David Thomasma, *For the Patient's Good* (New York: Oxford University Press, 1988).

III. Humanism, Humaneness and the Humanities

1. "Doch worin besteht die Menschlichkeit des Menschen?," Martin Heidegger, "Brief über den 'Humanismus'," in *Wegmarken* (Frankfurt/Main: Vittorio Klosterman, 1976), p. 319, *Gesamtausgabe*, vol. 9.

2. For the Romans, to live a humane life (*humaniter vivere*) was to live a life of leisure (i.e., *otium cum dignitate*) as befitted an educated, refined aristocrat. See Franz Beckmann, *Humanitas* (Münster: Aschendorff, 1952), p. 37.

3. Publius Terentius Afer (185 B.C.–159 B.C.), *Heautontimoroumenos*, verse 7. "I am a man, I hold that what affects another man affects me." *Terence*, trans. John Sargeaunt (Cambridge, Mass.: Harvard University Press, 1986), p. 125.

4. I am in debt to Gunther Stent for convincing me of the close relationship between etiquette and ethics during discussions at the Wissenschaftskolleg zu Berlin (December, 1988). For an account of the Greek distinction between etiquette (*euschemosyne*) and ethics (*ethika*) that underlies contemporary discussions, not to mention Greek discussions of medical ethics and etiquette, see Paul Carrick, *Medical Ethics in Antiquity* (Dordrecht: D. Reidel, 1985), pp. 88–93.

5. From at least the time of the Hippocratic corpus, the portrait of the good physician has encompassed more than moral virtues. For example, the author of "The Physician" says that a physician "must be a gentleman in character, and being this he must be grave and kind to all." *Hippocrates*, trans. W. H. S. Jones (Cambridge, Mass.: Harvard University Press, 1981), p. 311.

6. For an exploration of the role of notions of excellence and well-being in the constitution of concepts of disease and health, see H. T. Engelhardt, Jr., *The Foundations of Bioethics* (New York: Oxford University Press, 1986), pp. 156–201.

7. For the study of the ambiguity and richness of these terms in Latin, see Heinz Haffter, "Die römische Humanitas," in *Römische Wertbegriffe*, ed. Hans Oppermann (Darmstadt: Wissenschaftliche Buchgesellschaft, 1983), pp. 468–482. In Cicero in particular one finds a wide range of ways in which these cognate terms are used. Consider, for example, the following Loeb translations: *humanissime* is translated as "very kind" (Letters to Atticus XIII, 43), *humanitas* as "kindness" (Letters to Atticus XV, 1), *per humana* as "very courteous" (Letters to Atticus XVI, 12), and *humanitatis* as "kindly disposition" (Letters to Atticus XVI, 16c). *Cicero*, trans. E. O. Winstedt (Cambridge, Mass.: Harvard University Press, 1987), vol. 3, pp. 197, 293, 413, 435. *Humanitas* is also translated as "urbanity" (*De Oratore* III, 29) and *mollitudo humanitatis* as "the softness of a humane spirit" (*De Oratore* III, 161). *Cicero*, vol. 4, pp. 25, 127. And, for example, *sensus humanitatis* is translated as "a feeling of humanity" (*Pro Sexto Roscio Amerino* LIII, 154), vol. 6, p. 263. *Humanissimus et doctissimus* is translated as "highest possible sensibility and scholarship" (*Pro*

Caelio X, 24, vol. 13, p. 435). For a list of Latin synonyms, see *Historisches Wörterbuch der Philosophie*, ed. Joachim Ritter (Basel: Schwabe, 1974), vol. 3, pp. 1231–1232.

8. For a discussion of the ambiguities in French, see Shelby T. McCloy, *The Humanitarian Movement in Eighteenth-Century France* (New York: Haskel House, 1972), pp. 1–6.

9. The *Oxford Latin Dictionary* gives the following definitions of *humanitas*: "1. human nature or character; 2. the quality distinguishing civilized man from savages or beasts, civilization, culture; 3. humane character, kindness, human feeling." There is also the cognate term *humaniter*: "1. in a manner becoming a man, reasonably, moderately; 2. in a kindly or friendly fashion," as well as *humanitus*: "1. in the manner of human beings; 2. in a manner beocming to man, in a kindly way; reasonably, moderately."

10. Cicero, in order to indicate something like what we would mean by the liberal arts, uses the term *studia humanitatis*. Indeed, the Romans supported an equivocation between the *artes liberales* and the *artes humanae*. Franz Beckmann, *Humanitas* (Münster: Aschendorff, 1952), p. 39. But Cicero does not have a list of disciplinary areas in mind as we might, or as was the case in the Renaissance. The meaning is more general. *Studia*, the plural of *studium*, indicates strivings after, quests for, interests in something. The *Oxford Latin Dictionary* includes among the definitions of *studium*: "1. earnest application of one's attention or energies to some specified or implied object, zeal, ardour; inclination towards a thing, desire, fancy; . . . 7. intellectual activity, esp. of a literary kind, or an instance of it, study; (w. gen.) the study (of a particular subject); to make a study (of); a member of the imperial household acting as adviser on literary matters." The phrase *studia humanitatis* thus identifies a striving after and a "study" of the marks of the cultivated human. In *Pro Murena* 61, for example, Cicero says: "I will be a little more venturesome in disputing concerning the *studiis humanitatis*." Or in acknowledging that he is speaking to "a very erudite audience (*concursu hominum litteratissimorum*]", Cicero says that he will "enlarge upon *studiis humanitatis ac litterarum*" (*Pro Archia Poeta* i.2). In using these terms Cicero is shaping an ambiguous but powerful idea: an interest in the cultivated refinements of humans. "With Cicero the educated individual is recurringly addressed as *homo humanus*, and *humanitas* is equated with *doctrina*, *eruditio*, [and] *litterae* . . ." Beckmann, *Humanitas*, p. 39 (my translation).

11. Werner Jaeger, *Paideia: The Ideals of Greek Culture* (Oxford: Oxford University Press, 1943–45), 3 vols. Jaeger argues that the spiritual principle of the Greeks was not individualism but humanism, in the sense of education to the true human form and essence. See also Bruno Snell, "Die Entdeckung der Menschlichkeit und unsere Stellung zu den Griechen," in *Humanismus*, ed. Hans Oppermann (Darmstadt: Wissenschaftliche Buchgesellschaft, 1970), pp. 238–239.

12. The *Oxford Latin Dictionary* defines *humanus* as "1. of, belonging to, or involving, a human being or beings, human; human affairs; the human scene, life; also, the human race, the world; a human being; 2. human, of human beings; 3. (of conditions, etc.) that affect human beings, proper to man; 4. characteristic of human beings, human; 5. civilized, cultured, cultivated; 6. morally worthy of humanity, kindly, considerate, befitting the dignity of man, merciful, indulgent." There is also the cognate term *humane* (Latin): "1. in a manner becoming a man, reasonably; with the forbearance befitting a man, with moderation; 2. in a kindly or friendly manner."

13. Dietrich von Engelhardt, for example, notes that *humanitas* was among

the list of virtues that eighteenth-century physicians held should be a part of the character of the good practitioner. "Virtue and Medicine During the Enlightenment in Germany," in *Virtue and Medicine*, ed. Earl Shelp (Dordrecht: Reidel, 1985), p. 67.

14. Karl Büchner, *Vom Bildungswert des Lateinischen* (Wiesbaden: Franz Steiner, 1965), p. 52.

15. "I urge you not to be too unkind, but to consider carefully your patient's superabundance or means. Sometimes give your services for nothing, calling to mind a previous benefaction or present satisfaction. And if there be an opportunity of serving one who is a stranger in financial straits, give full assistance to all such. For where there is love of man [*philanthropia*], there is also love of the art." *Hippocrates*, "Precepts" VI, trans. W. H. S. Jones (Cambridge, Mass.: Harvard, 1984), vol. 1, p. 319. It is important to note that in many ways the attitudes of Greek physicians were something like those of tradesmen: they were interested in deporting themselves in a fashion that would establish their reputation and therefore attract patients. See, for example, Ludwig Edelstein, "The Professional Ethics of the Greek Physician," in *Ancient Medicine: Selected Papers of Ludwig Edelstein*, ed. O. Temkin and C. L. Temkin (Baltimore: John Hopkins, 1967), pp. 319–348.

16."The appearance of the goodness and loving-kindness (*philanthropia*) of our Savior, God" (Titus 3:4). See Helmut Koester, *History and Literature of Early Christianity* (Philadelphia: Fortress Press, 1982), p. 298.

17. The term *philanthropos* had a meaning in the Greek quite different from the English philanthropy. For example, the unknown author of Pseudo-Justin's book, *De monarchia*, contrasts a humanistic viewpoint with a religious viewpoint using the terms *philanthropos* and *philotheos*, where *philanthropos* has the sense of formal culture. Werner Jaeger, *Humanism and Theology* (Milwaukee: Marquette University, 1943), p. 87.

18. Like "secular" and "humanism," so, too, "humanitarianism" has a complex history and in certain quarters has taken on a sectarian cast. Moreover, the accepted meanings of the term are quite diverse. On the one hand, the *Oxford English Dictionary* defines humanitarianism in terms of humanitarian. Other than the first usage and its derivative meanings, which identify an individual who affirms the humanity (but denies the divinity) of Christ, the following are listed: "2. One who professes the 'Religion of Humanity', holding that man's duty is chiefly or wholly comprised in the advancement of the welfare of the human race: applied to various schools of thought and practice. 3. One who advocates or practises humanity or humane action; one who devotes himself to the welfare of mankind at large; a philanthropist. Nearly always contemptuous, connoting one who goes to excess in his humane principles. B.2. Devoted to humanity or the human race as an object of worship. 3. Having regard to the interests of humanity or mankind at large; relating to, advocating, or practising humanity or humane action; broadly philanthropic. Often contemptuous or hostile." Sometimes the antagonism against humanitarians stemmed from a failure to distinguish the scholarly and stylistic concerns of humanists from the philanthropic concerns of humanitarians. "In general the most serious confusion in the use of the word humanist has arisen from its appropriation by the humanitarians . . . Our educational policies, from the elementary grades to the university, are being controlled by humanitarians. They are busy at this very moment, almost to a man, proclaiming the gospel of service. It will be strange indeed if dissatisfaction with this situation is not felt by a growing minority, if a demand does not arise for at least a few institutions of learning that are humanistic rather than

humanitarian in their aims." Irving Babbitt, "Humanism: An Essay at Definition," in Norman Foerster (ed.), *Humanism and America* (New York: Farrar and Rinehart, 1930), p. 31, 51.

All of the foregoing meanings focus on the welfare of humans. However, the *Encyclopaedia of Religion and Ethics*, which reprints an entry from the early twentieth century, has humanitarianism place a major accent on the welfare of animals. "The principle of humaneness is based on the broad ground of universal sympathy, not with mankind only, but with all sentient beings, such sympathy being, of course, duly proportioned to the sensibility of its object. Humanitarianism is not to be confused with philanthropy — love of mankind — on the one side, or with zoophily — kindness to animals — on the other; it includes and comprehends them both . . . Humanitarianism, then, is the application of an evolutionary doctrine founded on the kinship of life, which unites the sentiment of East and West in the growing perception of fellowship and brotherhood between all living creatures; and a humanitarian is he who has substituted this wider sympathy for the partial benevolence which is restricted to the narrower circle of one's own countrymen or kin." James Hastings (ed.), (Edinburgh: T. & T. Clark, reprinted 1981) vol. 6, p. 837. According to the *Guide to Reference Books* (10th edition), the *Encyclopaedia of Religion and Ethics* first appeared between 1908 and 1927. The same shift of meaning from concern with humans to concern with animals can be noted in the term "humane society," which currently primarily identifies an interest in protecting the welfare of animals (following the interest of the Humanitarian League at the end of the nineteenth and beginning of the twentieth centuries; *Encyclopaedia of Religion and Ethics*, vol. 6, p. 838), though originally, according to the O.E.D., it identified the title of a society for the rescue of drowning persons founded on May 8, 1776.

19. Among the living languages, these ambiguities are not restricted to the English language. For example, Newald recognizes the ambiguity of the term *Humanität* by indicating that it encompasses "humanity, humaneness, human rights, human duties, human worth, and human love." Richard Newald, *Probleme und Gestalten des deutschen Humanismus* (Berlin: Walter de Gruyter, 1963), p. 20.

20. For example, Voltaire addressed Frederick the Great in a letter from the Hague on July 20, 1740 (as well as on other occasions) as "Your Humanity." *Posthumous Works of Frederic II, King of Prussia*, trans. Thomas Holcroft (London, 1789), VII, 124; quoted in Shelby McCloy, *The Humanitarian Movement in Eighteenth-Century France* (New York: Haskell House, 1972), p. 2.

21. Emil Ludwig, *Napoleon*, trans. Eden and Cedar Paul (New York: Modern Library), p. 322.

22. This ambiguity of the term humanity was especially pronounced in the eighteenth- and nineteenth-century French uses of *humanité*. It was used, *inter alia*, to indicate "a deeply felt concern over the welfare of one's fellow beings." Shelby McCloy, *The Humanitarian Movement in Eighteenth-Century France* (New York: Haskell House, 1972), p. 2. Toward the end of the eighteenth century, reform, revolution, and slaughter were all undertaken in the name of humanity. The term existed in German discussions as well. See T. G. Masaryk, *Ideale der Humanität* (Prag: Sudetendeutsche Buchgemeinde, 1935).

23. Paul O. Kristeller, "Humanism and Scholasticism in the Italian Renaissance," *Byzantion* XVII (1944–45), 346–374. Augusto Campana, "The Origin of the Word 'Humanist'," *Journal of the Warburg and Courtauld Institutes* 9 (1946), 60–73.

24. As an indication of the history of this term, there appears to have been a

late sixteenth-century controversy in Bologna involving a demand that the *professor humanarum litterarum* be included in the arts faculty. Augusto Campana, "The Origin of the Word 'Humanist'," *Journal of the Warburg and Courtauld Institutes* 9 (1946), 65.

25. Paul O. Kristeller, *Renaissance Thought* (New York: Harper, 1961), p. 10.

26. The interest in Greek and Roman literature that developed at the end of the eighteenth century in Germany led to the coining of the term "Humanismus," which was probably introduced by Immanuel Niethammer (1766–1848). "The designation humanism does not apply simply to the faction that wishes to protect the study of the so-called humanities *[Humanioren]* in schools of learning against encroachments that must be considered harmful. The term applies more properly and in a more eminent sense to the entire ancient pedagogy as such, which always had the character of being more concerned for the humanity than the animality of the student, and which continues to place its claims against modern education, which is predominantly directed to animality, even though this opposition remains a minority." Friedrich Immanuel Niethammer, *Der Streit des Philanthropinismus und Humanismus* (Jena: Frommann, 1808), p. 8 (my translation). See also Vito R. Giustiniani, "Homo, Humanus, and the Meanings of 'Humanism'," *Journal of the History of Ideas* 46 (April–June 1985), 171–174.

27. Horst Rüdiger, *Wesen und Wandlung des Humanismus* (Hamburg: Hoffmann & Campe, 1937), p. 13 [my translation].

28. "[H]umanists in this latter sense are those who, in any age, aim at proportionateness through a cultivation of the law of measure." Irving Babbitt, "Humanism: An Essay at Definition," in Norman Foerster (ed.), *Humanism and America* (New York: Farrar and Rinehart, 1930), p. 30.

29. In an essay on American education, Babbitt decries the loss of leisure in the American academy. In fact, he sees the phenomenon as world-wide. "Even at Oxford and Cambridge, and still more in our own college faculties, the humanist and man of leisure is being elbowed aside by the scientific specialist and the bustling humanitarian." Irving Babbitt, *Literature and the American College* (Boston: Houghton Mifflin, 1908), p. 251. Babbitt concludes that "it is only by a more humane reflection that we can escape the penalties sure to be exacted from any country that tries to dispense in its national life with the principle of leisure" (p. 263).

30. "The final appeal of the humanist is not to any historical convention but to intuition." Babbitt, "Humanism: An Essay at Definition," op. cit., p. 27.

31. "The virtue that results from a right cultivation of one's humanity, in other words from moderate and decorous living, is poise." "Humanism: An Essay at Definition," p. 29.

32. "The false pretensions of science must be wholly abandoned, and the problems of our destiny be examined by a wise judgment drawn from human experience, before we can hope for a sane and humanistic philosophy." Louis T. More, "The Pretensions of Science," in Norman Foerster (ed.), op. cit., p. 24.

33. H. T. Engelhardt, Jr., *The Foundations of Bioethics* (New York: Oxford, 1986).

34. Kristeller, *Renaissance Thought*, p. 8.

35. Immanuel Kant, *Zum ewigen Frieden* (Königsberg: Nicolovius, 1795).

36. Holyoake's secularism, as well as the various utilitarian movements of the nineteenth century, provide good examples of a secular humanitarian concern. Charles W. Goss, *A Descriptive Bibliography of the Writings of George Jacob Holyoake* (London: Crowther & Goodman, 1908).

37. In the fifth and fourth century B.C. the Greeks completed a process of secularization in the sense that their major religious ideas and symbols were to a large extent deprived of transcendent significance (they were secularized in the fifth sense described in chapter III above). One gets a sense of this secular attitude to the gods in Herodotus' account of the origin of their names. He claims that "wellnigh all the names of the gods came to Hellas from Egypt." *Herodotus*, trans. A. D. Godley (Cambridge, Mass.: Harvard University Press, 1981), vol. 1, p. 337 (II.50.1). Rist interprets Herodotus as claiming that Homer and Hesiod had invented the gods. For a study of the secular character of Greek thought and the appropriate qualifications on that secularity, see John M. Rist, *Human Value: A Study in Ancient Philosophical Ethics* (Leiden: E. J. Brill, 1982), especially pp. 6–10.

38. "You saw no form of any kind the day the Lord spoke to you at Horeb out of the fire. Therefore watch yourselves very carefully, so that you do not become corrupt and make for yourselves an idol, an image of any shape, whether formed like a man or a woman . . ." (Deut. 4:15–16).

39. "'For my thoughts are not your thoughts, neither are your ways my ways,' declares the Lord. 'As the heavens are higher than the earth, so are my ways higher than your ways and my thoughts than your thoughts'" (Isaiah 55:8–9).

40. Though an attempt was made philosophically to justify many of the 613 laws of the Torah, a number were seen simply to be the requirements of God, beyond human rational account. "And perhaps you might think these are vain things, therefore Scripture says: I am the Lord, i.e., I, the Lord have made it a statute and you have no right to criticize it." Yoma 67b, *Babylonian Talmud* (Soncino edition).

41. See, for example, Granville C. Henry, Jr., *Logos: Mathematics and Christian Theology* (Lewisburg, Penn.: Bucknell University Press, 1976).

42. Josephus Flavius (Josephus ben Matthias), *Against Apion* I, 42–44, in *Josephus*, trans. H. St. J. Thackeray (Cambridge, Mass.: Harvard, 1976), vol. 1, pp. 179–181.

43. One might recognize Hypatia (370–415), one of the last significant pagan philosophers, as a martyr for classical Greek learning. A mob of monks and lay Christians stripped her, dragged her into a church, killed her, and burned her body. She was eulogized by one of the pagan poets at the end of the era, Palladas (c. 350–450), as "Adorable Hypatia, Grace of speech, Unsullied Star of true philosophy." Quoted in John Sandys, *A History of Classical Scholarship* (New York: Hafner, 1958), vol. 1, p. 370.

The culture embodied in the *belles lettres* of the Greeks and the Romans celebrated the virtue of *sophrosyne* (which can be loosely translated somewhat as balance or temperance), which tended to count against the single-minded spirit needed to inspire martyrdom. Still, many individuals held tenaciously to being pagans, despite the substantial persecution they suffered. Some, like Phocas, preferred suicide to a forced conversion to Christianity. So, too, numerous Roman senators, who saw culture, paganism, and learning inextricably intertwined, struggled to the end to maintain the old traditions.

44. For example, the shema, which is said twice daily by orthodox Jewish males, affirms the singularity and oneness of God. It begins: "Hear, O Israel: The Lord our God, the Lord is one." Deuteronomy 6:4.

45. The Academy is described as being close to an altar to Eros, a god who was the object of special reverence in gymnasia, and whose festivals, the Erotia, involved gymnastic contests. "Before the entrance to the Academy is an altar to Love, with an inscription that Charmus was the first Athenian to

dedicate an altar to that god." Pausanias, *Attica* XXX, 1, in W. H. S. Jones (trans.), *Pausanias: Description of Greece* (Cambridge, Mass.: Harvard, 1978), vol. 1, p. 165. Pausanias, who lived in the second century A.D., produced what is equivalent to a traveler's guide to Greece and her monuments. The work is an indication of the extent to which, already in the second century, the Roman world looked backward to the splendid roots of Greek culture as to a golden age. There was already some of the antiquarian character in its interest in Greece that would mark the humanism of the Renaissance.

46. "The Lyceum has its name from Lycus, the son of Pandion, but it was considered sacred to Apollo from the beginning down to my time, and here was the god first named Lyceus." Pausanias, *Attica* XIX, 3, ibid., vol. 1, p. 95.

47. The Olympic games, a cultural event that united the Greeks, were first held in 776 B.C. They were performed in the nude, marking the profound Greek veneration of physical beauty and capacity. Held every four years, the games provided a common basis for reckoning time, and were celebrated until the 283rd Olympiad in A.D. 394, when the Christian Emperor Theodosius I (379–395) forbade their further celebration.

48. This paradigmatic struggle between the Greek and Jewish cultures, and the eventual liberation of the Jews from occupation, is remembered during Hanukkah.

49. Josephus, *Jewish Antiquities* XII, 241, vol. 7, p. 123. A similar account is provided in the First Book of Maccabees (Josephus may in part be paraphrasing Maccabees). "At that time there appeared in Israel a group of renegade Jews, who incited the people. 'Let us enter into a covenant with the Gentiles round about,' they said, 'because disaster upon disaster has overtaken us since we segregated ourselves from them.' The people thought this a good argument, and some of them in their enthusiasm went to the king and received authority to introduce non-Jewish laws and customs. They built a sports-stadium in the Gentile style in Jerusalem. They removed their marks of circumcision and repudiated the holy covenant. They intermarried with Gentiles, and abandoned themselves to evil ways." I Maccabees 1:11–15.

50. Hippocrates, "Decorum" V in *Hippocrates*, trans. W. H. S. Jones (Cambridge, Mass.: Harvard, 1959), vol. 2, p. 287.

51. Sir William Osler enjoined upon physicians the study and appreciation of the classics. For example, in a list of readings entitled "Bedside Library for Medical Students" he included Plutarch, Marcus Aurelius, and Epictetus. See Osler, *Aequanimitas* (New York: McGraw-Hill, 1919), p. 453.

51. Diogenes Laertius, *Protagoras* IX, 51, in *Lives of Eminent Philosophers*, trans. R. D. Hicks (Cambridge, Mass.: Harvard, 1979), vol. 2, pp. 463, 465.

53. Ibid., IX, 52, vol. 2, p. 465.

54. "Protagoras was the first to maintain that there are two sides to every question, opposed to each other, and he even argued in this fashion, being the first to do so." Diogenes Laertius, ibid. IX, 51, vol. 2, p. 463.

55. Protagoras of Abdera asserted that "all sense-impressions and opinions are true and that truth is a relative thing inasmuch as everything that has appeared to someone or been opined by someone is at once real in relation to him." Sextus Empiricus, *Against the Logicians* I, 60, trans. R. G. Bury (Cambridge, Mass.: Harvard, 1983), vol. 2, pp. 31, 33.

56. Sextus Empiricus, *Outlines of Pyrrhonism* I, 216, trans. R. G. Bury (Cambridge, Mass.: Harvard, 1976), vol. 1, p. 131.

57. It is impossible to determine in any detail the actual opinions of Protagoras. The introduction to his work *On the Gods*, where he argues that man is the measure of all things and that one cannot prove the existence of the

gods, led to his being expelled from Athens. Then "they burnt his works in the market-place, after sending round a herald to collect them from all who had copies in their possession." Diogenes Laertius IX, 52, vol. 2, p. 465. Though he qualifies the claim, and though the remaining fragments do not clearly establish the claim, Rist holds that Protagoras may have affirmed that moral rules should be the same everywhere. John M. Rist, *Human Value: A Study in Ancient Philosophical Ethics* (Leiden: E. J. Brill, 1982), p. 21.

58. Joseph Fletcher, *Morals and Medicine* (Boston: Beacon Press, 1960); *Situation Ethics* (Philadelphia: Westminster Press and London: SCM Press, 1966).

59. Laszlo Versenyi, *Socratic Humanism* (New Haven, N.J.: Yale University Press, 1963), p. 33.

60. Hippocrates, *On Ancient Medicine* III.

61. Laszlo Versenyi, *Socratic Humanism*, p. 61.

62. Hippocrates, *The Sacred Disease* V, in *Hippocrates*, trans. W. H. S. Jones (Cambridge, Mass.: Harvard University Press, 1981), vol. 2, p. 151.

63. For an excellent study of the development of the concept of humanism as well as an analysis of the ambiguities of the term, even in ancient times, see: Vito R. Giustiniani, "Homo, Humanus, and the Meanings of 'Humanism'," *Journal of the History of Ideas* 46 (April–June 1985), 167–195. I am very much in debt to this essay and to LeRoy Walters for calling the article to my attention. See also Vito R. Giustiniani, "Umanesimo: la parola e la cosa," in *Studia Humanitatis*, eds. Eginhard Hora and Eckhard Kessler (Munich: Fink, 1973), pp. 23–30.

64. John C. Rolfe (trans.), *The Attic Nights of Aulus Gellius* XIII.xvii.1 (Cambridge, Mass.: Harvard, 1978), vol. 3, p. 457.

65. John T. Noonan, Jr., *Contraception* (Cambridge, Mass.: Belknap Press, 1966).

66. Diogenes Laertius, *Lives of Eminent Philosophers*, II, 70, trans. R. D. Hicks (Cambridge, Mass.: Harvard University Press, 1980), vol. 1, p. 199.

67. Varro, *On the Latin Language* VIII, 31, trans. R. G. Kent (Cambridge, Mass.: Harvard, 1979), vol. 2, p. 395.

68. Martin Heidegger, "Brief über den 'Humanismus'," *Wegmarken* (Frankfurt/Main: Vittorio Klostermann, 1976), pp. 319f.

69. Marcus Fabius Quintilianus, *The Institutio Oratoria of Quintilian* XII, 25, trans. H. E. Butler (Cambridge, Mass.: Harvard, 1979), vol. 4, p. 397.

70. Ibid., XII, 27, vol. 4, p. 397.

71. Aristotle, *Politics*, trans. H. Rackham (Cambridge, Mass.: Harvard, 1977), VII.xiv.1335b10, vol. 21, pp. 623, 625.

72. St Thomas showed sympathy for Aristotle's argument in favor of restricting abortion to the first trimester, although St. Thomas held all abortions to be evil. However, St. Thomas argued that first trimester abortions did not involve the taking of the life of a person. See *Summa Theologica* I, 118, art.2; *Aristoteles Stagiritae: Politicorum seu de Rebus Civilibus*, Book VII, Lectio XII, in *Opera Omnia* (Paris: Vives, 1875), vol. 26, p. 484; *Summa Theologica* II, II, 64, art. 8; and *Commentum in Quartum Librum Sententiarium Magistri Petri Lombardi*, Distinctio XXXI, Expositio Textus, in *Opera Omnia*, vol. 11, p. 127.

73. Oath. *Hippocrates*, trans. W. H. S. Jones (Cambridge, Mass.: Harvard, 1984), vol. 1, p. 299.

74. Didache II.1, in *The Apostolic Fathers*, trans. K. Lake (Cambridge, Mass.: Harvard University Press, 1985), p. 311.

75. Owsei Temkin (trans.), *Soranus' Gynecology* (Baltimore: Johns Hopkins, 1956), p. 63.

76. Paul Carrick, *Medical Ethics in Antiquity* (Dordrecht: Reidel, 1985).

77. Tacitus (54–117), for example, records that ". . . the authority of their [the Germans] kings is not unlimited or arbitrary; their generals control the people by example rather than command, and by means of the admiration which attends upon energy and a conspicuous place in front of the line. But anything beyond this — capital punishment, imprisonment, even flogging — is permitted only to the priests, and then not as a penalty or under the general's orders, but as an inspiration from the god whom they suppose to accompany them on campaign." *Germania*, trans. M. Hutton, in *Tacitus* (Cambridge, Mass.: Harvard University Press, 1980), vol. 1, p. 141.

78. Gregory Vlastos, "The Rights of Persons in Plato's Conception of the Foundations of Justice," in *Morals, Science, and Sociality*, ed. H. T. Engelhardt and D. Callahan (Hastings-on-Hudson: Hastings Center, 1978), pp. 172–201.

79. The Protestant Reformation led to the decentralization of religious authority by placing an emphasis on each individual's direct relationship to the Deity. This led to accenting of individual decision and justification before God. This ethic resonated with remnants of the old pagan Germanic view of the individual and the individual's relationship to the community. This is not to suggest that Protestants were initially any more inclined to tolerate heresy or support free speech than were the Dominicans of the Holy Roman and Universal Inquisition. However, the logic of justification before God without the necessity of a human intermediary supported a sense of individualism that intersected synergistically with Anglo-Saxon common law when it was taken to the frontiers of America. The individualistic American language of rights recaptured the old pagan Germanic sentiments regarding the independent dignity of the individual in circumstances similar to those of pagan Germany.

Tacitus records that "It is well known that none of the German tribes live in cities, that even individually they do not permit houses to touch each other: they live separated and scattered, according as spring-water, meadow, or grove appeals to each man . . ." (*Germania*, p. 155). This description somewhat foreshadows the American frontiersmen who moved on further when the smoke of too many neighbors' houses could be seen, or the old Texan view that "your neighbors are too damn close when you can't shoot in every direction without fear of hitting someone." A decentralized Protestantism was the natural religion of such folk, and rights were seen as ways of keeping one's neighbors at a tolerable distance. It is not farfetched to see a continuity between the old Germanic view that "each freeman remains master of his own house and home . . ." (*Germania*, p. 169) and the American view that "The right of the people to be secure in their persons, houses, papers, and effects, against unreasonable searches and seizures, shall not be violated . . ." (U.S. Constitution, Amendment 4).

For a study of the influence of the old Germanic concept of freedom on political thought from the sixteenth through the eighteenth century, see Erwin Hölzle, *Die Idee einer altgermanischen Freiheit vor Montesquieu: Fragmente aus der Geschichte politischer Freiheitsbestrebungen in Deutschland, England und Frankreich vom 16.–18. Jahrhundert* (Munich: Oldenbourg, 1925).

80. The English word "right" has had a political and moral force quite different from the Latin equivalent, *potestas*. In great measure this is the case because rights language has served the special function in English history of setting limits to the claims of the king, who for a significant period of English history was seen as a part of a foreign occupying force. After the victory of

William the Bastard, the "Rights of Englishmen" were invoked to claim fair procedural justice and to limit central authority. They supported individual claims to the forbearance of society and made room for individual life over against the community's life.

81. The pagan philosophers, fearing death, fled to Persia. However, King Chosroes negotiated their safe return to Athens.

82. The Benedictines conducted their lives with a special focus on sacred learning. Each week a monk was chosen to read aloud during the common meals, and during Lent each monk was required to read a book from the monastery library. In this way, Benedict (A.D. 480–543) maintained remnants of the ancient *humanitas*, but now set within a quite different age. One of his contemporaries, Senator Magnus Aurelius Cassiodorus (A.D. 480–575), describes this age as *modernus*. The term *modernus* (from *modo*, "just now", on analogy with *hodiernus*, "of today"; cf. "modern" in the *Oxford English Dictionary*) is used by Cassiorodus to speak, among other things, of the modern *saeculum* that emerged after the Great Plague that swept the Roman Empire for four years beginning in 542. The very tenor and timbre of the world had changed. A new age had entered. John E. Sandys, *A History of Classical Scholarship* (New York: Hafner, 1958), vol. 1, pp. 269–271, 383.

83. As B. H. Streeter characterized the milieu out of which Christianity developed, "The Palestine Jew was the reverse of philosophically-minded." Chapter 7, "The Rise of Christianity", in *The Cambridge Ancient History*, ed. S. A. Cook, F. E. Adcock, and M. P. Charlesworth (Cambridge: Cambridge University Press, 1975), vol. 11, *The Imperial Peace A.D. 70–192*, p. 265. A number of qualifications are still in order, such as indicating the extensive metaphysical reflection in Jewish cabalistic literature and in Alexandrian Jewish theological reflections. However, Jewish religious thought did not enter into a sustained interaction with a secular metaphysical tradition, as did the Catholic Church. In the case of the Catholic Church, this produced a rationalistic theology, which culminated in Leo XIII's encyclical, *Aeterni Patris* (4 August 1879), which endorsed St Thomas's philosophy for Catholic schools.

84. *Babylonian Talmud*, Baba Mezia 59b (Soncino edition).

85. Because of the Christian incorporation of Greek thought and medieval theology's consequent confidence in reason, metaphysics was usually considered as a science that could be pursued through natural reason alone. For the Christian theologians of the Middle Ages, metaphysics was an element of the secular corpus of knowledge, independent of any special revelation.

86. Though this passage has its own theological meaning, the use of the term *logos* can only be understood against its background philosophical meanings in Greek thought and the special religious meanings it acquired in Jewish thought. Logos "has a history both in Greek philosophy and in Jewish Alexandrian theology. But, whereas in Greek philosophy the word means the divine Reason regarded as immanent in the cosmic process, the authors of the Septuagint use it to translate the Hebrew *Memra* and its poetic synonyms, which mean primarily the spoken word of the Deity. Hellenized Jewish thought attempted to fuse these two originally distinct meanings; and so arose the Christian use of the word as a name for the second Person of the Trinity, incarnated in Jesus of Nazareth." *Encyclopaedia of Religion and Ethics*, p. 134. See also Helmut Koester, *History and Literature of Early Christianity* (Philadelphia: Fortress Press, 1982), vol. 2, pp. 188–189.

87. Perhaps one of the major differences was the loss of a vital tradition of literary criticism. George Saintsbury, *A History of Criticism* (Edinburgh: Blackwood, 1961), vol. 1, pp. 373–4.

88. *Conciliorum Oecumenicorum Decreta* (Basel: Herder, 1962), p. 210 (author's translation).

89. Apollinaris was born in Lugdunum (Lyon) and became bishop of Augustonemetum (Clermont-Ferrand).

90. Sidonius, *Poems and Letters*, Book II.ix, trans. W. B. Anderson (Cambridge, Mass.: Harvard, 1980), vol. 1, pp. 451–457, 461.

91. Traditionally, the Roman Empire of the West is said to have ended in 476 with the forced abdication of Romulus Augustulus. Purists might argue that it continued, in that Julius Nepos, the former emperor and still claimant to the throne, had fled to Ravenna in August, 475, and survived until his assassination in 480. Even after that, the empire was nominally present, in that the emperor of Constantinople claimed to be sovereign of the entire empire. There was simply no longer a representative in the West. In fact, Odovacar actually petitioned Zeno, the emperor (474–491) in Constantinople (New Rome), for the traditional title of *patricius* and returned to the emperor the imperial insignia of Romulus Augustulus. Romania continued to exist with its sovereign, preserving much of the literature that would be the delight of the humanists of the Renaissance. The tradition of Constantinople has remained so vigorous that even today the Ecumenical Patriarch is styled the Patriarch of Rum.

92. During the development of education in the Middle Ages, the liberal arts were preserved and reshaped as the trivium (grammar, rhetoric, and logic) and the quadrivium (arithmetic, astronomy, geometry, and music). These are related only in part to the liberal arts as we now associate them with the humanities. Paul Abelson, *The Seven Liberal Arts* (New York: Russell & Russell, 1965; 1st printing, 1906).

93. For an attempt to construe St. Thomas and others of this period as humanists, *grosso modo*, because of their interest in human nature and the writings of the ancients (including the attempt to go back to original texts), see Werner Jaeger, *Humanism and Theology* (Milwaukee: Marquette University Press, 1943). Jaeger sees a humanistic aspect in St. Thomas' theocentric worldview.

94. For three years, between 1588 and 1591, early abortion was regarded as equivalent to murder. See Pope Sextus V, *Contra procurantes, Consulentes, et Consentientes, quorunque modo Abortum Constitutio* (Florence: Georgius Marescottus, 1588). Generally, following Aristotle, the soul was not held to enter a male fetus until forty days gestation and a female fetus until eighty or ninety days. *De Generatione Animalium*, 2.3.736a–b and *Historia Animalium*, 7.3.583b. For a gloss on the original case from the twelfth century, which entered into canon law in 1234 through the decretals of Gratian, and led to early abortion not being considered homicide, see *Corpus Juris Canonici Emendatum et Notis Illustratum cum Glossae: decretalium d. Gregorii Papae Noni Compilatio* (Rome, 1585), *Glossa ordinaria* at bk. 5, title 12, chap. 20, p. 1713.

95. St. Thomas Aquinas, *Summa Theologiae* 2a 2ae.64, 7.

96. In 1525 in his *Summula peccatorum*, Cajetan condemned as a mortal sin experimentation if it was done by deceit or on the poor. See Darrel Amundsen, "Casuistry and Professional Obligations: The Regulation of Physicians by the Court of Conscience in the Late Middle Ages," (Part I), *Transactions and Studies of the College of Physicians of Philadelphia* 3 (1981), 35. Similarly, in his *Summa Armilla* (1538) Bartholomaeus Fumus held that physicians acted sinfully if "they supply a doubtful medicine for a certain one, or do not practice in accord with the art, but desire to practice following their own stupid fancy, or make experiments and such like, by which the patient is exposed to grave danger." See ibid.

97. James McCartney, "The Development of the Doctrine of Ordinary and Extraordinary Means of Preserving Life in Catholic Moral Theology Before the Karen Quinlan Case," *Linacre Quarterly* 47 (Aug. 1980), 215–224. See also, Daniel A. Cronin, *The Moral Law in Regard to the Ordinary and Extraordinary Means of Conserving Life* (Rome: Typis Pontificiae Universitatis Gregorianiae, 1958).

98. The social factors that were concurrent with and influenced the development of the Renaissance included important economic and political forces. Among the more important was the emergence of powerful entrepreneurs whose financial status rivaled the status of the Church. Horst Rüdiger, "Die Wiederentdeckung der antiken Literatur im Zeitalter der Renaissance," in Herbert Hunger et al., *Geschichte der Textüberlieferung* (Zürich: Atlantis, 1961), p. 519. There were also important political changes that on the one hand strengthened nationalism and on the other shaped the character of the northern Italian states. Ephraim Emerton, *Humanism and Tyranny* (Gloucester, Mass.: Peter Smith, 1964). Humanism and the Renaissance were the heirs of the Empire and the Church. The Church's political significance was to be transformed by the Reformation and the development of nationalism. See Konrad Burdach, *Reformation, Renaissance, Humanismus* (Darmstadt: Wissenschaftliche Buchgesellschaft, 1963), especially p. 133.

99. Petrarch lived well in a century marked by pestilence, war, corruption, and chaos. His beloved Laura, for example, is reputed to have died of the plague in 1348. He lived, wrote, and gave intimations of the coming Renaissance during the period when the popes resided in Avignon, beginning with Clement V (1304–1314), who transferred the papacy there in 1309. Pope John XXII (1316–1334), Pope Benedict XII (1334–1342, who began the construction of the papal palace at Avignon), Clement VI (1342–1352, who purchased the entire city of Avignon), Innocent VI (1352–1362), Urban V (1362–1370), and Gregory XI (1370–1378, who excommunicated the entire city of Florence) all resided in Avignon. The papacy returned to Rome in 1377. Beginning with Urban VI (1378–1389), there was a pretender to the chair of St. Peter in both Rome and Avignon, and as of 1409, with Alexander V (1409–1410), there was a claimant in Pisa as well. Petrarch, who was a part of the papal court at Avignon, had two of his illegitimate children legitimated by papal edict. Evidently, neither of these children was borne by the fabled Laura.

100. The Pope's difficulties with the Councils of Constance and Basel can be seen as particular events in a long history of conflict between the bishop of Rome and other bishops, with such highlights as the Eastern Schism. Still, these difficulties are of special significance in marking the breakdown of the cultural synthesis focused on Rome that reached its highpoint in the thirteenth century.

101. The humanism of the Renaissance had élitist characteristics which bore some resemblance to those associated with the *humanitas* of ancient times. However, the accent had shifted to an intellectual élitism, with a focus on refined education and scholarly knowledge. It depended on the view that without a knowledge of ancient languages *humanitas* could not be achieved. Richard Newald, *Probleme und Gestalten des deutschen Humanismus* (Berlin: Walter de Gruyter, 1963), see especially pp. 1–66.

102. Paul O. Kristeller, "Humanism and Scholasticism in the Italian Renaissance," *Byzantion* XVII (1944–45), 350.

103. There was at times a near-fanatical devotion to the style of the ancients, especially Cicero. "The cult of Ciceronianism was so absolute that its followers would use no Latin expression not found in the works of Cicero. Thus Pietro

Bembo (1470–1547), who was cardinal and papal secretary to Leo X, would never speak of the Holy Ghost, and refers to the Virgin Mary only as *dea ipsa*." Moses Hadas, *Humanism: The Greek Ideal and Its Survival* (New York: Harper, 1960), p. 4. Such pretensions were entertained only by the upper classes. In fact, Lewis Mumford contends that "the humanist movement, by placing an emphasis upon textual scholarship and the dead languages to which this scholarship applied, re-enforced the widened separation of classes under capitalism." Lewis Mumford, *Technics and Civilization* (New York: Harcourt, Brace, 1934), p. 407.

104. The term *studia humanitatis* appears to have been reintroduced in the mid-fifteenth century. Thus, Peter Luder announced his lectures of 1456 in Leipzig as *studia humanitatis* and included poetry, rhetoric, and the works of historians. *"Id est poetarum, oratorum ac historiographorum libros publice legi."* Horst Rüdiger, "Die Wiederentdeckung der antiken Literatur im Zeitalter der Renaissance," in *Geschichte der Textüberlieferung*, ed. Herbert Hunger *et al.* (Zürich: Atlantis, 1961), vol. 1, p. 525. *Humaniora* as short for *studia humaniora* has also been in use since the seventeenth century. *Historisches Wörterbuch der Philosophie*, ed. Joachim Ritter (Basel: Schwabe, 1974), pp. 1216f.

105. "Man is the most fortunate of creatures and consequently worthy of all admiration." Giovanni Pico, *Oration on the Dignity of Man*, trans. Elizabeth L. Forbes (Lexington, Ken.: Anvil, 1943), p. 1.

106. Kristeller, "Humanism and Scholasticism in the Italian Renaissance," *Byzantion* XVII (1944–45), 353–354.

107. Nikolaus Copernicus, *De Revolutionibus orbium coelestium* libri VI (Norimbergae: Johannes Petrium, 1543). Two Copernican revolutions would come from East Prussia. The first was that of Copernicus, who lay on his deathbed in Frauenburg, East Prussia, just prior to the publication of his *De Revolutionibus*. The second was by Immanuel Kant, who metaphorically termed his philosophy Copernican: *Kritik der reinen Vernunft*, B. xvii.

108. Andreas Vesalius, *De humani corporis fabrica* (Basel: A. Operinus, 1543). Vesalius was a man of his times. As an aspiring humanist, he took pains to write the *De humani* in a Ciceronian Latin, which was inaccessible to many of his colleagues. See Ludwig Edelstein, "Andreas Vesalius, the Humanist," *Bulletin of the History of Medicine* 14 (December 1943), 547–561.

109. Rodericus Castro, *Medicus-Politicus: sive de officiis medicopoliticis tractatus* (Hamburg: Frobeniano, 1614).

110. V. Nutton, "Humanist Surgery," in *The Medical Renaissance of the Sixteenth Century*, eds. A. Wear, R. K. French and I. M. Lonie (Cambridge: Cambridge University Press, 1985), p. 81.

111. Ibid., p. 85.

112. Dietrich von Engelhardt, "Virtue and Medicine During the Enlightenment in Germany," in *Virtue and Medicine*, ed. Earl E. Shelp (Dordrecht: Reidel, 1985), p. 66.

113. In the latter part of the eighteenth century, one finds various usages of "*humanistisch*" to refer to schools, studies, and commissions. Vito R. Giustiniani, "Homo, Humanus, and the Meanings of 'Humanism'," *Journal of the History of Ideas* 46 (April 1985), 172. Wilhelm von Humboldt was a key figure in the development of the idea of a humanistic education. Horst Rüdiger, *Wesen und Wandlung des Humanismus* (Hamburg: Hoffmann & Campe, 1937), Chapter 8, "Wilhelm von Humboldt und der Neuhumanismus." Humboldt provided a philosophical synthesis focused around the idea of *Humanität*. Through his ideas and personality, he was able to focus the idealistic strivings of the time in a rebirth of interest in the Greeks and their culture. See Richard

Newald, *Probleme und Gestalten des Deutschen Humanismus* (Berlin: de Gruyter, 1963), pp. 31–39.

114. As has been noted, the term Humanismus appears to have been introduced by Fr. I. Niethammer in *Der Streit des Humanismus und Philanthropismus in der Theorie des Erziehungsunterrichts unserer Zeit* (Jena, 1808). Niethammer, in introducing and supporting his view of humanistic education, contrasts it with Philanthropinismus. He characterizes an education based on Humanismus as "not so much focused on the collecting of particular facts, but much more so on exercising the spirit" (p. 162, author's translation). In contrast, an education based on Philanthropinismus is "not so much focused on exercising the spirit in and for itself, but much more on arming it with the greatest amount of useful data" (ibid.). His view of education presupposes a dialectical interaction between *Humanismus* and Philanthropinismus.

115. Horst Rüdiger, *Wesen und Wandlung des Humanismus* (Hamburg: Hoffmann & Campe, 1937), p. 13.

116. The ideal American physician in the nineteenth century should cultivate a "pure and elevated style of conversation, urbanity and gentleness of manners, and kindness of heart." Thomas Sewall, "A Charge Delivered to the Graduating Class of the Columbian College, D.C. at the Medical Commencement, March 22, 1827" (Washington: 1828), p. 6. Quoted in Chester R. Burns, "American Medical Ethics: Some Historical Roots," in *Philosophical Medical Ethics*, ed. S. F. Spicker and H. T. Engelhardt, Jr. (Dordrecht: Reidel, 1977), p. 22.

117. Francis Abbot, *Report of Addresses at a Meeting Held in Boston, May 30, 1867, to Consider the Conditions, Wants, and Prospects of Free Religion in America* (Boston, 1867), pp. 37–40, quoted in Stow Persons, *Free Religion* (New Haven: Yale University Press, 1947), pp. 47–48.

118. See, for example, Francis Ellingwood Abbot, *The Way Out of Agnosticism or the Philosophy of Free Religion* (Boston: Little, Brown, and Co., 1890).

119. *The Universal Kinship* (London: George Bell, 1906), pp. 328–9.

120. "The third humanism is the creation of an ideal sentiment over against the surrounding materialism of post-war times . . . and against the positivist and historicist understanding given to the ancients by scholars during the last half of the nineteenth century." Horst Rüdiger, *Wesen und Wandlung des Humanismus* (Hamburg: Hoffman & Campe, 1937), p. 280 [my translation].

121. This passage is taken from a speech given by Werner Jaeger at the opening of a symposium entitled "Das Gymnasium" held in Berlin on April 6, 1925. This speech appeared as *Antike und Humanismus* (Leipzig: Quelle & Meyer, 1925), pp. 5–6.

122. Ernst Robert Curtius, *Deutscher Geist in Gefahr* (Stuttgart: Deutsche Verlags-Anstalt, 1932), p. 129. "The complete humanism finds its expression in Plato's feast, where wine and beauty, eros and flute-playing, reflective profundity and priestly consecration are bound together in one." Curtius, "Humanismus als Initiative," in *Humanismus*, ed. Hans Oppermann (Darmstadt: Wissenschaftliche Buchgesellschaft, 1970), p. 169 [my translation].

123. For an excellent study of the movement, see J. David Hoeveler, Jr., *The New Humanism* (Charlottesville: University Press of Virginia, 1977). For a contemporary critique of the New Humanists, see C. Hartley Grattan (ed.), *The Critique of Humanism* (Freeport, N.Y.: Books for Libraries Press, 1968; 1st printing 1930). In particular, Hartley Grattan accuses Irving Babbitt of being sectarian (p. 4) and Malcolm Cowley finds the New Humanism to be doctrinal in contrast with humanism proper, which he takes to be an attitude ("Humanizing Society," in *The Critique of Humanism*, p. 63).

124. Irving Babbitt, *Democracy and Leadership* (Boston: Houghton Mifflin, 1953; 1st printing 1924, p. 186).

125. The New Humanists saw individuals confronted with the task of disciplining their animal natures so as to realize their capacities as humans. This led to an endorsement of the old distinction between the higher and lower nature of individuals. Paul Elmer More, *On Being Human* (Princeton, N.J.: Princeton University Press, 1936), pp. 7–17.

126. There was an attempt to find and establish bridges between the New Humanist movement in the United States and similar movements in Europe. The latter were apparently closely tied to Roman Catholicism, Anglicanism, and French Royalism. See Gorham Munson, *The Dilemma of the Liberated* (Port Washington, N.Y.: Kennikat Press, 1967; 1st printing, 1930), pp. 79–106, and Louis J. A. Mercier, *Le Mouvement Humaniste aus Etats-Unis: W. C. Brownell, Irving Babbitt, Paul Elmer More* (Paris: Librairie Hachette, 1928). Munson, for example, observes: "The Europeans either come to rest on Catholicism (Chesterton, Belloc, Massis, Maritain), which for many Americans seems impossible, involving an act of too much faith, and furthermore they feel too *psychologically* distant from Rome; or the Europeans dedicate themselves to some political movement such as French royalism (Maurras and his disciplines) which to some extent perverts their classical attitude; or finally they fall back on some personal philosophy, scarcely more than a strong predisposition in favor of the disinterested activity of the mind (Benda) or else very much . . . full of idiosyncrasies (Wyndham Lewis)" (p. 105). For a brief comparison of British, American, and French humanism of the 1920s, see T. S. Eliot, "Experiment in Criticism," *The Bookman* 70 (November 1929), 225–233.

127. T. S. Eliot, "Religion Without Humanism," in *Humanism and America*, ed. Norman Foerster (New York: Farrar and Rinehart, 1930), p. 107.

128. Ibid., p. 110.

129. Abraham Flexner, *Medical Education in the United States and Canada, A Report to the Carnegie Foundation for the Advancement of Teaching*, Bulletin No. 4 (New York: Carnegie Foundation, 1910).

130. "Philology in the technical sense is science, not humanism." Abraham Flexner, *The Burden of Humanism* (Oxford: Clarendon Press, 1928), p. 8.

131. Ibid., p. 12.

132. Ibid., p. 22.

133. "Humanism," *Encyclopaedia Britannica*, 11th ed. (1910), p. 872.

134. Kristeller, "Humanism and Scholasticism in the Italian Renaissance," *Byzantion* XVII (1944–45), 356.

135. Albert William Levi, *The Humanities Today* (Bloomington: Indiana University Press, 1970), p. 29.

136. William J. Bennett, *To Reclaim a Legacy* (Washington, D.C.: National Endowment for the Humanities, 1984), p. 2.

137. Ibid., p. 2.

138. Ibid., p. 3.

139. One of the early representatives of this genre is Jacques Maritain, *Humanisme integral* (Paris: S. Aubier, 1936).

140. See, for example, M. Petrosyan, *Humanism*, trans. Bryan Bean and Robert Daglish (Moscow: Progress, 1972). Chapter 2 is entitled "Formation and Development of the Marxist-Leninist Theory of Humanism," and Chapter 5 "Communism: the Fulfilment of Genuine Humanism." The first section of Chapter 4 bears the title "The Anti-Humanism of Present-Day Capitalism."

141. See, for example, Jean-Paul Sartre, *L'existentialisme est un humanisme*

(Paris: Nagel, 1946). One might also want to consult Martin Heidegger, "Brief über den 'Humanismus'," (1949) in *Gesamtausgabe* (Frankfurt/Main: Vittorio Klostermann, 1976), vol. 9, pp. 313–364.

142. Bernard Murchland, *Humanism and Capitalism* (Washington, D.C.: American Enterprise Institute, 1984), p. 54.

143. Ibid., p. 57.

144. "Humanism," *Great Soviet Encyclopedia* (New York: Macmillan, 1975), vol. 7, p. 550.

145. Kate Soper, *Humanism and Anti-Humanism* (London: Hutchinson, 1986).

146. For an example of a defense of socialist humanism, see George Novack, *Humanism and Socialism* (New York: Pathfinder Press, 1973). Terms allied to humanism have also been used in the title of books concerning socialism, evidently to indicate a desideratum of socialist development. Andras Hegedus et al., *The Humanisation of Socialism: Writings of the Budapest School* (London: Allison & Busby, 1976).

147. Quoted in Raya Dunayevskaya, *Philosophy and Revolution* (New York: Delacorte, 1973), pp. 181f.

148. M. Merleau-Ponty, *Humanism and Terror* (Boston: Beacon Press, 1969), trans. John O'Neill, p. 97.

149. Hirsh provides an account of Althusser's difficulties with the French Communist Party because of his "theoretical anti-humanism." See Arthur Hirsh, *The French New Left* (Boston: South End Press, 1981), pp. 159–177.

150. See also Merleau-Ponty's defense of the Soviet Union, which was written in response to Arthur Koestler's criticisms. Merleau-Ponty (1908–1961) argues, among other things, that the West's use of humanism has been one-sided and disingenuous. M. Merleau-Ponty, *Humanism and Terror* (n. 148 above).

151. Kate Soper, especially pp. 9–23.

152. Claude Bonnefoy, "L'homme est-il mort? un entretien avec Michel Foucault," *Arts* 38 (15 June 1966), 8–9.

153. Here one must also include such critics of Jean-Paul Sartre's subjectivism and humanism as Lévi-Strauss. Arthur Hirsh, *The French New Left: An Intellectual History from Sartre to Gorz* (Boston: South End Press, 1981), pp. 148–151.

154. Jean-François Lyotard, *The Postmodern Condition: A Report on Knowledge*, trans. G. Bennington and B. Massumi (Manchester: Manchester University Press, 1986).

155. Louis Althusser, *Pour Marx* (Paris: François Maspero, 1966). See especially chapter VII, "Marxisme et humanisme."

156. Raya Dunayevskaya, "Humanism and Marxism," in *The Humanist Alternative*, ed. Paul Kurtz (London: Pemberton Books, 1973).

157. *Great Soviet Encyclopedia*, 3rd ed., vol. 7, p. 551.

158. Loren Graham, "How History and Politics Affect Closure in Biomedical Discussions," in *Scientific Controversies*, ed. H. T. Engelhardt, Jr., and A. L. Caplan (New York: Cambridge, 1987), p. 251.

159. Ibid., pp. 249–264.

160. See, for example, Leroy Augenstein, *Come Let Us Play God* (New York: Harper & Row, 1969). Expansive views of the capacities of medicine were anticipated by equally expansive views of the capacities of science. "For however far modern science and technics have fallen short of their inherent possibilities, they have taught mankind at least one lesson: Nothing is impossible." Lewis Mumford, *Technics and Civilization* (New York: Harcourt, Brace, 1934), p. 435.

161. Alvin Toffler, *Future Shock* (London: Bodley Head, 1970).

162. An ancestral version of the lecture appeared some three years before its presentation in C. P. Snow, "The Two Cultures," *New Statesman* (6 Oct. 1956), 413–414. The lecture itself was printed as *The Two Cultures and the Scientific Revolution* (Cambridge: University Press, 1962). A second edition was then published with a substantial reflective postscript, *The Two Cultures: and a Second Look* (Cambridge: University Press, 1964). Snow's lecture is in part a theme rediscovered. Matthew Arnold, in a previous Rede lecture, had defended the humanities against criticisms developed by the protagonists of the sciences. See Arnold, *Literature and Science* (Cambridge: Cambridge University Press, 1882). Arnold was responding to Thomas H. Huxley, among others, who had criticized the humanities on a number of occasions, but in particular in an address to the members of the Liverpool Institution in 1882. See T. H. Huxley, "Science and Culture," in *Collected Essays* (London: Macmillan, 1893), vol. 3, pp. 134–159. Huxley charged the humanists of his day with failing to appreciate the "criticism of life" which modern science made possible (ibid., p. 150). "Thus I venture to think that the pretensions of our modern Humanists to the possession of the monopoly of culture and to the exclusive inheritance of the spirit of antiquity must be abated, if not abandoned" (ibid., p. 152). For his part Arnold, in an expanded version of his Rede lecture, set out to defend the humanities to the "work-a-day world" of the United States. See "Literature and Science," in *Discourses in America* (New York: Macmillan, 1906), pp. 72–137. Arnold concluded that "the majority of men will always require humane letters; and so much the more, as they have the more and the greater results of science to relate to the need in man for conduct, and to the need in him for beauty," (ibid., p. 137). It is interesting to note that Huxley in "Science and Culture" stressed a need for what can best be described as the social sciences ("a clear understanding of the conditions of social life", ibid., p. 158); he conceived of social phenomena as the "expression of natural laws" (ibid., p. 158). For a further elaboration on these themes, but this time addressed to the three cultures (i.e., the humanities, the social sciences, and the natural sciences), see Wolf Lepenies, *Die Drei Kulturen* (Munich: Hanser, 1985).

163. J. Bronowski, *Science and Human Values* (London: Hutchinson, 1961; 1st printing 1956). "I have been developing an ethic for science which derives directly from its own activity" (p. 71).

164. Humanistic psychology emerged as a field of investigation and therapy because of concerns similar to those that occasioned the contemporaneous rebirth of interest in the humanities. In fact, humanistic psychology was seen as drawing on the core of humanism, where "the essence of humanism, in both psychological and ethical areas, is that man is fully acknowledged to be human — that is, limited and fallible — and that in no way whatever is he superhuman or subhuman . . . [E]thical humanism . . . goes hand in hand with the scientific method." Albert Ellis, *Humanistic Psychotherapy* (New York: McGraw Hill, 1973), p. 2. Against this background understanding of humanism, humanistic psychology has been construed as "the study of the whole individual, by logico-empirical means that are distinctly human, for the purpose of helping him live a happier, more self-actualizing, and more creative existence. It completely accepts people with their human limitations; it particularly focuses upon and employs their experiences and their values; it emphasizes their ability to create and direct their own destinies; and it views them as holistic, goal-directed individuals who are important in their own right, just because they are alive and who (together with their fellow humans) have the right to continue to exist and to enjoy and fulfill themselves." Albert Ellis, *Humanistic Psychotherapy*, p. 3. In the "Articles of Association" of the

American Association of Humanistic Psychology (1962) the field was described as "primarily an orientation toward the whole of psychology rather than a distinct area or school. It stands for the respect for the worth of persons, respect for differences of approach, open-mindedness as to acceptable methods, and interest in exploration of new aspects of human behavior. As a 'third force' in contemporary psychology, it is concerned with topics having little place in existing theories and systems: e.g., love, creativity, self, growth, organism, basic need-gratification, self-actualization, higher values, being, becoming, spontaneity, play, humor, affection, naturalness, warmth, ego-transcendence, objectivity, autonomy, responsibility, meaning, fair play, transcendental experience, peak experience, courage, and related concepts." American Association of Humanistic Psychology, "Articles of Association," p. 2, quoted in John B. P. Shaffer, *Humanistic Psychology* (Englewood Cliffs, New Jersey: Prentice Hall, 1978), p. 2. The reference to humanistic psychology as a "third force" derives from Abraham Maslow's characterization of humanistic psychology as an alternative to behaviorism and psychoanalysis (see Albert Ellis, *Humanistic Psychotherapy*, p. 2). Use of the term "humanistic psychology" dates from at least the late 1950s. See John B. P. Shaffer, *Humanistic Psychology* (Englewood Cliffs, New Jersey: Prentice Hall, 1978), pp. 1–8.

As a social phenomenon, humanistic psychology was associated with the encounter groups of the Esalen Institute of Big Sur, California. The field became associated with a critique directed in the 1960s against what many perceived to be the dehumanization of psychology and Western society and against an alienation by contemporary culture of individuals from true human values so that their full potential was not realized. A number of persons played an important role in the development of the field. For illustrations of some of their viewpoints see John F. Bugental (ed.), *Challenges of Humanistic Psychology* (New York: McGraw Hill, 1967); Abraham Maslow, *Motivation and Personality* (New York: Harper and Row, 1954); Robert Ornstein, *The Mind Field: A Personal Essay* (New York: The Viking Press, 1976); William Schutz, *Joy: Expanding Human Awareness* (New York: Grove Press, 1967); Frank T. Severin (ed.), *Humanistic Viewpoints in Psychology* (New York: McGraw-Hill, 1965).

John B. Schaffer gives the following summary of the major foci of humanistic psychology.

"1. Humanism is strongly phenomenological or experiential: its starting point is conscious experience."

"2. Humanistic psychology insists on man's essential wholeness and integrity."

"3. Humanistic psychology, while acknowledging that there are clear-cut limits inherent in human existence, insists that human beings retain an essential freedom and autonomy."

"4. Humanistic psychology is antireductionistic in its orientation."

"5. Humanistic psychology, consistent with its strong grounding in existentialism, believes that human nature can never be fully defined" (John B. Schaffer, *Humanistic Psychology*, pp. 10, 12, 14, 16, 17).

Humanistic psychology was also associated with sensitivity training groups (first known as T groups) which were formed to develop in corporate managers a sensitivity to the interpersonal aspects of their positions.

These developments, which have been gathered under the rubric of humanistic psychology, evolved concurrently with a perception upon the part of some that the culture of the West was in the grip of a technologically mediated tyranny. The goal of liberating human potentials was thus made a part of the counter culture movements of the 1960s and early 1970s. See, for example, Theodore Roszak, *The Making of a Counter Culture: Reflections on the Technocratic Society and its Youthful Opposition* (Garden City, N.Y.: Doubleday and London: Faber, 1969).

A result of the broad application of the adjective "humanistic" is that "humanistic" and its cognates are now applied in novel ways. There is talk of humanizing the workplace. "Using the word humanizing is an attempt to find a word which avoids the usual connotations associated with various words used around the world to describe the same phenomena. For instance, one tends to associate self-management with Yugoslavia, co-determination with West Germany and industrial democracy with Norway. Job satisfaction and worker participation seem to be used more widely in the United States and Great Britain. Humanizing the workplace is the title chosen to embrace a wide spectrum of issues, concepts, and aspects of all efforts to have work enhance human beings." Richard N. Ottaway, *Humanizing the Work Place* (London: Croom Helm, 1977), p. 11.

Proposals have been made in favor of humanistic education where the hope was that "The time may indeed be near when an adequately comprehensive perspective on human development and functioning may be related to a growing technology capable of bringing this about. A major hope must be that this will lead to a fuller liberation of that which is most transcendently human in all persons, rather than a more effective means of maintaining current inequalities in both society and the schools." Richard H, Weller (ed.), *Humanistic Education* (Berkeley, Cal.: McCutchan Publishing Co., 1977), p. 26.

Moreover, a very expanded sense of the humanities has now been established in some quarters: "The humanities may be considered either as a group of disciplines which are discrete and separate, each with its unique methods of investigation, or as an inter-related field of human expression. The former perspective is that of the traditional liberal arts scholar. The latter is a newer field which has excited those who wish to use the interrelationships of the humanities as a tool, or device, for self-understanding and self-examination as well as a means of becoming intimately acquainted with the arts." Robert C. Frazier et al. (eds.), *The Humanities: A Quest for Meaning in Twentieth Century America* (Dubuque, Iowa: Kendall/Hunt, 1982), p. vii.

165. J. H. Plumb (ed.), *Crisis in the Humanities* (London: Penguin, 1964). See, in particular, Ernest Gellner, "The Crisis in the Humanities and the Mainstream of Philosophy," pp. 45–81.

166. Eric Ashby, *Technology and the Academics* (London: Macmillan, 1958). For a criticism of the culture of technology, see Lewis Mumford, *The Pentagon of Power* (New York: Harcourt Brace Jovanovich, 1970).

167. Richard Schwarz, *Humanismus und Humanität in der modernen Welt* (Stuttgart: Kohlhammer, 1965).

168. R. S. Crane, *The Idea of the Humanities* (Chicago: University of Chicago Press, 1967), vols. 1 and 2.

169. This hope was supported, for example, by educators like William Arrowsmith who, in the spirit of the New Humanists, endorsed "the ancient, crucial, high art of teaching, the kind of teaching which alone can claim to be called educational, an essential element in all noble human culture, and hence a task of infinitely more importance than research scholarship." William Arrowsmith, "The Future of Teaching," *The Politic Interest* 6 (Winter, 1967), 53. On the other hand, there was also critique: "Surely, the truly humanistic educator must strive to create a world which does not demand of our students acts of madness as the price for spiritual wholeness. Our primary need then is not for a liberal education but for one which is actively committed to an end. If

we are to break out of the empty rhetoric of liberal educational reform, scholarship may need to become allied with activism." Louis Kampf, "The Humanities and Inhumanities," *Nation*, 207 (September 30, 1968), 312.

170. Though published in the 1970s, Ivan Illich's *Medical Nemesis* (New York: Pantheon Books, 1976) captures many of the concerns born of the 1960s engendered by the impression that medical technology had acquired a momentum of its own, apart from and estranged from the interests and concerns of humans.

171. Edmund D. Pellegrino and Thomas McElhinney, *Teaching Ethics, the Humanities, and Human Values in Medical Schools* (Washington, D.C, 1982: Society for Health and Human Values), p. 1. The Society for Health and Human Values, especially through an allied institution, the Institute on Human Values in Medicine (the latter being heavily funded by the United States Government through the National Endowment for the Humanities), played a major role in fostering the development of programs in the medical humanities in medical schools. The National Endowment for the Humanities, following its charter from the U.S. Congress in the National Endowment for the Humanities Act of 1965, understands that the term humanities "includes, but is not limited to, the study of the following disciplines: history; philosophy; languages; linguistics; literature; archaeology; jurisprudence; the history, theory, and criticism of the arts; ethics, comparative religion; and those aspects of the social sciences that employ historical or philosophical approaches." National Endowment for the Humanities, *Overview of Endowment Programs* (Washington, D.C., 1987), p. 3.

172. Pellegrino and McElhinney, *Teaching Ethics*, p. 22.

173. Ibid., p. 26.

174. Ibid., p. 51.

175. Edmund D. Pellegrino, *Humanism and the Physician* (Knoxville: University of Tennessee Press, 1979), p. 17. Pellegrino's publication is one of a genre of such publications on the humanities, including volumes like *Humanistic Perspectives in Medical Ethics*, ed. Maurice B. Visscher (London: Pemberton, 1973).

176. Pellegrino, *Humanism and the Physician*, p. 9.

177. I use the term Third Humanism, recalling Horst Rüdiger's usage, but conjoining it with the principal themes that define the so-called "New Humanism." Rüdiger, *Wesen und Wandlung des Humanismus* (Hamburg: Hoffmann and Campe, 1937), pp. 279–297; J. David Hoeveler, Jr., *The New Humanism* (Charlottesville: University Press of Virginia, 1977).

178. Pellegrino, *Humanism and the Physician*, p. 14.

179. John W. Dodds anticipates the transition from an interest in the medical humanities to bioethics in an essay that appeared in 1969, drawn from discussions held in 1966. "And finally, if the doctor in twentieth-century culture is scientist-humanist, should he not bring his immense prestige to bear upon some of the ethical problems which relate medicine to society?" "The Physician as Humanist in a Technological Society," in *Medicine and Culture*, ed. F. N. L. Poynter (London: Wellcome Institute, 1969), p. 35.

180. For a review of the development and state of humanities teaching in American medical schools, see Thomas McElhinney (ed.), *Human Values Teaching Programs for Health Professionals* (Ardmore, Penn.: Whitmore, 1981).

IV. Competing Foundations for Bioethics and Health Care Policy

1. Though here and elsewhere health care policy and bioethics are mentioned separately, as has already been noted, bioethics should be understood

as providing the foundations for a morally justified health care policy, as well as for a vision of human well-being insofar as this arises in health care.

2. Contemporary humanist movements have roots in the late nineteenth and early twentieth centuries' interest in a non-religious worldview based on what humans share: a secular humanism. F. C. S. Schiller is a good example. ". . . I would not disclaim affinities with the great saying of Protagoras, that *Man is the Measure of all things*. Fairly interpreted, this is the truest and most important thing that any thinker ever has propounded" (p. xvii). Schiller, unlike most secular humanists of today, also maintained an interest in humanism as a commitment to a literature marked by grace and felicity of expression. "If Humanism can restore against such forces [e.g., the philosophical influences of such as Kant and Hegel] the lucid writing of the older English style, it will make Philosophy once more a subject gentlemen can read with pleasure." *Humanism: Philosophical Essays* (Freeport, N.Y.: Books for Libraries Press, 1969; 1st ed. 1903), p. xxii.

3. Anthony Collins, *A Discourse of Free-thinking* (London: 1713), p. 104. The Enlightenment engendered a deist literature that was often critical of revealed religion, Christianity in particular. A good example is Thomas Paine's *Age of Reason*. This literature was strongly condemned. For example, D. I. Eaton, who republished Paine's *Age of Reason*, was sent to the pillory and then to a long imprisonment at Newgate. He was also prosecuted for blasphemous libel for publishing George Houston's translation of the Baron de Holbach's (1723–1789) *Histoire critique de Jésus-Christ* (1770), which first appeared in English in 1799. In his preface, Eaton argued for toleration, as did most deists of the time. "Nothing can be clearer, therefore, than that it is contrary to the true spirit of Christianity (if we take it from the mouth of its founder), to call in the aid of the civil power to its support. If it is an emanation from God, he is all-powerful, and will protect it. —If it is an invention of man, it is then, and only then, that it has to dread the effects of criticism." *Ecce Homo! or, A Critical Enquiry into the History of Jesus Christ; Being a Rational Analysis of the Gospels* (London: D. I. Eaton, 1813), p. v; the edition appeared without indication of author or translator.

4. See Gordon Stein, "Freethought: Past and Present," *Free Inquiry* 1 (Winter 1980), 13–15.

5. Naturalism has been a term used at least since Karl Marx to contrast naturalism or humanism on the one hand and idealism and materialism on the other. Raya Dunayevskaya, *Philosophy and Revolution* (New York: Delacorte, 1973), p. 53. See also Yervant H. Krikorian (ed.), *Naturalism and the Human Spirit* (New York: Columbia University Press, 1944). The New Humanists characterized naturalism as a "wasteland"; they saw man as distinct from nature, such that the true excellences of being human had no equivalent in nature. Moreover, individuals needed to discipline themselves in order to direct their animal natures properly. See Paul Elmer More, *On Being Human* (Princeton, N.J.: Princeton University Press, 1936), esp. pp. 1–42.

6. Charles Hartshorne, *Beyond Humanism* (Chicago: Willett, Clark, 1937), pp. 2–3.

7. Charles F. Potter, *Humanism: A New Religion* (New York: Simon and Schuster, 1930), p. 14. Potter, one of the original signatories of the Humanist Manifesto, was first a Baptist and then a Unitarian preacher. After his views brought him into conflict with the Church of the Divine Paternity, of which he was the minister, he founded the First Humanist Society of New York. Potter was one among many Unitarian ministers who played an important role in the development of humanism and who were signers of the humanist manifestos,

as well as the Secular Humanist Declaration. The effect of scientific theism on Unitarianism in the latter part of the nineteenth and the early twentieth centuries is to have identified many Unitarian congregations and fellowships with humanist and indeed secular humanist moral and metaphysical understandings. In this the Free Religious Association, founded in 1867, played a crucial role. "Free religion was most immediately influential in the transformation of Unitarianism from a Christocentric religion to a pragmatic, humanistic theism, retaining the Christian name but actually being Christian only in the sense of recognizing its dependence upon the religious patterns of Western culture." Stow Persons, *Free Religion* (New Haven: Yale University Press, 1947), p. 154. Among the nineteenth-century critics of the Unitarians, because of their initial reluctance to accept the tenets of the Free Religious Association, was George Holyoake, who argued, "we find Unitarianism willing to cast off its own free churches, and looking coldly on its progressive preachers, we are little attracted by it. Orthodox Unitarianism makes no progress. It has retrograded since the days of Priestley and Belsham." George Holyoake, *The Trial of Theism* (London: Holyoake & Co., 1858), p. 163. Holyoake also took pains to attack Unitarian ministers who "have fallen into the error of confounding Secularism and Atheism" (p. 163). For an account written from the perspective of a participant in the Free Religious Association's development, see O. B. Frothingham, *The Religion of Humanity* (New York: David D. Francis, 1873).

There is a history, nearly as old, foreshadowing the humanist movements of the twentieth century, to be found in the origins of Ethical Culture. The Ethical Culture movement was founded by Felix Adler (1851–1933). Adler, a former Reform Jewish rabbi, convoked the initial members of the movement on May 15, 1876. He had, however, already espoused many of its foundational ideas in a sermon at Temple Emanu-El on October 11, 1873, under the title "The Judaism of the Future" (see Benny Kraut, *From Reform Judaism to Ethical Culture: the Religious Evolution of Felix Adler* [Cincinnati: Hebrew Union College Press, 1979]). It was not until February 21, 1877, that the New York Society for Ethical Culture was incorporated. Adler's influence was also significant in Europe. With his inspiration the Deutsche Gesellschaft für ethische Kultur was established in 1892. See *Die ethische Bewegung in Deutschland: eine Festausgabe der Deutschen Gesellschaft für ethische Kultur zum fünfzigjährigen Jubiläum der amerikanischen Muttergesellschaft* (Berlin: Verlag für ethische Kultur, 1926). In 1894 Die Ethische Gemeinde was founded in Vienna and in 1896 The International Ethical Union (IEU) was formed. See Horace L. Friess, *Felix Adler and Ethical Culture* (New York: Columbia University Press, 1981).

8. Paul H. Beattie, "Is Secular Humanism a Religion?," *Free Inquiry* 6 (Winter 1985), 12–17.

9. Julian Huxley (ed.), *The Humanist Frame* (New York: Harper, 1961), p. 48.

10. Oliver L. Reiser, *The Promise of Scientific Humanism* (New York: Oskar Piest, 1940). The progressive sentiments of this genre of humanism are conveyed in Reiser's articulation of the one commandment of humanism: "Have faith in man and the potentialities of his intelligence" (ibid., p. 246). Reiser, one of the signers of the first Humanist Manifesto, characterized scientific humanism as "the last hope of mankind." Reiser, *World Philosophy* (Pittsburgh, Pa.: University of Pittsburgh Press, 1948), p. 19. See also Cyril Bibby, "Towards a Scientific Humanist Culture," in *The Humanist Outlook*, ed. A. J. Ayer (London: Pemberton, 1968), pp. 13–27.

11. Sidney Hook, "The Ground We Stand On: Democratic Humanism," *Free Inquiry* 1 (Winter 1980), 8–10.

12. Charles F. Potter, *Humanism: A New Religion* (New York: Simon and Schuster, 1930), p. 125.

13. Corliss Lamont, *The Philosophy of Humanism* (New York: Frederick Ungar, 1965; 1st ed. 1949), pp. 23–25.

14. John Dewey published a book one year after the first Humanist Manifesto that supports a humanist religion, though he does not use the term. *A Common Faith* (New Haven, Conn.: Yale University Press, 1934).

15. Paul Kurtz (ed.), *Humanist Manifestos I and II* (Buffalo: Prometheus, 1985), pp. 9–10. The first Manifesto, from which the quotation is taken, was originally published in *The New Humanist* (May/June 1933).

16. Ibid., p. 10.

17. Ibid., p. 17. The second Manifesto first appeared in *The Humanist* 33 (September/October 1973), 4–9.

18. In all of this, one must not forget that there is a rather substantial history of Christian humanism, of which a most distinguished example is the priest, bastard, and scholar Desiderius Erasmus (1467–1536). One might consider his scholarly edition of the New Testament as an undertaking in Christian rather than secular humanism. In contrast, his edition of Aristotle can be seen as an undertaking within the secular humanism of the time.

19. Torcaso v. Watkins, 357 US 488, 495 n.11, 6 L Ed 2d 982, 987, 81 S Ct 1680 (1961).

20. Smith v. Board of School Com'rs of Mobile County, 655 F. Supp. 939 (S.D.Ala. 1987). For an argument that American Constitutional law has been invidiously secularized, and that it should be restored to its "traditional Judeo-Christian apprehension of law," see Robert R. Melnick, "Secularism in the Law: The Religion of Secular Humanism," *Ohio Northern University Law Review* 8 (1981), 329–357.

21. J. David Hoeveler, Jr., *The New Humanism* (Charlottesville: University Press of Virginia, 1977), p. 188. Russell Kirk, for example, referred to Irving Babbitt as his mentor and held that Babbitt was "perhaps the strongest conservative author in the whole range of modern American letters." Russell Kirk, *A Program for Conservatives* (Chicago: Henry Regnery Co., 1954), p. 20. For another appraisal by Kirk of Babbitt, see *The Conservative Mind* (Chicago: Henry Regnery, 1953), p. 366–377.

22. Smith v. Board of School Com'rs of Mobile County, 655 F. Supp. 939 (S.D.Ala. 1987), 968f.

23. Smith v. Board of School Com'rs at 986f.

24. Smith v. Board of School Com'rs of Mobile County 827 F.2d 687 (c.11) 1987.

25. For a collection of essays by members of the Advisory Council of the British Humanist Association, see A. J. Ayer, *The Humanist Outlook* (London: Pemberton, 1968).

26. *Encyclopedia of Associations*, 20th ed. (1986), p. 1474.

27. See, in particular, point 9 of the first Manifesto, which endorses the "religious emotions" of the humanist (p. 9).

28. Edward L. Ericson, *The Humanist Way* (New York: Continuum, 1988), p. 10.

29. Ibid., p. 11.

30. Paul Kurtz, *Forbidden Fruit: The Ethics of Humanism* (New York: Prometheus, 1988), p. 188).

31. Ibid., pp. 215–288.

32. Ibid., pp. 182–183.

33. Gerald A. Larue, "Euthanasia: The Time is Now," 6–8; Derek Humphry, "Active Voluntary Euthanasia," 9–11, in *Free Inquiry* 8 (Winter 1988).

34. Kurtz, *Forbidden Fruit* (n. 30), p. 109.

35. Paul Kurtz, "A Secular Humanist Declaration," *Free Inquiry* 1 (Winter 1980), 3–6.

36. This ideal of the Secular Humanist Declaration reflects one of the first and cardinal demands of the Free-thinkers. "By Free-Thinking then I mean, The Use of the Understanding, in endeavouring to find out the Meaning of any Proposition whatsoever, in considering the nature of the Evidence for or against it, and in judging of it according to the seeming Force or Weakness of the Evidence." Anthony Collins, *A Discourse of Free-thinking* (London: 1713), p. 5.

37. For the purpose of this volume, I accept the general Kantian argument that human reason is limited to the realm of human experience. The only exception is that one may deny the existence of an object if its concept can be shown to be unavoidably contradictory in any possible universe.

38. "New Secular Humanist Centers," *Free Inquiry* 6 (Fall 1986), 14; and Vern L. Bullough, "The Need for Friendship Centers," *Free Enquiry* 6 (Fall 1986), 14–15.

39. Charles F. Potter, for example, states clearly that: "Humanists take the only logical position in an age of science, and are agnostics." *Humanism: A New Religion* (New York:· Simon & Schuster, 1930), p. 8.

40. See Immanuel Kant, *Grundlegung zur Metaphysik der Sitten*, Akademie Textausgabe (Berlin: Walter de Gruyter, 1968), vol. 4, p. 438. Kant's point is that we can consider ourselves from the perspective of a moral community, even though we are not members of any actual moral community. ". . . we think of ourselves as free, we transport ourselves into the intelligible world as members of it and know the autonomy of the will together with its consequence, morality . . ." Ibid., p. 453; *Foundations of the Metaphysics of Morals*, trans. Lewis White Beck (Indianapolis: Bobbs-Merrill, 1959), p. 72.

41. The ten-point Nüremberg Code was articulated as part of the Nüremberg Military Tribunals' decision in United States v. Karl Brandt *et al.*, published in *Trials of War Criminals Before the Nüremberg Military Tribunals Under Control Council Law* No. 10 (Military Tribunal I, 1947; Washington, D.C.: U.S. Government Printing Office, 1948–49).

42. As Merleau-Ponty phrased it, "Revolutionary justice appeals to the future as its standard." M. Merleau-Ponty, *Humanisme et Terreur* (Paris: Gallimard, 1947), p. 30.

43. Kurtz, *Forbidden Fruit*, p. 250. The closing paragraph of Rüdiger's 1937 study of humanism intimates how uncertain the prospects of humanism are and how great the gulf is between the justification of moral action and the motivation of moral action. "The lineaments of the future rise unclearly before our eyes: predictions are as vain as programs. But if it is possible in this or some other way — perhaps it will be still possible for particular spirits to overcome the division between 'spirit' and 'soul' and to breathe life into the 'singular form' before its ruins in their collapse 'bury mankind'. It is destiny, which is hidden to rational insight, that will in the end decide" (Rüdiger, *Wesen and Wandlung*, p. 297 [my translation]).

V. A Secular Health Care Policy: Of This World but not Opposed to the Other

1. St. Thomas Aquinas, *Summa Theologica* I, Q. 1, art. 1. *The Basic Writings of Saint Thomas Aquinas*, ed. Anton C. Pegis, vol. 1 (New York: Random House, 1945), p. 6.

2. The Roman Catholic Church has as a matter of faith declared that the existence of God can be proven by reason alone. "If anyone shall have said that it is not possible to know certainly the one and true God who is our Lord and Creator by the light of natural human reason through those things that have been made, may he be anathema." *Constitutio dogmatica de fide catholica, Canones*, II. *De revelatione*, 1, from the Fourth Session of the Vatican Council, 24 April 1870 (my translation). For the Latin original, see *Conciliorum Oecumenicorum Decreta* (Basel: Herder, 1962), p. 786.

3. Edwin F. Healy, S.J., in the first chapter of his book on medical ethics (a volume on Roman Catholic medical ethics), states: "All men, then, are called upon to obey the natural law. Hence it matters not whether one be a Roman Catholic, a Protestant, a Jew, a pagan, or a person who has no religious affiliations whatsoever; he is nevertheless obliged to become acquainted with and to observe the teachings of the law of nature. In the present volume all the obligations which are mentioned flow from the natural law, unless the contrary is evident from the contest." *Medical Ethics* (Chicago: Loyola University Press, 1956), p. 7.

4. "The revolutionary working class has produced a new morality, which is based on a scientific insight into the progress of social development, into the world-historical role of the working class as the grave of capitalism and as the creator of the new socialist society, and into the goals and tasks of the struggle of the working class." Georg Assmann *et al.* (eds.), *Wörterbuch der marxistisch-leninistischen Soziologie* (Berlin: Dietz, 1977), p. 444.

5. David Hume, for example, in 1739 argued that morality "consists not in any matter of fact, which can be discover'd by the understanding." *A Treatise of Human Nature* (Oxford: Clarendon Press, 1964), Book III, sec. 1, p. 468.

6. G. E. Moore, *Principia Ethica* (Cambridge: University Press, 1965), p. 10.

7. For a provocative illustration see: H. T. Engelhardt, Jr., "The Disease of Masturbation: Values and the Concept of Disease," *Bulletin of the History of Medicine* 48 (Summer 1974), 234–48; see also H. T. Engelhardt, "Clinical Problems and the Concept of Disease," in *Health, Disease, and Causal Explanations in Medicine*, eds. L. Nordenfelt and B. I. Lindahl (Dordrecht: Reidel, 1984), pp. 225–233.

8. Most actual attempts to ground bioethics or health care policy philosophically are mixed in their foundations. In order to avoid the confusions likely to result from references to mixed examples, the accent of this chapter will be primarily on displaying possibilities for argument. Unlike the previous chapters which focused on the history of the development of a number of ideas (e.g., secularity, humanism, and secular humanism), here the accent is on the kinds of philosophical considerations that support a secular humanist account of health and medicine.

9. Kant envisaged an individual who rejects all commitment to charity. Kant recognized that this is not logically inconsistent: a criterion he employed to distinguish moral from immoral actions. That is, Kant attempted to deliver a system of morality founded on what can be willed without contradiction as a universal law. This approach was meant to derive morality from the very notion of a rational agent. However, one can consistently affirm the eschewal

of charity as a universal law of nature. "What concern of mine is it? Let each one be as happy as heaven wills, or as he can make himself; I will not take anything from him or even envy him; but to his welfare or to his assistance in time of need I have no desire to contribute."

Because his usual test for contradiction (or irrationality) would not suffice, Kant expanded his argument to include "contradictions in will."

"For a will which resolved this would conflict with itself, since instances can often arise in which he would need the love and sympathy of others, and in which he would have robbed himself, by such a law of nature springing from his own will, of all hope of the aid he desires." Immanuel Kant, *Foundations of the Metaphysics of Morals*, trans. L. W. Beck (Indianapolis: Library of Liberal Arts, 1959), p. 41: *Grundlegung zur Metaphysik der Sitten*, Akademie Textausgabe (Berlin: Walter de Gruyter, 1968), vol. 4, p. 423.

10. Here one would need to include every philosophy that has claimed to establish a morality on the basis of rational arguments available to persons as such.

11. F. B. Livingstone, "The Distributions of the Abnormal Hemoglobin Genes and Their Significance for Human Evolution," *Evolution* 18 (1964), 685.

12. H. T. Engelhardt, Jr., *The Foundations of Bioethics* (New York: Oxford University Press, 1986), pp. 157–201.

13. Richard H. Post, "Population Differences in Red and Green Color Vision Deficiency: A Review, and a Query on Selection Relaxation," *Eugenics Quarterly* 9 (March 1962), 131–146.

14. Since the treatment of diseases and of ill-persons is a social endeavor embedded in both formal and informal social structures, disease categories are as much determined socially as individually. This is to say the least an involved issue, which thankfully falls beyond the focus of this work. See H. T. Engelhardt, Jr., *The Foundations of Bioethics* (New York: Oxford University Press, 1986), pp. 184–195.

15. Humanist Manifesto II states, for example, "Ethics is *autonomous* and *situational* . . . [it] stems from human need and interest . . . Human life has meaning because we create and develop our futures." Well-being is thus an individual and cultural creation. Paul Kurtz (ed.), *Humanist Manifestos I and II* (Buffalo, N.Y.: Prometheus, 1973), p. 17.

16. Paul Kurtz (ed.), *Humanist Manifestos I and II* (Buffalo, N.Y.: Prometheus, 1973), p. 25.

17. Joseph Margolis, "The Concept of Disease," *The Journal of Medicine and Philosophy* 1 (1976), 238–55.

18. The Secular Humanist Declaration states: "Nor do we believe that any one church should impose its views of moral virtue and sin, sexual conduct, marriage, divorce, birth control, or abortion, or legislate them for the rest of society." *Free Inquiry* 1 (Winter 1980/81), 5. Here again one finds an instance where, from different arguments, secular humanism and Secular Humanism support the same conclusions.

19. Joseph Fletcher, *Situation Ethics* (Philadelphia: Westminster Press and London: SCM Press, 1966).

20. Paul Kurtz (ed.), *Humanist Manifestos I and II* (Buffalo, N.Y.: Prometheus, 1973), p. 28.

21. "A Secular Humanist Declaration," *Free Inquiry* 1 (Winter 1980/81), 7.

22. Joseph Fletcher, *Morals and Medicine* (Boston: Beacon Press, 1960).

23. Joseph Fletcher, *The Ethics of Genetic Control* (Garden City, N.Y.: Doubleday Anchor, 1974).

24. Joseph Fletcher, "Morality Without Religion," *Free Inquiry* 1 (Winter

1980/81), 39.

25. See, for example, Marvin Kohl (ed.), *Beneficent Euthanasia* (Buffalo: Prometheus Books, 1975); Marvin Kohl, "Euthanasia and the Right to Life," in *Philosophical Medical Ethics*, ed. Stuart Spicker and H. T. Engelhardt, Jr., (Dordrecht: D. Reidel, 1977), pp. 73–84; Kohl, *Infanticide and the Value of Life* (Buffalo: Prometheus Books, 1978); and Kohl, "Moral Arguments for and Against Maximally Treating the Defective Newborn," in *Euthanasia and the Newborn*, ed. R. C. McMillan *et al.* (Dordrecht: Kluwer, 1987), pp. 233–252. Given the Humanist Manifesto II's statement that "Ethics stems from human need and interest," one would not expect a categorical condemnation of euthanasia as long as it is not undertaken against the wishes of the individual involved. Paul Kurtz (ed.), *Humanist Manifestos I and II* (Buffalo, N.Y.: Prometheus, 1973), p. 17.

26. "A Secular Humanist Declaration," point 4, *Free Inquiry* 1 (Winter 1980/81), 5.

27. See, for example, the treatment of the religious significance of suffering by the Council of Trent, Session XIV, 25 November 1551, especially Chapter 8, "*De satisfacionis necessitate et frutu*" and chapter 9, "*De operibus satisfactionis.*" Denziger, pp. 1689–1693.

28. Paul Kurtz, *In Defense of Secular Humanism* (Buffalo, N.Y.: Prometheus Books, 1983).

29. One should note that such a commitment need not be seen as integral to Orthodox Christianity. Thus, at Vespers and in the Divine Liturgy one prays: "A Christian ending to our life, painless, blameless, peaceful; and a good defence before the dread Judgment Seat of Christ." Isabel F. Hapgood, *Service Book* (Englewood, N.J.: Antiochian Orthodox Christian Archdiocese, 1983), 6th ed.

30. Gerald Kelly, "The Duty of using Artificial Means of Preserving Life" *Theological Studies* II (1950), 203–20.

31. Robert Nozick perceptively draws the distinction between respect of free choice as a constraint on human action, and what values we might assign to acting freely or to free choice. *Anarchy, State, and Utopia* (New York: Basic Books, 1974), pp. 30–34.

32. Because of this grounding of a morality for moral strangers in terms of the decision of individuals to negotiate peaceably, only those entities that can negotiate are persons in the strict sense with an unimpeachable claim to respect: As a result, the moral status of not only fetuses but infants and severely senile adults is derivative. In addition, definitions of death oriented on higher brain centers will be the most plausible. For a discussion of these issues, see H. T. Engelhardt, Jr., *The Foundations of Bioethics* (New York: Oxford, 1986), pp. 202–249.

33. Ludwig Wittgenstein, *Philosophical Investigations*, trans. G. E. M. Anscombe (Oxford: Basil Blackwell, 1963), § 371.

34. "Elemente zu einer Grammatik," Immanuel Kant, *Prolegomena zu einer jeden künftigen Metaphysik*, Akademietextausgabe IV, p. 323.

35. In commenting on the status of grammatical, categorial, or transcendental knowledge, Stanley Cavell notes that such knowledge is "meant to provide us with not more knowledge of matters of fact, but the knowledge of what would count as various 'matters of fact'. Is this empirical knowledge? Is it a priori? It is a knowledge of what Wittgenstein means by grammar — the knowledge Kant calls 'transcendental'." "Availability of Wittgenstein's Later Philosophy," in George Pitcher (ed.), *Wittgenstein: The Philosophical Investigations* (New York: Doubleday, 1966), p. 175.

36. G. W. F. Hegel, *The Philosophy of Right*, § 303.

37. Ibid., § 270, Zusatz.

38. See, for example, Aristotle's *Politics* 7.4.1326b and *Nicomachean Ethics* 9.10.1170b. It is one of the ironies of history that Aristotle, the tutor of Alexander, who would create one of the first large-scale states of the ancient world, wrote his *Politics* with a nostalgia for the city-states of a past era. He gave us few helpful suggestions about how one might morally compass within a large-scale state a number of divergent moral communities.

39. In playing on the history of Latin words associated with *humanitas*, one might also recommend the term *personiter* to identify that mode of action in accord with the constraint to respect the choices of innocent persons.

40. See, for example, Katherine F. Drew (trans.), *The Lombard Laws* (Philadelphia: University of Pennsylvania Press, 1973), and Drew (trans.), *The Burgundian Code* (Philadelphia: University of Pennsylvania Press, 1972).

41. Lea, in his classical treatise on torture, indicates that under ancient Germanic law free persons were immune from torture, unlike individuals in the Mediterranean world generally and later the Christian world. This inviolability of the individual led to a quite different sense of propriety and deportment on the part of individuals. "For the cringing suppliant of the audience chamber, abjectly prostrating himself before a monarch who combines in his own person every legislative and executive function, we have the freeman of the German forests, who sits in council with his chief, who frames the laws which both are bound to respect, and who pays to that chief only the amount of obedience which superior vigor and intellect may be able to enforce . . . This personal independence of the freeman is one of the distinguishing characteristics of all the primitive Teutonic institutions." Henry Charles Lea, *Torture* (Philadelphia: University of Pennsylvania Press, 1866; reprinted 1973), pp. 24–5.

42. In their old Germanic communities, individuals appear generally to have been consulted on the actions of their leaders. The consent of the assembled freemen was necessary for the resolution of significant issues. In all of this they deported themselves in a way that suggested authority flowed from the individuals to the community. "On small matters the chiefs consult; on larger questions the community; but with this limitation, that even the subjects, the decision of which rests with the people, are first handled by the chiefs . . . It is a foible of their freedom that they do not meet at once and as if commanded, but a second and a third day is wasted by dilatoriness in assembling: when the mob is pleased to begin, they take their seats carrying arms." *Germania*, in *Tacitus*, trans. M. Hutton (Cambridge, Mass.: Harvard University Press, 1980), pp. 147, 149.

43. Dudo of St. Quentin (ca. 970–1043) records an interchange between Rollo, the First Duke of Normandy (ruled 911–932), and Charles the Simple (ruled 898–929), King of France, when the former was persuaded to do homage to the king. When he was told to kiss the emperor's foot, he asked one of his comrades to do so in his place. The man forthwith lifted the king's foot to his mouth, laying the king flat on his back. Peter Foote and David M. Wilson, *The Viking Achievement* (London: Sidgwick & Jackson, 1980), p. 79.

44. "That the individual shall have full protection in person and in property is a principle as old as the common law . . ." Samuel Warren and Louis Brandeis, "The Right to Privacy," *Harvard Law Review* 4 (1890), 193.

45. See, for example, Erwin Hölzle, *Die Idee einer altgermanischen Freiheit vor Montesquieu: Fragmente aus der Geschichte politischer Freiheitsbestrebungen in Deutschland, England und Frankreich vom 16.–18. Jahrhundert* (München: R. Oldenburg, 1925), pp. 59–101.

46. Natanson v. Kline, 186 Kan. 393, 404, 350 P.2d 1093, 1104 (1960).

47. The retreat was signaled by the Supreme Court in its July 3, 1989, decision in Webster v. Reproductive Health Services, US SupCt, No. 88–605.

48. The United States of America at its inception had a secular character, due in great measure to the deist and general secular sentiments of many of its founders. Though the Constitution in no way established a religion and through the First Amendment forbade the federal establishment of a religion, the United States generally understood itself as a Christian nation. This has been affirmed by the Supreme Court, which has opined that "we are a Christian people." Church of the Holy Trinity v. United States, 143 US 457 (1892), and United States v. Macintosh, 283 US 605 (1931). In the former case, the Court even held that the Christian religion was part of the common law of Pennsylvania (at 470). It is only recently that the Constitution has been viewed in a fully secular fashion. See, for example, Tessim Zorach v. Andrew G. Clauson et al., 343 US 306, 96 L ed 954, 72 S Ct 679 (1951); Roy R. Torcaso v. Clayton K. Watkins, 367 US 488, 6 L ed 2d 982, 81 S Ct 1680 (1961); and School District of Abington Township v. Edward L. Schempp et al., William J. Murray et al. v. John N. Curlett et al., 374 US 203, 10 L ed 2d 844, 83 S Ct 1560 (1963).

49. From the very beginning, and even prior to Locke's (1632–1704) influence, the Americans saw themselves as conveying authority to the government through actual contract or covenant. One might think of the Mayflower Compact, through which the signers on November 11, 1620, stated that "[we] do by these Presents, solemnly and mutually in the Presence of God and one of another, covenant and combine ourselves together into a civil Body Politick, for our better Ordering and Preservation, and Furtherance of the Ends aforesaid; And by Virtue hereof to enact, constitute, and frame, such just and equal Laws, Ordinances, Acts, Constitutions and Offices, from time to time, as shall be thought most meet and convenient for the General good of the Colony . . ." The Americans, who wrote a number of constitutions, had no difficulty seeing civil rights justified in an actual historical contract.

50. For a definitive study of the limits of the authority conveyed to the central government by the compact styled the Constitution of the United States, see Alexander H. Stephens, *A Constitutional View of the Late War Between the States: Its Causes, Character, Conduct and Results* (Philadelphia: National Publishing Co, 1868, 1870), 2 vols. For another treatment of some of the controversies over the central government's authority, see Charles Warren, "Legislative and Judicial Attacks on the Supreme Court of the United States—a History of the Twenty-fifth Section of the Judiciary Act," *American Law Review* 47 (Jan. 1913), 1–34 and (Mar. 1913), 161–189.

51. It is interesting to note that, in a vain attempt to prevent the dissolution of the Union, the American Congress on 2 March 1861 passed by the required two-thirds majority an amendment that would have barred the Federal Government from interfering with the "peculiar institution." This is the only amendment that was submitted to the states for ratification signed by a president. It received sufficient votes despite the absence of many Southern senators, and no doubt would have been adopted, had the prime cause of the war been slavery. The proposed Thirteenth Amendment read: "No amendment shall be made to the Constitution which will authorize or give to Congress the power to abolish or interfere, within any State, with the domestic institutions thereof, including that of persons held to labor or service by the laws of said State."

52. There is a contrast between the Preamble to the American Constitution and the body of the document only if one does not recognize that the authors for the most part presumed that the formal procedural structures they

established would free men to act so that the result would be the establishment of justice, the ensuring of domestic tranquillity, and the promotion of the general welfare.

53. The American constitution and the founding of the law in Iceland (A.D. 930) share in common an appeal to consent for authority. David Friedman, "Efficient Institutions for the Private Enforcement of Law," *Journal of Legal Studies* XIII (June 1984), 379–397; "Private Creation and Enforcement of Law: A Historical Case," *Journal of Legal Studies* VIII (March 1979), 399–415. For the Icelanders, the law was seen as grounded not in reason, but as derived from the authority of human agreement. Pagan Icelandic law came into existence for the very practical purpose of maintaining peace and order. It was not seen as justified in a content-full vision of justice. Remarkably, Icelandic law went out of existence as a pagan institution when the last pagan law-sayer, Thorgeir, argued that, rather than Christians and pagans possessing different laws and thus being out of law with each other, Christianity should be established with special protections for the rights of the pagans. P. G. Foote and D. M. Wilson, *The Viking Achievement* (London: Sidgwick & Jackson, 1980), p. 60. Original accounts of old Icelandic law and customs are available in *Njals Saga*, the *Gragas*, and the *Laxdaela Saga*. In this regard, the pagan Germanic approach, the perspective of Reykjavik, contrasted with Greek and Roman reflection that often attempted rationally to ground the law in particular conceptions of justice. Instead, as in English customary law, which formed the background assumptions of English common law (i.e., the law common to the counties of England), one appealed to precedents (taken for the purposes of this volume as analogous to past agreements), not reason, in order to establish how the law is to be understood. For example, consider the following remark about English law. "Sir, the law is as I say it is, and so it has been laid down ever since the law began; and we have several set forms which are held as law, and so held and used for good reason, though we cannot at present remember that reason." Yearbook 36, Henry VI, folio 25b–26 (Fortescue, C. J.). Ancient Icelandic law similarly depended on customary understandings. With respect to Iceland, consider a tenth-century Icelandic woman who is reported to have secured a summary divorce to her advantage on a technicality by sewing her husband a shirt that would blow open, revealing his nipples. "Thord came over. Gudrun told him about the shameful treatment she had received and asked him how she could get back at Thorvald. Thord smiled and said: 'For this I have good advice. Make him a shirt with a wide neck opening and then declare yourself divorced from him.' Gudrun had no objection to this and no more was said. Gudrun declared herself divorced from Thorvald that very same spring and went home to Laugar. After that a settlement of Thorvald's and Gudrun's property was made, and she got half of all the wealth; and by that time her half share amounted to more than before. They had lived together for two years." A. Margaret Arent (trans.), *The Laxdoela Saga* (Seattle: University of Washington Press, 1964), p. 85. In all this, the point is illustrative rather than strictly historical: to show systems of governmental authorities based on consent.

54. Outside considerations of constitutional law, rights to privacy can be understood in terms of the four torts associated with invasion of privacy: (1) intrusion on an individual's seclusion, solitude, or private affairs; (2) public disclosure of embarrassing facts; (3) placing an individual before the public in some false fashion; and (4) use without permission of an individual's name or likeness. Edward J. Bloustein, "Privacy as an Aspect of Human Dignity," in *Philosophical Dimensions of Privacy*, ed. Ferdinand Schoeman (Cambridge:

Cambridge University Press, 1984), p. 158. In this book I am not referring to rights to privacy in any of these senses. Instead, my focus is on the rights of individuals over against their governments, which have been expressed in American law as constitutional rights of privacy. It is very likely that the notion of rights to privacy gained currency in legal literature through Samuel Warren and Louis Brandeis in 1890 in "The Right to Privacy," *Harvard Law Review* 4, 193–220, where the accent was primarily on issues of tort law. Some thirty years later as a Supreme Court Justice, Brandeis gave expression to his view regarding rights to privacy in a dissenting opinion: "The makers of our Constitution undertook to secure conditions favorable to the pursuit of happiness. They recognized the significance of man's spiritual nature, of his feelings and of his intellect. They knew that only a part of the pain, pleasure, and satisfactions of life are to be found in material things. They sought to protect Americans in their beliefs, their thoughts, their emotions and their sensations. They conferred, as against the Government, the right to be let alone — the most comprehensive of rights and the right most valued by civilized men." Olmstead v. United States, 277 U.S. 438, 478 (1928), (Brandeis, J., dissenting). For a general study of the development of concepts of privacy in the law, see Tom Gerety, "Redefining Privacy," *Harvard Civil Rights-Civil Liberties Law Review* 12 (Spring 1977), 233–296.

55. The constitutional concept of rights to privacy as limits on governmental intrusions was best articulated in decisions such as Griswold v. Connecticut, 381 U.S. 479, 85 S.Ct. 1678, 14 L.Ed.2d 510 (1965); Eisenstadt v. Baird, 405 U.S. 438, 92 S.Ct. 1029, 31 L.Ed.2d 349 (1972); and Roe v. Wade, 410 U.S. 113 (1973). There is no question that the possible exception made for "compelling state interests" is troubling, given the arguments in this chapter. The concept of privacy is now in retreat: see In re Cruzan 58 LW 4916 (June 25, 1990).

56. The crucial importance of the Ninth Amendment was accented by Justice Arthur Goldberg in his concurring opinion in Griswold v. Connecticut, 381 U.S. at 493. Generally, rights to privacy have been seen to involve the First, Fourth, and Fifth Amendments, in addition to the Ninth. See John E. Nowak, Ronald D. Rotunda, and J. Nelson Young, *Constitutional Law* (St Paul, Minn.: West, 1983), pp. 1412–1414.

In defending his viewpoint, Goldberg argues that the Ninth Amendment is "almost entirely the work of James Madison. It was introduced in Congress by him and passed the House and Senate with little or no debate and virtually no change in language. It was proffered to quiet expressed fears that a bill of specifically enumerated rights could not be sufficiently broad to cover all essential rights and that the specific mention of certain rights would be interpreted as a denial that others were protected." Griswold v. Connecticut at 488.

"In sum, I believe that the right of privacy in the marital relation is fundamental and basic — a personal right, retained by the people, within the meaning of the Ninth Amendment. Connecticut cannot constitutionally abridge this fundamental right, which is protected by the Fourteenth Amendment from infringement by the States." Griswold v. Connecticut at 499. For a study of the jurisprudential roots of a constitutional right to privacy, see David M. O'Brien, *Privacy, Law, and Public Policy* (New York: Praeger, 1979), esp. pp. 177–199.

57. Bennett B. Patterson, *The Forgotten Ninth Amendment* (Indianapolis: Bobbs-Merrill, 1955), pp. 1–2.

58. Individuals often falsely compare the controversies regarding abortion with those regarding slavery. But this flies in the face of history. The Romans

recognized that their erudite Greek slaves were persons in the moral sense, even though they treated them as lacking legal rights. (Thomas Wiedemann, *Greek and Roman Slavery* [Baltimore: Johns Hopkins University Press, 1981].) Indeed, the traditional Western justification of slavery presupposed that slaves were individuals who were conquered in war or whose ancestors were persons conquered in war. (Hugo Grotius [1583–1645], *De Jure et Belli ac Pacis*, Book III, Chaps. 7–8.) So, too, Southern theories of slavery acknowledge slaves as persons capable of eternal salvation (Fred A. Ross, *Slavery Ordained of God* [New York: Lippincott, 1859]). Indeed, in some Southern states such as Texas, slaves were recognized as having the status of villeins at old feudal law (A. E. K. Nash, "Texas Justice in the Age of Slavery: Appeals Concerning Blacks and the Antebellum State Supreme Court," *Houston Law Review* 8 [1981], 438–456).

59. It is worth noting that hereditary slavery was recognized by a number of Southerners as violating natural law, and that there was moral opposition in the South, especially in Texas, to the holding of slaves. Consider the following statement by Judah Benjamin almost two decades before he joined the Confederate Cabinet. "The position that slavery is a contravention of the law of nature is established by the concurrent authority of writers on international law and of adjudications of courts of justice, from the era of Justinian to the present day . . ." (Eli N. Evans, *Judah P. Benjamin* [New York: Macmillan Free Press, 1988], p. 38). In contrast, consider St. Paul's advice, "Slaves, obey your earthly masters with respect and fear, and with sincerity of heart, just as you would obey Christ . . . And masters, treat your slaves in the same way. Do not threaten them, since you know that he who is both their Master and yours is in heaven, and there is no favoritism with him" (Ephesians 6:5, 9). Also, "All who are under the yoke of slavery should consider their masters worthy of full respect, so that God's name and our teaching may not be slandered" (I Tim. 6:1). So, too, "Slaves, obey your earthly masters in everything; and do it, not only when their eye is on you and to win their favor, but with sincerity of heart and reverence for the Lord" (Col. 3:22). St Peter repeated the same advice: "Slaves, submit yourselves to your masters with all respect, not only to those who are good and considerate, but also to those who are harsh" (I Peter 2:18). Also, Philemon appears to be a letter concerning the return of a fugitive slave, Onesimus. The New Testament need not be seen as approving of slavery. It is, however, tolerant of slavery and offers the conditions for Christians holding slaves and being held as slaves. If nothing else, the New Testament must be regarded as opposed to liberation theology (which is perhaps a symptom of the fundamental secularization of Christianity). For early Christianity, slaves were to accept their status. "But let them rather endure slavery to the glory of God, that they may obtain a better freedom from God. Let them not desire to be set free at the Church's expense, that they be not found the slaves of lust." Ignatius to Polycarp, IV. 3, in *The Apostolic Fathers*, trans. Kirsopp Lake (Cambridge, Mass.: Harvard University Press, 1965), vol. 1, p. 273. This toleration sprang naturally from a willingness to accept injustice and martyrdom in order to witness to a transcendent religious commitment. There was little interest in liberating this world.

60. "To guard against transgressions of the high powers herein delegated, we declare that every thing in this bill of rights, is excepted out of the general powers of government, and shall forever remain inviolate . . ." The Texas Constitution of August 28, 1845, art. 1, sec. 21, *Documents of Texas History* (Austin: Steck, 1963), p. 150. The current Constitution of Texas, written after the brutal occupation subsequent to the loss of the Southern

War of Independence, has preserved this passage; see art. 1, sec. 29. However, the moral corruption consequent on unrestrained immigration from those States that participated in the aggression of the Late Unpleasantness has led to some minor additions and clarifications of the amendments. Chief among these has been the disallowal of bail for some non-capital offenses. See Article I, Section 11. Perhaps even this can be justified, given the central government's constraint on the generous use of the hangman's rope.

61. Here is not the place to look to the philosophical foundations and significance of constitutions or original societal compacts. However, there are good reasons for regarding constitutions somewhat as charters for corporations, so that initial rules can be established regarding who may enter subsequently as shareholders and with what rights to vote or to draw on common resources. None of this can be given a full account without revising the received understanding of the state. Nor is this the place to explore this issue in detail. For more on this matter, see H. T. Engelhardt, Jr., *The Foundations of Bioethics* (New York: Oxford, 1986), pp. 135–145.

62. In *The Foundations of Bioethics* (pp. 127–135) I distinguish among private, communal, and general ownership. The border between general and other ownership will often be unclear, or TEYKU. See pp. 98f. In such cases, matters are best decided by majority vote, since this recruits as much authority as possible to resolve a dispute about things. However, the authority limiting character of persons will never allow majoritarian vote to set aside areas of rights to privacy.

63. If the foundation of a secular morality is mutual respect in peaceable negotiation, then property will derive from the capacities one has prior to any negotiation, the products one has made, alone or with consenting others, and the common wealth that results from communal undertakings. There will remain major difficulties in showing how any particular individual or particular society can exhaustively own natural resources. However, the line between state property and private property should be no more mysterious than the line between property owned by IBM and the property owned by its employees and shareholders. One should generally be able to decide who owns what by looking at the process of acquisition and transfer. Much would need to be said here about how to draw the line between private and public property, and the implication of this line for the provision of health care. See H. T. Engelhardt, Jr., *The Foundations of Bioethics* (New York: Oxford, 1986), especially pp. 127–135, 336–374.

64. See in particular, *Protection of Human Subjects*, 45 Code of Federal Regulations, 46.116(a).

65. National Commission for the Protection of Human Subjects of Biomedical and Behavioral Research, *The Belmont Report* (Washington, D.C.: U.S. Government Printing Office, 1978).

66. Phillip Hammond has argued, for example, that "The rhetoric of procedure thus becomes the new common or civil religion." "Pluralism and Law in the Formation of American Civil Religion," in Robert Bellah and Phillip Hammond, *Varieties of Civil Religion* (San Francisco: Harper & Row, 1980), p. 160.

67. In the absence of fraud and coercion, the market reflects the definition of justice given in Justinian's *Institutes*, restating Ulpianus, where justice is defined as "the constant and perpetual wish to render everyone his due" (*justitia est constans et perpetua volunts jus suum cuique tribuens*). Flavius Petrus Sabbatius Justinianus, *The Institutes of Justinian*, trans. T. C. Sanders (West-

port, Conn.: Greenwood Press, 1970), Book I.1, p. 5. Each person is given what that person has implicitly agreed is his.

68. Common property may be disposed of as determined in the agreement (e.g., constitution) uniting participants (e.g., citizens) in a common endeavor.

69. Alvin Toffler, *Future Shock* (London: Bodley Head, 1970), p. 267.

70. What has been provided is the intellectual solution to a puzzle: can a secular morality be justified in general terms, even after the collapse of the modern endeavour of justifying a content-full moral vision on the basis of reason alone? The considerations are about justification and not about motivation, though the conclusions justify certain forms of coercion, a genre of justified motivation. As such, this volume is a special endeavour in controversy theory: it addresses the possibility of resolving moral controversies between moral strangers with moral authority. See H. Tristram Engelhardt, Jr., and Arthur L. Caplan (eds.), *Scientific Controversies: Case Studies in the Resolution and Closure of Disputes in Science and Technology* (Cambridge: Cambridge University Press, 1987). I am specially in debt to Tom Beauchamp's article, "Ethical Theory and the Problem of Closure," pp. 27–48.

71. I have introduced the neologism *personitas* to underscore the result of a reflection on *humanitas* (see pages 125 and 188). In order to provide a secular moral understanding open to moral strangers outside of any particular moral tradition, including any particular interpretation of the moral significance of human nature, the concept of *humanitas* must be rendered universal. Reflection on the notion of humanism, especially at its root notion of *humanitas*, leads one essentially to revise the notion, yet to maintain elements of this notion, which are moments of the new or higher notion, *personitas*, which more clearly states the truth of the prior notion, *humanitas*. That is, the attempt to understand the universal significance of humanism leads one to consider the central moral significance of humans, that they are persons. Then in turn, that which is most truly human and specifically human, the *humanitas*, is better understood in terms of its higher truth *personitas*.

What was an aristocratic, male-oriented notion developed in the West became first free of its original bonds to a particular class, gender, and culture, and was then transformed into a notion free of bonds even to the particularities of human nature itself.

All of this is, in somewhat Hegelian jargon, a dialectical development. Reflections on humanism begin within a particular tradition that has its roots in Greek thought and its notion of *paedeia*. These reflections flourish in the Roman civilization of the ancient world and are reinvigorated in the European Renaissance. They are again reanimated in order to master the emerging technologies of the nineteenth and the twentieth centuries. Throughout these reflections on humanism, there is an interest in speaking to all about what is most exemplarily human. However, that which is most exemplarily human is not merely human. It is that which marks us as persons, as entities able to reach across moral visions and to will a general moral fabric based on mutual respect. The more one reflects on *humanitas*, the more it becomes clear that the bond between this notion and the particularities of Western culture, even the particularities of being human, are too parochial, too incomplete and limiting to give an adequate account of the universalist nisus of the notion of *humanitas*, of that which distinguishes us as humans. That which distinguishes us as humans (i.e., that we are persons) is in the end more important than the terribly important, but still logically contingent, fact that we persons are also humans. The fact that we are persons transforms the significance of all we are as humans.

72. The prospect of genetic engineering offers a heuristic by which to appreciate the contingent character of human nature. Human nature, after all, is the outcome of spontaneous mutations, natural selection, catastrophic events, and various constraints set by the laws of physics, chemistry, and biology, as well as by the initial conditions and circumstances of the universe. Human nature is also something that persons can judge, criticize, and in the end reshape. It is in this sense that the particularity of species membership carries no morally necessary implications. To say that species membership has no necessary moral significance in the articulation of the general character of a secular ethics for moral strangers is not to say that non-human species have equal moral standing with humans. The members of non-human species have moral standing with human persons only if they also are persons.

73. It is necessary for morality to have a contingent element. In a view from nowhere, outside of any particular moral perspective, morality has no content. It can only gain content within a particular moral perspective. Hegel makes this point well in his contrast between morality (*Moralität*), which aspires to universality, and the ethical life (i.e., *Sittlichkeit*), which is particular and rich in content. "In an ethical community, it is easy to say what man must do, what are the duties he has to fulfil in order to be virtuous: he has simply to follow the well-known and explicit rules of his own situation." (*Hegel's Philosophy of Right*, trans. T. M. Knox [Oxford: Clarendon Press, 1965], p. 107, § 150.) To have a content-full understanding of humanism and of *humanitas*, one must be within a particular, contingent, but content-full tradition. Otherwise, one will find only a universal but contentless account of *humanitas*, which will evanesce into *personitas*.

74. The intellectual need to justify a general, secular health care policy can thus be met: a secular bioethics is possible. It is secular in being partisan to no particular moral tradition or perspective. It is open to the world, to this age in general. It is humanistic in finding an excellence of humans, on which moral strangers can focus, which can guide them in a virtuous life, and ground a morality. The excellence of humans is that humans can be persons. Moreover, the histories of secularity and of humanism can be seen to lead to a notion of secular humanism, which provides the general foundation for secular bioethics. In short, a common morality can be found and justified. The only difficulty is that it lacks moral content. Better something than nothing. After all, this book begins with despair about the capacities of moral reasoning. Despite good grounds for much of the despair, one still finds a basis to save something of the Enlightenment dream of a generally justifiable secular morality.

75. Here the reader must turn to tradition, culture, or God's good grace to find a particular morality and the content it affords. But this involves issues beyond the compass of this volume.

Index